LIBRARY CLASSIFICATION

LIBRARY CLASSIFICATION

By

Dr. P.Vidya Sagar

M.A., B.Ed., M.L. I.Sc, M.L. I.Sc.
Librarian
Y.V.R. Siddartha College of Education
Vijayawada (A.P.)

SONALI

SONALI PUBLICATIONS
NEW DELHI-110002

Edition : 2024

ISBN 81-88836-85-0

Published by

SONALI PUBLICATIONS
4228/1, Ansari Road,
New Delhi-110 002 (India)
Phone: 23266109, 23279245 • Fax: 91-11-23253475

Printed By :
Navya Digital, Delhi - 110092

PREFACE

The major treads that had been conspicuous in the fabrication of classification theory were these—dichotomy, the unity of knowledge, the hierarchical order, the principle of filiation and gradation by speciality. The other bibliographic systems had their own philosophical antecedents, and though their authors might insist that they had been busying themselves with classification of printed materials rather than organization of knowledge the fact remains that in reality they were merely adapting the former to the latter, with such thinkerings of *notation* provision for *form categories* and other relatively minor adjustments as would make their efforts more nearly adequate to library conditions and needs.

A part of a series of works concerned with investigating systems for the "intellectual organisation of information." This volume examines the development and potential value of the Colon Classification. The book also includes a 'panel discussion', which involves scholars from several different specializations commenting and posing questions regarding the system and Ranganathan responding to these. This work is probably intended for casual or beginning students, rather its audience would be professionals specifically concerned with classification systems and their development and theory.The focus of this book is the development of library classification. Because of the authors intellectual background and perspective, much of this work is framed within concepts and theories taken from Ranganathan and the theoretical basis of the Colon Classification scheme. This work would be useful to the study of library classification and the development of faceted classification schemes.

Editor

CONTENTS

1

Concepts of Library Classification

Subject

An organized or systematized body of ideas, forming a coherent group and a segment (or an area) of the universe of knowledge. A subject is also referred to as "Discipline".

Extension of a Subject

The extension of a subject may extent to:

1. Several volumes in a multivolumed work; or
2. To only a single volume; or
3. Part of a volume; or
4. Chapter of a part; or
5. Section of a chapter or a paragraph; or
6. A sentence; or
7. Even a word

Kinds of Subjects

Subjects like sentences in grammar are of three kinds:

1. Simple;
2. Compound; and
3. Complex

Simple Subject

A Basic Subject is said to be a Simple Subject.

Basic Subject

A subject without any Isolate as a component (Ranganathan).

Isolate Idea

Any idea or idea complex fit to form a component of a subject, but not by itself fit to be a subject (Ranganathan). It is the concept being studied in the subject.

Example

Rural Sociology – Here, 'Sociology' is a Basic Subject; and 'Rural' is an Isolate Idea.

BASIC SUBJECT

Main and Non-Main Basic Subjects

Initially a Basic Subject was equated with the Main Subject. At a later stage, the Basic Subjects were categorized into two types: Main and Non-Main Basic Subject. The main Subjects are described as the first order array of classes which are mutually exclusive and totally exhaustive of the whole field of knowledge. The Non-Main Basic Subjects were described to be of 3 kinds: (1) Canonical Divisions (traditional subdivisions of a Main Class); (2) Systems (Schools of thought); and (3) Specials (Specializations).

New Approach to the Study of Basic Subjects

In one of his papers Dr. Ranganathan indicated the use of chain procedure in understanding the concept of Basic Subject. In deciding about a Basic Subject he states: "Look up for the uppermost link in Chain of Classes, which has to be used in a Class Index or Subject Heading in order to remove homonym. The Class represented by the link may be taken to be the Basic Class".

Example

MA	Home Science
MA-(44)	Indian style, Home Science
MA-(44,N)	Modern, Indian style, Home Science

Fusion of Isolates

According to Mr. V. V. Parthasarathy the essential mode of formation of a new Basic Subject as suggested by the above criterion, appears to be the fusing of isolates derived on the basis of a characteristic or a succession of characteristics to an existing Basic Subject. Further, the above criterion requires that the sequence of the characteristics, the isolates based on which are to be fused into a Basic Subject should parallel the sequence of characteristics decided for the subjects going with the Basic Subject.

On the Basis of Mode of Formation of a Subject

At a later stage, Prof. Neelameghan studied the derivation of Basic Subjects by modes of formation of Subjects.

Types of Basic Subject

According to Prof Neelameghan, the Basic Subject can be categorized into two Broad Groups:

1. Primary Basic Subjects; and
2. Non-Primary Basic Subjects

The list of Basic Subjects is also referred to occasionally as the 'layout' of the scheme

PRIMARY BASIC SUBJECT

These were earlier described as "Main Basic Subjects' or simply 'Main Subjects'.

These can broadly be categorized into two kinds:

1. Traditional Primary Basic Subjects; and
2. New Primary Basic Subjects.

A subject included in the schedule of Primary Basic Subjects.

Fission of the original Universe

The division by fission of the universe of subjects produces a fewer number of major groups of subjects, which when arranged in a helpful order are termed as Primary Basic Subjects.

Fission

'Fission' is one of the various modes of formation of subjects. It is a process of division or splitting or breaking up into parts. Earlier this process was described as 'Dissection'. Dissection involves an 'outside agency', where as, fission represents an 'internal processes' of division without the involvement of an outside agency.

Enumeration

The order of Primary Basic Subject in Colon Classification (CC) is based on convention. The purpose of library classification is to arrange various subjects in a sequence helpful to majority of the readers. The readers refer to books in terms of subjects known and established by tradition. This may be the reason why all the classificationists divided knowledge by conventions established by scientists and educators. This Bliss referred to as 'scientific and educational consensus'.

Logical Background

The Primary Basic Subjects can broadly be grouped into two distinct groups. The first group constitutes 'sciences' where there is progression from the abstract discipline of B-Mathematics to the concrete one ending with the subject that deals with the living body of man. The culmination is in the discipline of Spiritual Experience and Mysticism which comprehends knowledge of intuitive and trans-intellectual origin. This discipline forms, as it were, a peak. As we move down from that discipline to the discipline Law, there is a recession from naturalness to artificiality. The disciplines on the other side of the peak constitutes the Humanities and Social Sciences. Ranganathan had already explained in detail the graduation of subjects in CC.

Reiser's View

Prof. Neelamghan mentioned that "the sequence of Natural Sciences, Humanities, and Social Sciences is in general conformity with the principle of Decreasing Predictability and Increasing Richness of Contents" as described by Mr. O.L. Reiser. For example, the subjects in the field of Mathematical Sciences with relatively the highest predictive quality but with little "content" are placed at one end of the spectrum, while the subs in the field of Social Sciences with relatively poor predictive quality but with rich "content" are placed at the other end of the sectrum. The Humanities have an intermediate degree of predictive quality and richness of content.

List of Primary Basic Subjects

B	Mathematics
C	Physics
D	Engineering
E	Chemistry
F	Chemical technology
G	Biology
H	Geology
I	Botany
J	Agriculture
K	Zoology
KX	Animal husbandry
M	Useful arts
	Spiritual experience and Mysticism
N	Fine arts
O	Literature
P	Linguistics
Q	Religion
R	Philosophy
S	Psychology
T	Education
U	Geography
V	History
W	Political Science
X	Economics
Y	Sociology
YX	Social work
Z	Law

Pure-Applied Sequence

Among the (Traditional) Primary Basic Subjects, we can find that, that 'Pure disciplines' are followed by 'applied disciplines'.

Examples

- Physics *followed by* Engineering

- Botany *followed by* Agriculture
- Zoology *followed by* Animal Husbandry.

NEW PRIMARY BASIC SUBJECT

Apart from the Primary Basic Subjects, there are some New Primary Basic Subjects added from time to time. These are mainly formed by the following 3 modes of formation:

1. Distillation;
2. Fusion; and
3. Clustering.

Distillation

In this mode, a pure discipline is evolved as a Basic Subject out of its appearance as an isolate idea in action in diverse compound subjects going with diverse host Basic Subjects or occasionally even with one particular Basic Subject only. Thus, there are two kinds of New Primary Basic Subjects formed by Distillation mode. These are:

Distillation 1; and

Distillation 2.

Distillation 1

A Distilled Primary Basic Subject of kind 1 is a pure discipline evolved out of its appearance as an isolate idea denoting a *practice in action in diverse subjects*. This subs going with such Primary Basic Subjects are usually found to deal with either a 'service' or a 'methodology'.

Example

1. Management Science: Management has been occurring as an isolate idea in numerous Primary Basic Subjects which indicates a practice-in-action. The study of this concept in depth in diverse Primary Basic Subjects helped to distill out certain basic principles of management and specialized studies of these principles in the course of time lifted it to the level of a Primary Basic Subject.

List of Distilled Primary Basic Subjects: 1

The New Primary Basic Subjects dominantly dealing with a 'Service'

I	Information Science
IX	Universe of subjects : Structure and Development
2	Library Science
3	Book Science
3V	Reading method
3X	Notes taking
4	Mass communication
4T	Journalism
5	Exhibitionology
6	Museology
7	Systemology
9b	Career
9c	Metrology
9d	Standardisation
9f	Research methodology
9g	Evaluation technique.

Distillation 2

A Distilled Primary Basic Subject of Kind 2 is a pure discipline evolved from one particular Primary Basic Subject only.

The subject distilled out must be occurring earlier as a command subject going with a particular Basic Subject. Due to intensive study and with the resultant literary warrant, the compound subjects need to be considered as a specialization by itself. In course of time, it attains a totally independent status and thus becomes New Primary Basic Subject.

List of Distilled Primary Basic Subjects: 2

Following is the list of some of the New Primary Basic Subjects formed by Distillation 2:

BT	Statistical calculus
BTT	Operational Research
BTV	Information Theory
BV	Cybernatics
DT	Draughtmanship
FV	Foundry

FX	Welding
HUB	Geology
GT	Cytology
GTX	Histology
GC	Microbiology
GWA	Molecular Biology
LTa	Physical Exercises
LU1	Social Medicine
LU5	Public Health
LU6	Hospital
LU7	Sanitorium
LY1	Nursing
LYT	Anaesthesiology
MZX	Astrology
PX	Applied Linguistics
SX	Applied Psychology
VX	Historical Source
WT	Public Administration
WAY	International Politics
XY	Economics in action.

Fusion

Inter-Disciplinary Research

Inter-disciplinary research is a common phenomenon these days. The inter-disciplinary research results in inter-disciplinary subjects. Such Subjects naturally have embedded in themselves principles of both the Host Primary Basic Subjects.

Initial Location

In the beginning the classificationist may place an interdisciplinary subject among subjects going with one of Primary Basic Subjects that has the 'Core entity'.

As a New Primary Basic Subject

In due course, the Inter-disciplinary subject may develop its own normative principles and theory. Specialised studies in the new field will generate sufficient literary warrant which will prompt the classificationist to segregate from the Primary Basic Subject with which it has been initially associated and telescope it the level of Primary Basic Subjects.

Position

The Fused Primary Basic Subject is placed as an adjunct to the Primary Basic Subject where it was accommodated earlier as an isolate idea. If there are two or more Fused Primary Basic Subjects occurring as adjuncts, their sequence is determined by principles like Canon of Scheduled Mnemonics, etc.

List of Fused Primary Basic Subjects

BYC	Astrophysics
BYE	Astrochemistry
BYG	Astrobiology
EX	Chemical Engineering
F	Chemical Technology
GWB	Biomechanics
GWC	Biophysics
GX	Biochemistry
GYT	Biometry
GYV	Biocybernetics
HV	Geophysics
HWT	Geochemistry
JYT	Agrometry
LUD	Medical Technology
LYT	Medicometry
PUG	Biolinguistics
PUS	Psycholinguistics
PUV	Sociolinguistics
PYT	Mathematical Linguistics
PYV	Linguistic cybernetics
TYT	Educametry
TYV	Educational Cybernetics
WYT	Politimetrics.

XYT Econometrics
XYV Economic cybernetics

Clustered Primary Basic Subjects

Inter Disciplinary Research

Clustering is another mode of formation of New Primary Basic Subjects from inter-disciplinary research. In the process of investigation of a phenomenon or entity, a large number of specialists are drawn from different subject fields to study the various aspects. The preliminary results of such a study and the data obtained in different Basic Subjects or Compound Subjects going with the different Basic Subjects are published in one and the same document disjunctively for further investigation or elaboration independently by the specialists in the respective subjects.

Scope

This mode of formation features clustering of entities around a nodal idea because of their relation to each other, or their simultaneity of occurrence or for convenience in treatment or discuss (–Neelameghan).

Varieties of Clustered Primary Basic Subject

There are 3 varieties of Clustered Primary Basic Subjects;

1. Area Study;
2. Generalia Person Study; and
3. Entity/Phenomenon study

Area Study

In an Area Study, the input studies may cover subjects falling in the Natural Sciences, Humanities, as well as, Social Sciences. Therefore an Area Study is placed in between 'Generalia' and 'Universe of Subjects'. Among the different Area Studies, the preferred sequence is spatial contiguity of the areas forming the focus of study.

Generalia Person Study

Some individuals are encyclopaedic in range of influence or recorded thought. Their contributions may range from subjects in the Natural Sciences, the Humanities as well as Social Sciences. Thus, such persons are to be put under 'Generalia'.

Examples

w	Generalia person
	(IPI) isolates
	Note: To be derived by (CD) (*Illustrative*)
w, M6	*Gandhi studies*

or

w, G

(Alphabetical Device is also suggested as an alternative method).

Entity or Phenomenon Study

Prof. Neelamghan divided the subject involved in the entity or phenomenon study into two groups:

1. Those with a 'wide Range of Input'; and
2. Those with a 'Restricted Range of Input'.

Wide Range of Input

Any entity or phenomenon can be focus of study with inputs from different subject-fields. The array divisions of the Primary Basic Subject 'Entity or Phenomenon Study' is obtained by Subject Device.

Examples

X	Study of entity/phenomenon (from the viewpoint of diverse subject fields ranging over the natural sciences and social sciences).
	Note: Divisions by (SD) *(Illustrative)*
X(C1,6)	Study of time

Restricted Range of Input

These studies were observed to be coming dominantly from specialists in the natural science subjects.

Examples

A	Natural Sciences
A X	Study of entity/phenomenon from several different angles
	(Input mainly from natural sciences)
A X B	Environmental Sciences

AXD Soil sciences

AXF Hydrosciences

AxG Ocean sciences

Non-Primary Basic Subject

These are Basic Subjects other than the Primary Basic Subjects. These are derived from the Primary Basic Subjects by the following modes of formation:

Primary Basic Subject	— By Fission	→	Secondary Basic Subjects —	Non-Primary Basic Subjects
	— By Lamination 2	→	Compound Basic Subject —	
	— By Agglomeration	→	Agglomerated Basic Subject —	

SECONDARY BASIC SUBJECT

Some of the Primary Subjects are having Certain traditionally recognized sub-fields. These were described by Ranganathan earlier as Canonical Divisions. The mode of formation of these subjects is by 'Fission';. The fission of most of these Primary Basic Subjects occurred longback and the specialists have been referring of these subjects in particular order.

Host Primary Basic Subjects having Secondary Basic Subjects:

S.No.	Subject	Class Number
1.	Mathematics	B
2.	Physica	C
3.	Engineering	D
4.	Chemistry	E
5.	Geology	H
6.	Medicine	L
7.	Useful Arts	M
8.	Fine Arts	N
9.	Philosophy	R
10.	Geography	U

Secondary Basic Subject

As the Secondary Basic Subjects are conventional divisions of a Primary Basic Subject, no specific characteristic of division can be explicitly stated. The divisions of a Primary Basic Subject are called as Secondary Basic Subject.

Secondary Basic Subject: in CC, ED 7:

B1	Arithmetic
B2	Algebra
B3	Analysis
B4	Group theory
B5	Trignometry
B6	Geometry
B6T	Topology
B6V	Mathematical logic
B7	Mechanics
B8	Physico-mathematics
B83	Potential function
B85	Wave function
BT1	Probability
BT2	Distribution
BT3	Sampling
BT4	Test of significance
BT5	Design of experiment
BT6	Analysis of variance and co-variance
BT7	Theory of attribute
BT8	Correlation and regression
BTC	Forecasting
BTE	Multivariate analysis
BTF	Statistical quality control
BTH	Sequential Analysis
BTM	Time series analysis
BTN	Acturial analysis
BTT1	Linear programming
BTT2	Non-linear programming

BTT3	Dynamic programming
BTT4	Theory of games
BTT5	Queuing theory
BTT6	Sequencing theory
BTT7	Replacement theory
BTT8	Inventory control
C1	Fundamentals of physics
C2	Properties of Matter
C3	Sound, Physics of
C4	Heat, Physics of
C47	Thermodynamics
C5	Heat radiation
C57	Electronics
C6*Z	Electricity and magnetism
C6	Electricity
C7	Magnetism
D1	Civil Engineering
D12	Foundation Engineering
D13	Building Materials studies
D18	Structural engineering
D2	Building engineering
D2T	Hydraulic engineering
D3	Irrigation engineering
D4	Track engineering
D5	Environmental engineering
D51	Safety engineering
D53	Public Health Engineering
D55	Water Supply Engineering
D56	Sweage Engineering
D58	Pollution Engineering
D5T	Production engineering
D6	Power Engineering
D7	Service Engineering
D71	Workshop practice

D73	Communication engineering
D75	Illumination engineering
D76	Ventilation engineering
D761	Aircondition engineering
D762	Refrigerator engineering
D77	Accustic engineering
D78	Control systems engineering
D7A	Instrumentation engineering
D7H	Industrial engineering
D7H1	Materials handling
D7H7	Packaging engineering
D7H8	Maintenance engineering
D8	Commodity production engineering
E1	General chemistry
E2	Physical chemistry
E3	Analytical chemistry
E4	Synthetic chemistry
H1	Minerology
H2	Petrology
H3	Structural geology
H4	Geomorphology
H5	Stratigraphy
H6	Paleontology
H61	Paleobotany
H62	Paleozoology
H7	Economic geology
LTO1	Physical exercise
LTO2	Indoor games (Collective treatment)
LTO5	Outdoor games (Collective treatment)
LT-1*Z	Ball games
LT	Tug of war
LTC	Throwing game
LTE	Aiming games
LTF	Chassing Games

LTJ	Wrestling games
LTK	Boxing games
LTM	Ice and snow games
LTN	Water sports
LX3	Pharmacology
LX34	Toxicology
LX5	Pharmacopia
LX6	Pharmacy
M1	Book production and distribution
M2	Wood working trade
M3	Masonry
M4	Materials protection trade
M6	Metal working trade
M7	Textile weaving
M8	Dress making
M92	Tailoring
M95	Footwear making
M97	Laundry services
M9C	Optician's services
M9P	Auditorium services
MA	Home science
MA3	Food craft
MG	Hotel and catering services
MH	Beauticulture
MH1	Hair dressing
MH3	Manicuring
MK	Hostellery
MM	Entertainment and Hobby
MV1	Land Military science
MV5	Air Military science
MX1	Business letter writing
MX3	Notes and minute taking
MXN	Typewriting
MXP	Shorthand writing

Nn	Ornament making
Ns	Lapidiary art
Nt	Bead work
Nv	Numismatic art
Nt	Graphic art
N3	Calligraphic art
N5	Drawing
N6	Painting
N7	Engraving
N8	Etching
N91	Needle work
N93	Embroidery work
N95	Lace work
N97	Tapestry
NA	Architecture
NAT	Interior decoration
NAX	Furniture design
NB	Town planning
NC	Plastic art
ND	Sculpture
NF	Glass art
NH	Ceramic art
NJ	Inlay art
NL	Mossaic art
NR	Music
NRV	Musical instruments making
NS	Dance
NT	Theatre
NU	Puppet play
NV	Shadow play
NW	Photography
NX	Cinematography
R1	Logic
R2	Epistemology

R3	Metaphysics
R4	Ethics
R5	Aesthetics
R6	Indian philosophy
R7	Greek philosophy
R8	Other schools thought
U1	Mathematical geography
U2	Physical geography
U3	Biogeography
U5	Anthropogeography
U6	Political geography
U7	Economic geography
U8	Travel

Secondary Basic Subject

It can be observed that some of the Secondary Basic Subjects of Order 1 are fissioned further to form Secondary Basic Subjects of Order 2.

Example

Atmospherology *fissioned* to:

Meteorology,

Aeronomy,

Ionosphere studies, etc.

Compound Secondary Basic Subject

Whenever a Speciator is attached to a Secondary Basic Subject, it results as a Compound Secondary Basic Subject

Example

Economics – Public Finance – Socialism.

COMPOUND PRIMARY BASIC SUBJECT

Specials Compound Primary Basic Subject

Specialisation

Another feature of Primary Basic Subjects is that of specialization. Certain sub-areas of a Primary Basic Subject may become classes of specialization on account of social necessity or intensive research.

Specialists

The class of people doing specialization are called specialists. Then field of activity is restricted, but more intensified. It will be helpful for them, if all the documents of their field of specialization are in close proximity. This necessitated a special treatment for the specials.

Origin of the Specials

Unlike systems, specials are of recent origin. Such Basic Subjects came into prominence during the last few decades.

Definition

Ranganathan defined special as 'restriction of the field of a Primary Basic Subject to a particular range of the incidence of any of its characteristics likely to belong to the unrestricted state of a subject'.

Host Primary Basic Subjects

The following are the Primary Basic Subjects in CC, Ed 7 having special Compound Primary Basic Subjects:

Subject	Class Number
Physics	C
Chemistry	E
Botany	I
Zoology	K
Medicine	L

Example

L	Medicine
9F	Female
L-9F	Female Medicine
List of Special	Compound Primary Basic Subjects in CC, Ed 7
C-92	Transport phenomena
C-9B*Z	Microphysics
C-9B	Molecular physics

(Contd.)

L	Medicine
C-9C	Atomic physics
C-9D	Nuclear physics
C-9E	Particle physics
C-9F	Cosmic ray physics
C-9H	Pressure physics
C-9H1	Cosmic ray physics
C-9H2	Law pressure physics
C-9H4	High pressure physics
C-9J	Temperature physics
C-9J1	Absolute zero, Physics of
C-9J2	Law temperature, Physics of
C-9J4	High temperature, Physics of
C-9L	Physics of potential
C-9L2	Low potential, Physics of
C-9L4	High potential, Physics of
EX-9G	Biochemical engineering
I-9H	Creeper, Botany of
I-9J	Climber, Botany of
I-9K	Insectivorous plants
J-9B	Dry farming
J-9C	Soilless farming
J-9D	Strub farming
J-9E	Dwaft Tree farming
J-9F	Turf farming
K-9B	Embroyology
K-9C	Young animal
K-9J	Zoo zoology
K-9K	Sanctuary zoology
KX-9C1	New born animal, Animal Husbandry of
KX-9F	Old animal, Animal Husbandry of
KX-9H	Female animal, Animal Husbandry of
L-9B	Human Embroyology
L-9C1	New born child medicine

L	Medicine
L-9C5	Pre-adolescent medcine
L-9D	Adolescent medicine
L-9E	Adult medicine
L-9F	Old age medicine
L-9G	Male medicine
L-9H	Female medicine
L-9J	Eunuch medicine
LT-9C	Children's game
LT-9F	Games of oldage
LT-9H	Games of women
LT-9J	Games for physical handicapped.

2

Philosophies of Classification

History

At the close of the 19th century librarians began to think seriously about the problem of the arrangement of their book stocks and they related classification more to physical books (i.e., books as artifacts) than to their thought content. At that time, the major treads that had been conspicuous in the fabrication of classification theory were these – dichotomy, the unity of knowledge, the hierarchical order, the principle of filiation and gradation by speciality. Before we define these treads we may broadly state that the *traditional library classification is a story of adaptation of existing philosophical systems to library materials and needs*. Early in the 19th century Thomas Jefferson had turned to Bacon for the Philosophical basis of a book classification that was adopted by the Library of Congress. Melville Dewey bethought himself of Harris' "inverted Baconian" and adopted it as the framework of his own scheme. The Expansive Classofication of Charles Ammi Cutter, especially in the evolutionary or developmental pattern of its subordinate classes, shows the influence of Comte and Spencer. The other bibliographic systems had their own philosophical antecedents, and though their authors might insist that they had been busying themselves with classification of printed materials rather than organization of knowledge the fact remains that in reality they were merely adapting the former to the latter, with such thinkerings of *notation* provision for *form categories* and other relatively minor adjustments as would make their efforts more nearly adequate to library conditions and needs.

"The efforts of classifiers from Francis Bacon onwards were directed towards finding a new relational system of classification to replace that of Aristotle." Aristotle's pattern of knowledge classification was that he "divided knowledge into three parts – the Theoretical, which aims at knowledge for its own sake; and the Productive, which aims to be used in making things useful or beautiful. Practical knowledge included Ethics, Politics, Economics and Rhetoric, while Productive knowledge covered Politics and the Arts." His Theoretical knowledge is akin to the modern conception of Science. Francis Bacon in the *Advancement of Knowledge* gave a new interpretation to Aristotle's basic dichotomy. He denied that knowledge could be divided into theoretical, practical and productive, and instead suggested a division into history, poetry and philosophy. It is however found that the basic groupings of Aristotle's Physics and Mathematics appeared almost unchanged in Bacon's classification. "By the beginning of the eighteenth century, however, the Aristotelian scheme was generally dropped. Instead, a *simple enumeration* of basic disciplines occurred." The traditional basic disciplines, current at that time, henceforward formed the 'raw material' out of which classifications of science were constructed. The problem on which nineteenth century classification was concerned was to discover how these disciplines, traditional fields of study, were to be arranged, rationally grouped and ordered.

Fields of knowledge were divided by the 'scientific and educational consensus', as Bliss calls it. In other words, the common consciousness of educated society had already divided knowledge into suitably homogeneous blocks. Natural historical development of knowledge had already assembled areas of subject matter with some care and accuracy, and had further performed at least part of the process of carefully dividing these areas into sub-classes.

Thus, the nineteenth century classificationists depended on the enumeration and grouping of traditional fields of study, which were current at that time and the process of classification they followed was that found in the older works on Logic which concerned itself also with the process of division. It aimed at mutual exclusiveness and between one species of genus and another as is illustrated in the one species of genus and another as is illustrated in the *Tree of Porphyry* in which a species is derived from a genus by the discovery of *difference*. The Aristotelian concept of hierarchy was followed as the basic principle of classification. In doing so the traditional book classification failed to adapt itself to constantly changing needs, uses and points of view.

Before we discuss the structure and principles of *hierarchical classification* we may incidentally note that the nineteenth century classificationists grouped, divided or arranged the sciences by *subjective* characteristics. Bacon's primary division depended on the way the mind approached phenomena – by memory or by reason. This was a break with the Aristotelian method. Although Aristotle's primary grouping was subjective, yet he further divided groups of entities by means of attributes of the entities themselves. The subjective mode of dividing the sciences is slosely linked with the choice of traditional disciplines as the raw material of classification.

Hierarchical Structure of Classification

Hierarchical classification, derived from the philosophies of Plato and Aristotle, is the *arrangement of things (objects, concepts, etc.) into genera, species, and subspecies, according to their similarities and differences.*

The *main principles of hierarchical classification* are:

1. A hierarchical classification proceeds by the assembly of the groups of sciences or of the principal fields of knowledge into main classes or divisions which are dictated by the theory of knowledge accepted. Such *classes* have great *extension* and the small *intension*.
2. The process is continued by differentiating qualities (*differentia*) within each main class, and thus subclasses or subdivisions are made.
3. Each subdivision in turn is divided by further differentiated qualities to produce still further subdivisions, and by still others to make sections and subsections, until further subdivision is impossible or imparticable.
4. Every subdivision of a class is subordinate to the class heading and the sum of these subdivisions is the whole meaning of the class term, but each single set of subdivisions.

Aristotelian Predicables

The Five Predicables identified by Aristotle are:

1. **DEFINITION:** It signifies the "essence" of a thing i.e., set of fundamental attributes which are necessary and sufficient conditions for any concrete things to be the thing of that type. Essence is that which makes a thing what it is and not something else. 'Definition' is the enumeration of the essential attributes of a term. We must give in a definition the briefest possible statement of such qualities as are sufficient to distinguish the class from other classes.
2. **GENUS:** A genus, used in its intensive meaning, denotes the qualities belonging to all of the genus, and sufficient to mark them out. It is identified by the "essence" common to a number of things that among themselves exhibit differences in other properties. It is a series of objects or idea which can be divided into two or more groups called species.

   The SPECIES means the sum of the qualities common to all the individuals forming part of the species, and sufficient to mark them out from the rest of the genus as well as from other things. It is evident, therefore, that there must be more qualities, implied in the meaning of the species than of the genus, for the species must contain all the qualities of the genus, as well as a certain additional quality or qualities by which the several species are distinguished from each other.
3. **DIFFERENCES:** It may be defined as the quality or sum of qualities which mark out one part of a genus from the other part or parts. Thus, difference (Latin differentia) is the quality added to the genus to form the species. It is the characteristic attribute which distinguishes one species from all other species in the same genus.
4. **PROPERTY:** It is a quality common to every member of the genus, but which is not confined to that genus and is not essential to the definition of genus. It is an attribute peculiar to a subject, but not part of its "essence". Thus, it is a property of the genus "triangle" to have the three internal angles equal to two right angles; this is very remarkable circumstance, which is true of triangles, but it is not make part of the genus, or is not employed in defining a triangle, because the possession of three straight sides is a sufficient mark.

5. **ACCIDENT:** It is a quality which may or may not be possessed by any member of the genus. Its possession is a pure accident and has not fundamental connection with any member of the genus. The word means that which falls or happens by chance, and has no necessary connection with the nature of a thing. An accident it not formally derivable from the definition. For example, the colour or size of a rag is an accident of the rag. Some writers distinguish separable and inseparable accident.

The GreekLogician, Porphyry (Porphyrius) omitted *definition* from his Latin version and substituted species which is defined as that portion of the genus distinguished by a given *differentia*. According to porphyry, therefore, theFive Predicables are *genus, species, differentia, property* and *accident*.

The first three predicables as defined by Porphyry are illustrated in the well-known Tree of Porphyry, where we observe a succession of genera and species—Substance, Body, Living Being, Animal and Man. Of these Substance is the *summum genus*, or all-embracing class, because it is not regarded as a species or any higher class; Man is the infima-species, because it is a class not divided into any lower class, but only into individuals, of whom it is usual to specify Socrates and Plato. Body, Living Being, and Animal are called *subaltern genera* and species, because each is a species as regards the next higher genus, and a genus as a regards the next lower species. The qualities implied in the adjectives Corporeal, Animate, Sensient (i.e., capable of feeling) and Rational are the successive differences which occasion a division of each genus into species.

In the Tree of Porphyry a species is derived from a genus by the discovery of a difference, so that genus is shown to divide into two species, one of which possesses the difference and the other does not. This sort of division is called *dichotomous*. It will be discussed later that dichotomous division is quite useless for the purpose of book classification.

It will be evident that the negative parts of the genera, *viz.*, Not corporeal Substance, Non-organic Body etc. are capable of subdivision, which has not been carried out in order to avoid confusing the reader.

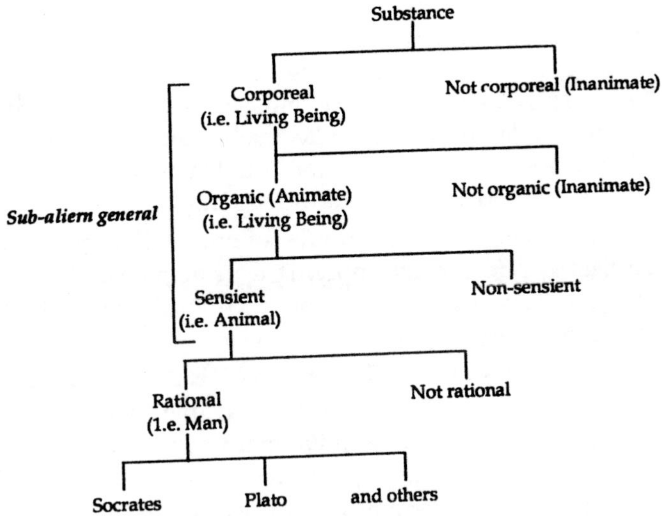

Figure 2.1. The Tree of Porphyry

Extension and Intension

The term Substance has great *extension* (denotation) and small intention (connotation). The *extension* or denotation of a term is the aggregate of objects covered by the term. The *intension* or *connotation* of a term is the aggregate of qualities implied by that term—the minimum qualities necessary for its definition.

It follows that in any schedule, formed by adding differences to the genera, the terms in the order of the hierarchy gradually increase in intension and decrease in extension. A genus has always greater extension than its species and, similarly the species have always greater intension than their genus.

The value of the Tree of Porphyry. Porphyry's Tree is an illustration of his theory that all things are interdependent. As a classification it is very incomplete. Many biological steps are missing. The Tree is of value as an example of a hierarchy i.e., a series divided into ranks or orders and a clear illustration of a method of subdivision, known as *dichotomy*, a division where at each step every class is subdivided into only two sub-classes, one positive and the other its contradictory or correlative negative.

Prophyry's Tree conforms to the formal rules of division e.g. (1) Each step must be based on a single characteristic or principle of division and (2) co-ordinate classes must be mutually exclusive and (3) co-ordinate classes must be collectively exhaustive. Coordinate classes are classes of the same order, equal in rank or degree. They form arrays of classes or the same order of rank.

N.B.: It will be explained in subsequent sections how division of a subject is effected by applying a principle of Division (or characteristic as is often called) to produce subclasses in which the principle is manifested in varying degrees.

Division of classes and library classification. Older ideas of book classification owe much to the principle that classification should start with knowledge in its totality and divide it up into classes, as illustrated in Porphyry's Tree. Nineteenth century book classification—Dewey Decimal, Library of Congress classification—rejected the notion of dichotomous division; but nevertheless learned heavily on the idea of starting with large subject fields and dividing them up, using one characteristic or principle of division at a time, so that eventually they had attempted to list all departments of knowledge in a systematic sequence moving from the very general to the highly specialized, in a series or chains of regulated steps.

Division, as will be seen in the next section, is complementary to classification. In this connection we may note that *logical classification* is a grouping of individuals into groups, according to their points of resemblances and differences. In logical Division we begin with a higher class and proceed to lower classes—*i.e.*, we proceed from the more general to the less genera. For this reason Division is called *Deductive Classification*. In Division or Deductive Classification we proceed from the more general to the less general, while in (Inductive) Classification we proceed from the less general to the more general. As we have already noticed hierarchical classifications are developed deductively, beginning with the assumption of unity of all knowledge and *dividing* knowledge progressively by adding distinguishing characteristics to the intension of each class. Multidimensional classifications tend to be developed inductively by isolating definable classes at the lowest level and *combining* them according to the relationships that are important in the particular situation.

The ideas borrowed from the rules of formal logic assume that in a general classification designed to cover all departments of knowledge, a collection of books will be broken up into organized subject groups using one characteristic at a time. The characteristics used in division will enable us to assemble things according to their degree of likeness or to make a specific class. To use a formal logical phrase a classification practically proceeds from terms of great extension (*denotation*) and small intension (*connotation*) to terms of great intension and small extension. Each class is said to be a species of the one immediately above it (*superordinate class*) in the hierarchical chain and a genus in relation to the one below (subordinate class). This process, in which one characteristic only is used as the dividing principle at each stage will enable us to enumerate all branches of knowledge in the form of an organized "family tree".

It will be seen that book classificationists do not follow Porphyry's dichotomy. When the classificationist makes his scheme he wants to show *all the co-ordinate classes based, on the same principle of division* (array of classes) that can be derived from the major inclusive class in one operation. He is not content to go through the process of dichotomy, deriving one species at a time by seeking the difference again and again. He looks instead for some quality of subject which all the books in a class possess in varying degree or measure, or in different ways and uses this quality as a criterion of arrangement. The subject 'Education', for example, might be divided up according to 'educand' or class of persons to be educated (e.g. pre-school child, adult, etc.).

Classification and Division: Their Complementary Nature

In classifying *subjects* we recognize that different subjects share some common attributes and this makes them members of a class, e.g. that Economics, Political Science, Law are all *Social Sciences*; similarly, Insurance, Banking, Transport are all *Commerce*, etc. These examples suggest that classification is an *inductive* one of building broader classes from narrower classes, working from particular to the general. This is exactly what the term *classification* does imply, particularly in Logic. Nevertheless, it is found in practice that library classifications are usually constructed by the opposite process of *Division*, working deductively from the general to the special : for example, dividing Library Economy into its subclasses, Cataloguing, Classification, Book Selection, Book Charging, etc., and then dividing them into further subclasses or sections, and so on.

The reason for this is mainly that it is easier to begin from accepted main classes, based upon educational and scientific consensus, like Economics, Psychology, Chemistry, etc., which reflect generalizations which have already been made from long experience. To begin with the analysis of the larger classe is a labour-saving device, though this device has certain dangers, for it trends to make classes appear rigid.

Library classification is primarily the classification of the thought content or subject content of books and a vital preliminary in the process is that of subject analysis or division.

Steps of Division

Characteristics is the focal point of the process of division and classification implies the discovery and identification of successive differences. The following rules of division govern the process of classification:

1. Each step must be based upon a single principle of division of characteristic; in other words, the use of characteristics, natural or artificial, must be consistent at each stage of division, one principle of division being exhausted before another is introduced. This insistence that a division be based upon a single principle or characteristic avoids the fallacy of *cross division* or overlapping. Again the characteristics used must be essential and relevant to the purpose of the classification.
2. The process of division must be gradual, the least amount of difference possible in the class being used at each stage. The resulting division should be as minute as practicable. This helps in keeping the closely related material as continuous as the materials themselves permit. Each chain of classes should suitably modulated, so that no links are omitted.
3. Divisions of a class (the derived class *in an array*) i.e., the *coordinate classes* must be mutually exclusive, or discrete. This

principle is really a corollary of the preceding rule in that cross division usually results from the presence of more than one principle of division operating at the same time.

4. Co-ordinate classes or divisions of class (the derived class in an array) should be collectively exhaustive of their immediate universe; *i.e.*, co-extensive with the *summum genus.* In other words, the sum of the constituent divisions or species should be equal to the genus and nothing should be omitted which should be included in that genus. Take for example, the two classes 'Corporeal Body' and 'Non-Corporeal Body' in the Tree of Porphyry. These two co-ordinate classes or divisions of the genus 'Substance', taken together exhaust or cover up the extension or denotation of the genus 'Substance'. We should, however, note that this rule of exhaustiveness should be considered in relation to the state of existent knowledge.

These rules define the formal conditions to which a classification should conform, but they are not sufficient for practical or theoretical purposes. The practical or theoretical requirements can only be defined by reference to the purpose and use to be made of the classification. The method of division and the extent of subdivision are governed by the purpose.

Library Classification and Logical Division

In the practice of classification the original *'universe'* of knowledge at the top of the family tree, the subject field to be divided, is one of the main classes, which Dr. Ranganathan defines as the fairly homogeneous, conventional regions of knowledge, which together form the first order array of classes, which are mutually exclusive and totally exhaustive of the field of knowledge.' This universe is divided and subdivided into whatever detail is required. In theory, the process of division is logical, i.e., each genus is differentiated into a species by means of a particular characteristic of division, each term is divided in only one way, and all the subdivisions of any term are true species of the parent genus.

The *'entities'* (concrete and conceptual existents) in each main class have many attributes, and some of these can serve as characteristics for the *'logical division'* of the main class into sub-classes or groups. The groups so derived can then be ranked in a helpful order.

Limitations of Logical Division in Library Classification

1. A library classification schedule is full of examples of classes whose relation to their subclasses is not that of a genus to its species; e.g. Elbow is a part of the arm (in Human anatomy); London is a part of England; it is not a kind of England; for the relation between England and London is quite different from that between a genus and its species. In a classification of documents by their subject content restriction or recognition to the single relation of genus/species would be unrealistic. All different relations—part, operation, constituent etc. should be recognized.
2. In logical division the characteristics, to be truly generic, should partake of the 'essentia' nature of the genus. The genus 'Soldier' for example, could be divided by 'Mode of fighting' /artillery, infantry, etc.), by 'Rank' (commissioned, non-commissioned, etc.), 'conditions of service' (regular, conscript, etc.)—all these being distinctive of military science. But, to introduce a characteristic, viz. 'Social background' ('working class', 'professional class'. etc.) would not be legitimate in logical division, since this principle is not essentially a military one and its use would make class formation a matter of mere combination of arbitrary characteristics.
3. In logical division he successive characteristics by which a genus is divided should reflect one consistent notion, e.g. if Soldier were divided by 'Mode of fighting' it would be improper to proceed with the characteristic 'Rank'; for rank is not peculiar to any one mode of fighting.

   In library classification, however, the formation of classes by combination of quite distinct characteristics is inevitable. This is not possible according to the formal rules of logical division.
4. Logical division assumes the possibility of mutually exclusive classes. In library classification, the physical documents frequently overlap in subject content; a book classified as Egyptian archaeology may include incidental data on modern

Egyptian life. J. Mills points out that for practical purposes, mutually exclusive classes are quite feasible, provided a facet formula [For discussion see the Chapter on Colon Classification] in each subject is strictly adhered to; e.g. if the facet formula is used for 19th Century English History it becomes History – Place – Period; here the class 19th Century History (meaning the class "Documents exclusively or largely concerned with the topic 19th Century History, without reference to any particular place") definitely excludes the class 19th Century English History.

5. In logical division the choice of characteristics is restricted to those reflecting generic qualities, and these are quite inadequate.
6. As to the order of application of characteristics, logical division gives no guidance. Whether Soldier is divided by Rank before conditions of service, or vice-versa, depends on extra-logical considerations—i.e., the purpose of the classification.
7. As to the arrangement of the classes produced by the operation of division, logical division gives no guidance; e.g., whether the general should precede the special, or the abstract precede the concrete, or what order a coordinate class should follow.

3

RELATION BETWEEN CLASSIFICATION & SUBJECT CATALOGUING

Introduction

In England the majority of libraries use the classified catalogue. For them the classification chosen is obviously vital, because the better the classification the better the catalogue. The whole idea of a classified catalogue is that should show not only each desired subject but also its relationship to other subjects and how they complement each other, as well as being an additional guide to the user who cannot identify the required subject.

In reference libraries the classified sequence is vital to a good information service. A closed library which is not arranged on classified lines cannot give a true information service without a classified catalogue which has been guided to show not only main classes but also the various subordinate classes and general lines of division.

Such a classified catalogue cannot work on its own and it must have indexes to accompany it. These are discussed later in this chapter. The best general guide to the classified catalogue is J. H. Shera and M. E. Egan. The classified catalogue. In addition see Needham 128-130, the introduction to Sayers chapter twenty six and a new edition of Ranganathan Classified catalogue code.

The syllabus, in demanding conversance with the relationship of classification to subject cataloguing, implies a much wider study than merely the classified catalogue.

The other major form of catalogue is the dictionary catalogue where words predominate, and there are lists of subject headings. However L Jolly states in Principles of catalogue 'all subject headings catalogues are based on a system of classification. The cataloguer...cannot hope to enumerate all possible specific headings within a subject except by a process of consecutive subdivision. The more thorough his analysis of the relationships of different terms, the more accurate will be his definitions'. Jolly goes on to state his objections to classification in general. Despite his subsequent justification of dictionary cataloguing, it remains true that classification acts as a guide for subject heading work and does aid the right decision about choice and specificity of entry.

One further point is the relationship of classification to indexing. In general subject indexing, the emphasis is on alphabetic order. It must be relised that classicication cannot exist without an alphabetic guide to subjects. It is useful to consider not only indexing by itself, but also the compilation of indexes to classification schemes. This is a devolution from part one examination studies, but must be more thoroughly understood. First comes what *Sayers* called the 'specific' index of Brown's sc. This term is itself a misnomer, for it suggests a specific location for topics, which in Brown it is not. It is a one place index which does not show any other aspects of the subject, but presupposes that the classification has brought all aspects of all subjects together. This is false because, for example, in certain cases the concretes are in one place (as with ROSES), in others (such as MANAGEMENT) they are widely scattered. This means in fact that the 'specific' index is an incomplete relative index.

The latter is a repetition of the schedules, a mistake to be avoided since it lengthens the index, makes it more difficult to consult and does not serve any useful purpose.

Indexing in Classification

Chain indexing evolved from the need to eliminate repetitions, and to ensure that all steps of the classification were systematically indexed, while at the same time cutting out wasteful steps. Ranganathan in cc has used what is now known as chain procedure in his scheme. There have been frequent descriptions of chain indexing, but the best in J Mills in Library Association record 57 (4) April 1955 173-178. Note however the limitation which has been placed on the method since the Cranfield Research Project. Cranfield showed that failure to invert the terms in certain cases caused delays and failure in the faceted classification. The researchers therefore abandoned strict chain procedure and improved their performance with faceted classification. The limitations on chain indexing are that it is less valuable for very detailed indexing of a limited field.

This general discussion on indexing in classification leads to discussion of the use of indexes to the classification scheme. First they are auxiliary to a scheme and not substitutes for a scheme. This is what Bliss called the 'subject index illusion'—that it doesn't matter where material is classified as long as it is indexed properly. This, as Bliss pointed out, is nonsense. A good index will find a specific topic, but it does not show the inherent relationships of that subject and how they can be followed up.

Another general mistake is to use the index to the schedules as a subject index to the library. This is wrong because few libraries follow schemes exactly, the index is rarely up to date in terminology and it does nothing to reflect the stock of the library.

From indexing in classification some further consideration must be given to coordinate indexing techniques. The nature of coordinate terms has already been shown. Here we are concerned with the methods of applying the terms. There is, for example, what we might call content indexing. Basically this is an analysis either of the title or of brief notes of contents of an article, with promotion of the words to form an alphabetical list of subjects. This method is popular in content indexing and does provide some form of subject guide. It employs a kind of dictionary technique and does not endeavour to show relationships. However, more sophisticated systems have evolved and it is from these that some relationship to classification can be deduced.

Two expressions which must be fully understood are 'item on term' and 'term on item'. In 'item on term' methods, also called 'invested system, 'the item numbers of documents are all entered on the relevant term cards. Thus if documents 24, 36 and 40 all refer to prestressed concrete. These document numbers will be written on both the card headed PRESTRESSING and the card headed CONCRETE.

This simple ' item on term' method is very popular in this country and PEEKABOO is being used by several firms for indexing items on concrete (a subject badly treated by most classification schemes). However the method is really only feasible where the terms are simple and generally mutually exclusive. The relationships between documents as terms cannot be shown, and it is therefore of comparatively little value for complex searches.

For the latter purpose the sequential 'term on item' method is more useful. In this each document card has every term entered on it, or alternatively a notation for every term. This means that every time a query is placed *all* documents have to be searched. It is a slower method, but is becoming more popular with the increasing use of mechanization, and in the United States sequential scanning is now used with the majority of systems.

4

The Designing of Classification Schemes

Overview

Before dealing with the broad principles of arrangement of terms or classes in a classification scheme in orderly rows or columns we may touch upon the various schemes (or, written or printed schedules of terms) designed for providing a set of guiding rules to fix the position of a newly emerging class in correct filiatory position among the already existing classes. We have dealt with conventional main classes and stated that the making of a library classification should begin with the literature and should use as its raw material the concepts manifested in the literature. Dr. S.R. Ranganathan mentions the following five species of schemes for classification: (1) Enumerative classification; (2) Almost-Enumerative classification; (3) Almost-Faceted classification; (4) Rigidly-Faceted classification; and (5) Freely-Faceted classification. In fact, we can trace the evolution from the enumerative scheme to the analytico-synthetic one (Faceted classification).

An *Enumerative scheme* for classification, according to Dr. Ranganathan, 'consists essentially of a single schedule enumerating all subjects—of the past, the present and the anticipatable future'. The class number of an enumerative scheme consists of semantically rich digits and is 'monolithic'. Examples of purely enumerative schemes of classification are Library of Congress Classification (commonly abbreviated as L.C.) and Riders' International Classification.

An *Almost-Enumerative scheme* for classification 'consists of a large schedule enumerating most of the subjects of the past, the present and the anticipatable future, and in addition, a few schedules of common isolates'. Such a scheme enumerates not only basic subjects, but also compound subjects. Examples are Brown's '*Subject Classification*' and *Dewey Decimal Classification*.

An *Almost-Faceted Scheme* for classification 'consists of a large schedule enumerating most of the subjects of the past, the present, and the anticipatable future, and a few schedules of common isolates and also some schedules of special isolates'. Examples are *Universal Decimal Classification* (commonly known as UDC), Bliss's *Bibliographical classification.*

A *Rigidly-Faceted Classification* is classification with pre-determined faces; e.g., *Colon Classification* of Ranganathan.

A *Freely-Faceted Classification* is analytico-synthetic classification guided by postulates and principles. Colon Classification is a typical example.

Broad Principles of Arrangement

Book classification traditionally started by dividing the Universe of Knowledge (which Dr. Ranganathan terms Universe of Subjects) into a restricted number of 'main classes' or disciplines. The conventional main classes adopted by different classificationists in constructing their schemes have been dealt with in Chapters 7-10. Traditional methods of constructing classification schedules were based on a close analogy with logical classifications, where the classification structure is a hierarchy formed by the successive application of characteristics of division thus enumerating all branches of knowledge in the form of an organized family tree, the branches of knowledge being part of the more general class to which it belongs. The classification based on the rules of logical division moves in systematic stages from general to specific subjects. The main purpose of traditional schedules is the definition of terms and categories and is concerned with relations between genus and species—the thing and its kind.

Steps for Making Classification Scheme

Subject analysis or division: The preliminary step in the process of construction is that of subject, analysis or division. We have already discussed the rules of division, and these rules, though by themselves are quite inadequate as a basis of library classification are nevertheless of considerable interest. Division of a subject is affected by applying a characteristic (Principle of Division) to produce sub-classes in which that principle is manifested in varying ways or degrees. Literature, for example, is first divided by the characteristic of Language to obtain subclasses such as 'English Literature', 'French Literature', etc., and then by Form-poetry, drama, fiction, essays, oratory, letters, satire and humour—to obtain foci within each subclass; e.g. French poetry, English drama, etc.; French poetry, French drama, etc.

Determining the Order within Each Hierarchy

Any given hierarchy consists of terms of increasing intension, derived from the *summum genus* by the application of a succession of characteristics. Traditional classification had laid down a number of canons which give useful guidance to classificationists. It is useful, for example, to use well defined and consistent characteristics of division. The derived classes in array should be muturally exclusive and collectively exhaustive of their immediate universe. Each chain of classes should be suitably modulated, so that no links are omitted.

The term in each array form a series of co-ordinate classes. The total sub-classes resulting from the application of single characteristic is called *Facet* (by Ranganathan). For example, we may have *Language Facet* of literature class; *Literary Form Facet* of literature class. The items in the facet are called *co-ordinate terms in an array*. These co-ordinate terms bear the same relation to the main subject or the immediate super-ordinate class (or proximate genus). But they do not bear any relation to one another. This poses a problem to the classificationists viz. which item should precede or follow another. It thus becomes necessary for the classificationist to decide on a helpful order within a major class and among the series of co-ordinate classes in each array or terms. The choice of order will be dictated by the nature of the subject matter.

The individual member of sub-class within a facet is called a *focus; e.g.*, in D.C. 'English Literature' is a focus in the Language Facet of the literature class; 'English poetry' is a focus in the Literary Form Facet of the class English literature.

[In dealing with the latest trends in the construction of classification schemes we shall discuss *facet-analysis* as well as other steps in the construction of a modern scheme]

Every array of terms in a classification is liable to require expansion. New entities co-ordinate with the old may have to be added. Classificationists are to make provisions for them in their schemes.

The structure of traditional enumerative bibliographical, schemes is rigid and offers a fixed hierarchy in each subject field and, as such, the enumerative schemes have always found it difficult to keep pace with changes in the field of knowledge. In fact, each subject field is often only of several hierarchies which might exist. The exact classification of many documents is thus prevented, for if a scheme shows subject B as subordinate to subject A, and subject C as subordinate to subject B, we cannot classify A plus C without using B as an intermediary, for traditional classification is dependent on the genus to species relationship.

Analytical Approach

The difficulties encountered due to 'knowledge explosion' and interdisciplinary subject matter led to the formation of new methods and the construction of both general and specific schemes, which emancipated book classification from the strict genus to species relation produced by following the rules of logical division. The new methods are based upon an analytical approach which seeks to recognize the basic facets, or categories, produced by the application of characteristics of division to each subject field, and to provide for the combination of concepts from these categories in such a way that any subject may be specified; it is, therefore, possible to classify accurately, through the use of a faceted scheme the micro documents.

Both the older and newer schemes of library classification have much in common in that, for instance, both rely on the application of characteristics of division to a subject field and both recognize the supreme importance of finding out the most important characteristics for the purposes of a helpful order. Yet, they have a great gulf of difference.

Analytico-Synthetic Classification

Faceted Classification: The new methods are chiefly associated with the name of Dr. S.R. Ranganathan, the doyen of Indian librarianship, and many of them were put forward, in a tentative form, in his Colon Classification, which first appeared in 1933 (now in its 6th edition). Dr. Ranganathan stressed that classification should be entirely synthetic. Instead to attempting to list all subjects like an enumerative scheme book classification, he argued, should merely enumerate basic concepts, arranging these in appropriate categories or facets (each facet of any subject being a manifestation of *Five Fundamental Category*). Every subject will consist of the amalgamation of a number of these concepts. In Colon Classification, for example, in the class Medicine two groups of terms are first formed before starting the subdivision, viz. 'organ' (e.g. morphology, physiology, disease, hygiene). Other groups of terms also were introduced to express 'symptoms' of disease (e.g. fever, inflammation), its 'agents'.

The Colon Classification, by dividing its terms into categories or facets, and making notational provision for linking facets together, was able to bring together terms in a co-ordinate relationship to designate a complex idea', as Taube puts it.

Colon scheme of classification is faceted and the core of a faceted classification is a series of schedules in which the terms encountered in a given field of knowledge are grouped into distinct categories. In order to form compound subjects, terms form two or more categories are combined. However, the construction of schedules for a bibliographical classification involves a good deal more than a simple sorting of terms into categories.

A faceted scheme differs from a completely enumerative classification in that while the latter would try to provide the classifier with a complete class-mark for a subject, a completely synthetic or faceted scheme would instruct the classifier to break down the subject into its component parts and then to build the required class mark by linking together the parts.

Facets and Foci. The classificationist, in making such a synthetic scheme would need to survey the literature of each subject field and to divide it up according to different characteristics. In any class, the total division arising from the application of a single characteristic constitutes one facet. The individual units of each facet, isolated by the dividing process, are described as *foci* or *isolates*. Dr. Ranganathan found these concepts ('Facets' and 'Focus') and the terms in which they are expressed to be more elegant than the traditional "Train of characteristics' and 'part of the class number corresponding to a single train of characteristic'.

Steps of Designing Modern Classification

C. D. Needham in his 'Organizing knowledge in libraries' mentions seven stages in the making of a modern classification scheme for a particular subject. These are as follows:

Analysis

"The first job of a maker of subject classification scheme will be to examine a representative sample of documents in that subject, covering all topics within the subject and all levels—such as could be found in a bibliography of the subject—listing concepts as they arise. In this way all simple concepts will be discovered and they will be concepts actually arising in documents—they will have *literary warrant*. Concepts in this un-organized state are often called *isolates*."

Creation of Facets

"The isolates are then grouped according to proximate relations. The sum total of isolates formed by the division of a subject by one characteristic of division is called a facet. Facet should be mutually exclusive, i.e., based on only one characteristic of division. The individual units of each facet, isolated by the dividing process, are described as foci which should be exhaustive according to the literary warrant. In other words, all foci should be listed and there should be room for expansion as new foci arise."

Arrangement of Co-ordinate Divisions

Deciding on the Combination Order of Facets: Needham discusses that the scheme will consist of simple concepts which will have to be combined or synthesized to accommodate the complex subjects found in documents. "A combination order (or citation order as it is sometimes called) must therefore be laid down, i.e., a combination order of facets. Without this documents on the same subject may be classed at different places." Needham cites the example Sixteenth-century English literature and remarks that a person classifying such a document may, unless he is given an indication of combination order, place it in the Period facet of the Language facet. The knowledge as to the combination order (first, language, second, period, in this case) is very important, for it determines the extent of collocation. The best combination order for a subject will depend to some extent on the needs of users. In the field of literature, for example, 'students normally confine their studies to the Literature for a particular language, rather than Period or Form, hence language should take precedence in the combination order for compounds; within a particular language they normally study Period rather than Form and therefore the combination order should be Language—Period—Form.

Arrangement of Facets in the Scheme: Schedule Order

"The final decision before the notation is added is the relative order of the facets in the scheme itself." It is traditional for 'general' to precede 'special'. Needham observes "If we wish to achieve the order of increasing speciality, then the order of facets in the scheme must be reverse of the combination order. For example, if the combination order in Education is Grade—Subject, then the schedule order must be Subject—Grade." (Some recent schemes have however, abandoned the order of increasing speciality.

Steps in the Construction of a Faceted Scheme

The construction of modern schedules for a bibliographical classification involves a good deal more than a single sorting of terms into categories. Vickery analyses the steps admirably in his 'Classification and indexing in science'.

The first problem is that of delimiting a field of knowledge. In science and technology it appears more helpful to build each field of knowledge around a 'thing'—a natural substance or organism, a man-made product or human idea.

"All the substances are either simple chemical elements or compounds of such elements, so subjects in documents are either simple concepts or compounds of such concepts." (Needham). For example, Influence of English Literature on Bengali short story; Hindi drama etc.

Analysis of Subject: Each kind of 'thing' or substance has connected with it a series of other categories – groups of terms with which it is regularly associated in compound subjects found in literature. The categories applicable in each particular field of science must be listed. The second step in constructing a faceted classification is to collect all such terms and to group them into categories. Certain categories may occur in more than one field of knowledge.

Some examples of categories useful in science and technology may be given thus: Substance, state, property, reaction, operation, device, organ, agent, handling, apparatus, process, and so on. Attempts have been made to draw up a comprehensive list of 'fundamental' categories which are applicable to any field of knowledge. Ranganathan, for example, recognizes only five fundamental categories : Personality, Matter, Energy, Space and Time (PMEST).

After completing the 'analytical' side of the classification work – analysing the subjects encountered in literature into their constituent terms and categories we may turn to the 'Synthetic' side.

Synthesis: In synthesizing we must identify and display the relations between the terms and between categories.

Synthesis refers to the creation of compound subjects by combining simple elements. Number-building refers specifically to notational aspects.

Grouping in a Helpful Order: The third step is to group the terms within each category of a field of knowledge in a helpful order – an order which will display both generic relations between the terms and other relations between the collateral species of each particular genus.

Establishing Relation Between Categories: The fourth operation is to establish relations between categories. Partically this involves establishing, for each field of knowledge, the most logical and helpful order in which the categories should be combined into a compound subject.

These two operations complete the establishment of the relations existing between concepts, between the 'entities' or terms of a classification—the central theoretical problem of classification.

These relations, again, are to be displayed in as effective and as simple a way as possible.

Establishing a Standard Order for Citing Terms: The sorting of terms into categories is undertaken in order to elucidate the relations between terms. The grouping of terms into facets helps us to establish unequivocally a standard order for citing terms in a compound subject.

We may note here that a faceted scheme can achieve a helpful order in chain by applying first of all the characteristic which produces the most concrete of the facets and by subordinating the more abstract facets to it in the order of decreasing concreteness.

Hospitality in Chain and Array can be successfully achieved in a faceted scheme. Hospitality in chain is, in the world of Mills, 'the simultaneous specification of all the facets of a subject, if necessary, and the ability to specify new facets in their correct sequence.

In a faceted classification all possible compounds are specifiable. The notation maintains the preferred order and, as such, foci from all facets are specifiable simultaneously and in correct sequence. Every facet is qualifiable by all less concrete facets. Any compound made up simultaneously of foci from each facet is specifiable in the order required by the facet formula.

Order within each Hierarchy

Helpful Order and Consistent Sequence

In the preceding chapter we have discussed that older classificationists, influenced by the principles of philosophical classification laid great stress on the importance of *main class* in a scheme of book classification and on the need to arrive at a satisfactory *main class order*. Cutter and Brown, for example, attempt to explain the principles behind the order which they selected for the main classes of their respective schemes. Modern classificationists, however, concentrate rather less on the notion of main classes and give more time to the question of achieving a *helpful order* or arrangement within each class, though the order of arrangement of the main disciplines is not unimportant.

In this chapter we are to discuss how the sub-classes or groups of subjects or even specific subjects into which the main class is divided can be marked in a helpful order. Each group itself it a fresh 'universe' which can be divided by another characteristic. Successive division by a train of characteristics results in a chain of classes. In determining the most helpful by the concept of chain and array. 'A chain', in the words of Mills, 'is a line or lines of classes which moves, step by step, from a general subject to a specific one'.

'Helpful order', explain Palmer and Wells, 'displays subjects in such a way that a person approaching a group of subjects at any point is led by the order itself to the specific subject he needs.' Very few readers think in terms of specific subject, but in terms of more general subjects which comprise the specific subject sought; for example, a reader actually requiring a book on 'personnel administration' may request for a book on 'business administration' or 'commerce'. Again, readers may require related materials in most cases in pursuit of their specific subject of study or research. Specific subjects should, therefore, be accurately defined and an order should be established in the classification of library materials so that it may lead to the specific subject sought, no matter what the point of approach is. This order demands a system which arranges subjects in an order of *decreasing extension*, so that the general subject, which may include material on the specific subject, is followed by the specific subject itself. Specificity of subject is, however, relative.

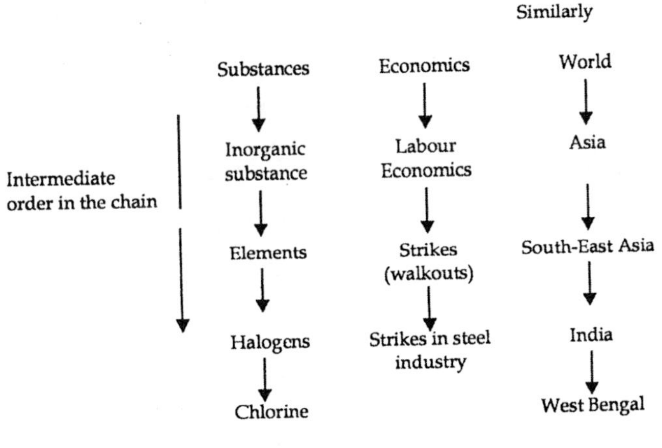

Figure 4.1. Order of subjects in decreasing extension

Dr. Ranganathan formulates two canons for the chain of classes, viz. Canon of Decreasing Extension, and Canon of Modulation. "While moving down a classification, its first link to its last link, the intension of the classes should increase, and the extension of the classes should decrease. This is the canon of Decreasing Extension.'

Each chain of classes should be suitably modulated, so that no links are omitted. Dr Ranganathan's Canon of Modulation states, "A chain of classes should comprise one class of each and every order that lies between the orders of the first link and the last link of the chain." Ultimately modulation depends on (a) the relevant characteristics allowed in a train of characteristics and (b) the sequence of application of those characteristics.

Dr. Ranganathan defines the specific subject of a book as 'that division of knowledge whose extension and intension are equal to those of its thought content.' We have earlier defined what is extension (denotation) and what is intension (connotation) of a subject. In earlier chapters we have also discussed that any given hierarchy consists of terms of increasing intension derived from the summum genus by the application of a succession of consistent characteristics of division. In fact, as Sayers states in a formal way 'Classification should proceed from terms of great extension and small intension to terms of great intension and small extension.'

"An array is a row of topics of foci which are co-ordinate in importance, or of equal rank." Thus in Law the first order of array may be Internationa Law, Constitutional Law, Criminal Law, Martial Law, Private Law, Church Law and so on. In Mathematics, the first order of array may be Arithmetic, Algebra, Analysis, Trigonometry, Geometry, Mechanics, Potentials, Astronomy.

Schematic Chart of Chain and Array

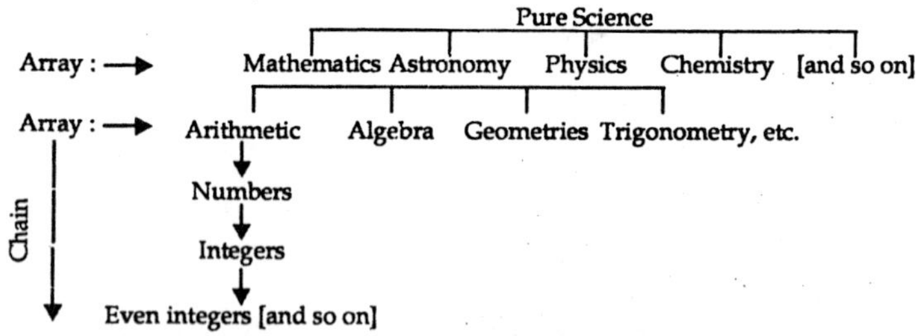

Figure 4.2. Derived Classes in Array

It may be noted that the derived classes in an array should be *mutually exclusive* and *collectively exhaustive.*

The helpful and consistent sequences in an array are discussed in the next sub-section.

Bliss holds that the order for any subject which should be most useful to readers is to put the general works first, followed by works on general subjects treated specially, then by works on special subjects treated generally, and lastly, by works on special subjects treated specially. Examples may make this clear:

1. The general treated generally ...A text book on Medicine
2. The general treated specially . . . Medicine : its surgical aspects
3. The special treated generally ... The stomach : a general handbook
4. The special treated specially . . . Surgery of the stomach

It is clear from the above example that the most helpful order for any subject which leads to the specific subject sought and gives an overall picture of the ramifications of the subjects demands a system of classification which arranges the subjects in an order of decreasing extension. The general principle followed here is that while arranging books according to subjects we give names to the groups into which we divide them for convenient reference. These names are called *terms of classification,* by which we call the classes, divisions and sections.

We must remember in this connection that in approaching knowledge a workable system of book classification should display the entire field of knowledge or of a subject with such clarity that one may see their subjects in their relative values, their extent, varying, aspects, interrelations, sequence and gradations. Its divisions and subdivisions should be inclusive. Further it should be flexible so that new subjects may be added in relation to subjects already in the schedule. In order words, hospitality in chain and hospitality in array should be secured.

Arrangement of Co-ordinate Divisions

We next proceed to discuss about the most useful order among the series of co-ordinate classes formed by the terms in each array.

We have already discussed the first of the two steps in the arrangement of library – the breaking down of a class into a number of co-ordinate divisions by the consistent application of a characteristic of division. We have also discussed about the helpful order of the subclasses or groups of subject.

The choice of order among the series of co-ordinate species (derived from a genus), formed by the terms in each array will be dictated by the nature of the subject matter. Dr. Richardson and Dr. S. R. Ranganathan have, however, put forward certain general possibilities.

Dr. Richardson has listed nine possible orders : (1) Logical – form the complex to the simplest; (2) Geometrical – according to the position of things in space; (3) Chronological – according to the position in time; (4) Genetic – according to likeness in origin; (5) Historical – a combination of many of the preceding characteristics; (6) Evolutionary – from simple to complex; (7) Dynamic – order of power; (8) Alphabetical; (9) Mathematical – order by means of a notation.

Dr. Ranganathan has used different terms for the second, third and ninth of the above orders listed by Richardson, and he has added (10) Decreasing extension and (11) Increasing concreteness. In his Elements of Library Classification Dr. Ranganathan has formulated his principles ('Canons', as he calls them) in simple language. He calls the chronological principle as 'Principle of later in time', which provides that, 'if one of the two classes belongs to an earlier point of time than the other, then that one must have precedence over the other'. Dr. Ranganathan also recommends 'Geometrical principle' which he terms 'The principle of special contiguity'. It provides for the arrangement of a number of geographical areas, not lying within one another, in accordance with their contiguity. For example, Austria, France and Italy can be arranged in order of their position in space thus : France, Italy, Austria : or Austria, Italy, France.

The evolutionary order may be illustrated by the groups of Biological organisms in 'Soil Science', e.g. Bacteria, Fungi, Actinomycetes, Algae, Protozoa, Fauna, etc., and the Chronological order by the operation facet of 'Soil Science', e.g. Survey, Reclamation, Drainage, Terracing, Irrigation, etc. In his examples of helpful order for 'Education' Dr. Ranganathan gives precedence to Elementry

Education to Secondary Education on grounds that it belongs to an earlier stage of educational evolution.

Dr. Ranganathan's Canon of Decreasing Extension which applies to the arrangement in chain particularly, lays down that of two classes that of greater extension (or, denotation) will have precedence over the other of less extension; For example, 'Botony' will have precedence over 'Flowering plants', for it includes the latter.

The Principle of increasing Concreteness (mainly applicable in the arrangement in chain) laid down by Dr. Ranganathan provides that the less concrete (i.e., more abstract) of two classes of different degree of concreteness will have precedence over the other'. We quote from Dr. Ranganathan for examples:

"Education

Curriculum

Mathematical Curriculum

. . . .

Mathematical Curriculum for secondary schools."

In place of Richardson's 'Mathematical principle' Dr. Ranganathan formulates the 'Principle of Cononical Sequence', which, in his own words, can he stated thus : "When no other principle is available to assist in finding a helpful sequence among a set of given classes, any traditional or Conventional or Canonical sequence may be adopted".

Dr. Ranganathan formulates another principle, which he calls 'Canon of Consistent Sequence'. The Canon states "When the same categories occur explicitly or implicitly in different places they must be arranged in the same sequence in all the places". In other words, 'whenever similar classes occur in different arrays, their sequences should be parallel in all such arrays, whenever insistence on such a parallel does not run counter to other more important requirements' -(Prolegomena). As example, Dr. Ranganathan mentions the legal systems of different religious communities. By following the Canon of Consistent Sequence the legal systems of different religions can be arranged as the religions themselves. If the major religions are arranged chronologically thus: Hinduism, Judaism, Christianity, Mohammedanism, the corresponding legal system should be arranged in the following sequence: Hindu Law; Jewish Law; Christian Law, Muslim Law.

He has also formulated the Principle of Increasing Complexity.

Any of the above orders which proves to be the most useful for the particular array may be chosen, and must be mechanized by notation so that it shall be consistently followed.

5

Universal Decimal Classification

Overview

The new scheme entitled Manuel du Repertoire Bibliographique Universel was published in 1905. It was a colossal work of some 2000 pages, published in parts from 1899 to 1905. The Manuel was the first complete international edition of the UDC. It was so called because it provided the basic classification schedules for the great card subject-index (the Universal Bibliography) then being compiled in Brussels. It is also because of this that the UDC is sometimes called the System of the Brussels Institute.

Since 1905 several versions of the UDC have appeared: 2nd edition (also in French) during 1927-33; 3rd edition (in German) during 1933-53. The 4th edition (in English) was started in 1936 but is still not completed. An abridged English version, however, was issued in 1948, which has gone into its 3rd edition in 1961. the abridged edition is also available in French and German.

Three other full editions are in progress: the 5th edition (French) 1939, the 6th edition (Japanese) 1950, and the 7th edition (Spanish) 1955.

The IIB changed its name in 1931 into institute International de Documentation and in 1938 it became a federation, with membership of national bodies, and assumed its present name: Federation International de Documentation (FID). Its seat is now in The Hague, and there is a full-time Secretary General.

After the first World War the FID became responsible for the central organization of the UDC, and various national bodies have assumed responsibility for their own edition.

Principles

The principles underlying the UDC are (a) to follow the general pattern of the DC schedules, i.e. the division of the whole human knowledge into ten main branches, each further subdivided decimally to the required degree, (b) to retain the use of the decimally conceived numerals and (c) to introduce numerous synthetic devices-an auxiliary apparatus of connection and relation signs, lacking in the DC, whereby all types of compound subjects can be represented through combination of symbols.

The last principle has justified the epithet Universal. As has been said in the 'Introduction' to the abridged edition, "It is a Universal Classification in that an attempt is made to include in it every field of knowledge, not as a patch-work of isolated, self-sufficient specialist groupings, but as an integral pattern of correlated subjects. This universality at the conceptual level is supported by notational devices, which permit the linking of simple main numbers (for simple ideas) either with other main numbers or with auxiliaries denoting Place, Time, and similar commonly recurring Categories — in each case forming combined or compound numbers". The universality also lies in the fact that the UDC removes the occasional American and European bias found in the DC.

Another modification of the DC is that whilst the UDC like the DC is a general classification, not a composite of special classifications, teh UDC makes distinct provision, through its Points-of-vie devices, for a mechanism whereby the structure of the general scheme may be adjusted to the needs of a special classification.

DESIGN

Collocation

The basic outline is that of the DC. Therefore, the weakness in the collocation of subjects as obtained in the DC is found to a large extent in the UDC. For example, Economics, Commerce and Business are separated; so are Language and Literature, although through notational device, as will be seen later, these subjects can be brought together.

The UDC, however, modifies parts of the DC's original outline. In Philosophy, for example, there is no clash between the topics placed in the DC at 40 (School of Philosophy) and at 180/190 (Individual Philosophers); class 140 is reserved strictly for Philosophic Systems, while Philosophers are arranged in one alphabetical sequence at 190. again, class 159.9 psychology replaces the separate classes 130 and 150 of the DC. Class 9: History shows a distinct modification and marked improvements. In the DC the order is: Would history-Periods of world history-Travel and Geography-Biography-Ancient history-Modern history. In the UDC the sequence is:

The Homeland (comprehensive studies of any country)	908
Geography and Travel	91
Biography	92
History	93
World	930.9
Ancient	931
Medieval and modern	94/99

Evidently the UDC collocation is more helpful.

Adjustments

The improvement upon the DC as seen in the UDC is that some adjustments have been made to endow the modified system with features of a faceted scheme. The inflexible structure of the DC makes it difficult to connect closely related concepts or aspects of a subject. The UDC makes this connection possible. The basic defect of the DC—enumeration of compounds, is removed to a great extent and consequently the size of the schedule is reduced, so much so that the abridged English edition, consisting of some 250 pages can replace the two big volumes of the DC (16th ed.)

The adjustments consist in separating tables of recurrent and generally subordinate concepts, such as Form. Time, Place, Language, Point of view, and providing distinctive symbol other than numerals to represent each of the concepts.

The adjustments are but synthetic devices greatly enhancing the number-building capacity of the original DC. The Common Auxiliaries (series of divisions recurrent throughout the whole field of knowledge) are clearly an extension of the idea underlying the DC's Form and Geographic divisions. The Special Auxiliaries are an extension of the DC's idea of subdivisions recurrent within a particular subject, e.g. the linguistic divisions under each language.

Schedules

The UDC, therefore, consists of two categories of schedules: (a) the main tables in which are set out the main classes 1 to 9 and the various series of special auxiliaries; (b) the Auxiliary tables in which are set out the common auxiliaries and connecting symbols.

Auxiliaries: Common

The following are the categories of common auxiliaries. Each category has its distinctive notation, so that it becomes clear which category is combining with the main subject.

(i) Addition and Consecutive extension, represented by + (plus) and / (stroke) signs respectively. The + sign is used to designed two or more co-ordinate topics whose UDC numbers are not consecutive. For example, 622 + 669 Mining and Metallurgy; 655.1 + 686.1 Paper manufacture, Printing and Bookbinding.

The / stroke sign called "to" is used when some consecutive UDC numbers imply a broad subject or an aggregate of subjects. For example, 592/599 systematic zoology; 22/38 Christian religion.

The + and / signs thus connect commonly associated concepts or a range of concepts for which the UDC does not provide a single comprehensive number.

(ii) Relation, represented by: (colon) or by [ ] square brackets. Any two or more concepts, otherwise separately listed in the schedules, may come together into some relationship other than mere co-ordination: Colon is the device to link such concepts. Examples: 63:31 Agricultural statistics; 338:62 Economics of the Engineering industry. Highly specialized compounds can be synthesized by the use of ":". For example, Science in the curriculum of secondary schools 373.5: 371.214:5 (373.5 is Secondary schools, 371.214 is Curriculum, and 5 is Science).

Colon may be replaced by [ ] square brackets, when the second class number signifies a subordinate concept. For example, to represent 'Office Organisation is Banks' we may use [ ], if the concept 'Banks' is subordinated to the concept 'Office Organisation' ; the number will be 651 [332.1].

(iii) Language, represented by = equals. This category of auxiliaries is used to specify the language in which a subject dealt with in a book is written. The = equals signs may be interpreted as 'written in'. After this sign the language scheduled will provide the number for individual language. For example, Library administration written in the German language: 025.4 = 30 (30 has come from 430 German language).

Polyglot or multi-lingual is represented by = 00; e.g. Polyglot Bible: 22=00.

The original language and the language of translation are specified in this way-Aristotle's Politics, in German: 321.01 = 75 = 30.

(iv) Form, represented by (0) called 'Brackets 0'. The table of Form auxiliaries corresponds with the table of form divisions of the DC, with the striking feature that the two inner forms 'Theory and philosophy' and 'Study and teaching' are excluded, which, however, can be specified by a : colon added to 1 and 37 respectively.

It may also be noted that using: colon with the Form facet indicator, complex concepts of form can be represented. For example, Socialism, treated in the form of a novel in English: 335 (0 : 820-3).

(v) Place, represented by ( ) brackets. From this table of auxiliaries we get the numbers for places corresponding to the DC's 'Divide like 930-999'. Thus, 385 (54) is Indian railways.

(100) is world, e.g. 342.4 (100) Constitutions of the world.

(-0) indicates zone, e.g. (-04) Frontiers, so Defence operations on Indian frontiers is 355.45 (54.04).

(-1) indicates Orientation, points of compass, e.g. South India: (54-13).

(-2 to -5) indicates political, administrative units, areas etc., e.g. Rural India (54-202), British colonies (42-5).

(-6) indicates groupings of independent states; alliances, etc.

(-7) Spheres for private and (semi) public enterprise, e.g. (-77) Underdeveloped areas.

(-8) Source and destination.

(2) indicates places characterized by physical features, divisions being derived from the class 55. 'For example, (212) Temperate regions, (22) Islands. With a : colon any number of this facet may be related to a country; thus (22:4) is Islands of Europe.

(vi) Race and Nationality, represented by (=), called 'Brackets equals'. This auxiliaries of this table serve to signify ethnological relationship, or racial aspect. These are based on the common auxiliaries of language. For example 784.4 (=4) Folk songs of the French people; (71=4) French Canada.

(vii) Time, represented by " " inverted commas. By this category of auxiliaries the UDC seeks to specify all facets of time.

Years, months and days are represented by simple numerical statement in the sequence of year, month and date; e.g. "1970. o4. 02" and "1970. 10. 29" are respectively 2nd April 1970 and 29th October 1970.

Single years are represented by 4 figures. Thus, "1970" is 1970, "0820" is A. D. 820, "0058" is A. D. and "0005" is A. D. 5.

Decades are represented by 3 figures. Thus, "197" is the nineteen seventies, "085" is the 850's.

Centuries are represented by 2 figures. Thus, "19" is 20th century, "05" is the 6th century A. D.

Dates before the birth of Christ are represented by figures with a -hyphen preceding them. For example, is 34 B. C. "-034" is 340's B. C., "-04" is the 5th Century B. C.

Besides dates, the Time auxiliaries also specify other aspects of time, such as ages, past, future, seasons, months of the year, durations and intervals, phenomenological divisions. Examples:

"04/14" Middle ages.

"313" Future-Future of Library Science 02 "313".

"321" Spring-Springtime flowers 635.9"321".

"33.04" April-April rains 551.578 "33.04".

"403" Short-term-Short-term examinations 371.27"403".

(viii) Alphabetical and (non-decimal) numerical sub-division. This auxiliary is to specify individual members of a class.

The appropriate names or initials (in brackets, if desired) and/ or numerals are to be added. To individualise by numerals alone, the symbol 'No'. has to be prefixed.

For example, 92 (Wells) or 92 Wells or 92W: Bibliography of Well; 820 (Shak) Shakespeare's works.

06.3 AIG A conference, the initials of which are AIG.

625.711 (42) A4 The Great West Road of England known as A4.

656.4.02 (541.2) No. 34 Calcutta Tram Services Route No. 34.

Auxiliaries: Special

Special auxiliaries are represented by-hyphen, .0 point noght, and ' apostrophe. These auxiliaries serve to signify analytical subdivisions of some special classes, particularly in the fields of science and technology. Of these, the auxiliaries with the - hyphen as the symbol or facet indicator, are the most widely applicable. Under 621, -1/9 are auxiliaries denoting machinery details:

621-1 General characteristics.

621-2 Fixed and moving parts.

621-3 Valve gear parts; valve motion.

621-4 Form and shape of products.

621-5 Operation, control and regulation.

621-6 Machinery, plant according to fuel used.

621-7 Servicing, maintenance, etc.

621-8 Machinery, plant or apparatus according to motive force or power.

These auxiliaries are extensively applied in all sections of 6 (other than 61).

In the fields dealing with the arts and humanities, .0 numbers are used in a much greater degree. For example, .01 aesthetics may be applied to a number of classes, and hence.

7.01 Art aesthetics.

72.01 Architectural aesthetics.

78.01 Musical aesthetics.

8.01 Literary aesthetics.

With 8 Literature, .07 is used to bring Literature and Language together. Therefore, 8.07 is Linguistics. This special subdivision is applicable to any specific literature to get the specific language. Thus, 820 is English literature, 820.07 is English language, which, again, may be further subdivided as 41. for example, 820.07-5 English grammar; 891.44.07-5 Bengal grammar.

The ' apostrophe is however, not analytical but synthetic in function. Its use is clearly seen in class 546 Inorganic chemistry, and 547 Organic chemistry. Organic and inorganic compounds are synthetically represented with the help of ' apostrophe, and these are not enumerated in the schedules. For example,

546.12 Halogens.

546.33 Sodium.

546.34 546.33'12 Sodium-Halogen compounds.

Again,

547.29 Carboxylic acid.

547.26 Alcohol and their esters.

547.29'26 Carboxylic-acid esters.

NOTATION

Structure

The UDC, notation follows the fundamental structure of the DC, having retained the use of decimally conceived Arabic numerals. But the three-figure base is dropped, and the zero (0) has been given ordinal value. Thus 1 is Philosophy, 16 Logic, 8 Literature, 82 Western literatures (European literature), 820 literature.

When numerical figures, without any auxiliary notation intervening, are more than three in number, a point is inserted after every third place. This is just a convention serving as a visual aid. Thus,

6	Technology.
62	Engineering.
621	Mechanical and Electrical engineering.
621.3	Electrical engineering.
621.316	Distribution and Control of power supply.
621.316.923	Fuse.

Brevity and Simplicity

Brevity is affected by the same factors as in the DC. Simplicity is affected by the use of the auxiliary symbols. When close classification is attempted, numbers often become long and cumbersome. For example,

333.1:331.762 (=96) [677] (73) "183" Wages of Negro unskilled labour in textile industries in the US during 1830's. But in a general library such complex number may only be occasionally necessary to be built. In practice it will be found that normally the use of more than one auxiliary is not necessary. Usually colon linkage and the auxiliaries denoted by ( ) brackets will suffice.

The length of the notation is a big disadvantage in applying the UDC to a specific subject field. The narrow base from which the notation is derived causes the formation of lengthy class numbers. Frequently the number of a particular discipline is in three figures before any subdivision is introduced.

Hospitality in Array and Chain

As in the DC, the decimal device provides for infinite hospitality to both array and chain divisions of the UDC. The alphabetical and non-decimal numerical devices also greatly contribute to the hospitality in array. Also, the symbol zero is made available to specify a division, and thereby to extend an array by one class. For example, 94 Medieval and Modern history, 940 European history : 82 European literature, 820 English literature.

Hospitality to Compounds

As has already been shown, the UDC provides for hospitality to compounds through the Common and Special Auxiliaries. The Auxiliaries have given the UDC such a power of synthesis, or number-building capacity that almost any compound subject can be notationally represented.

Hospitality to Alternative (Flexibility)

The notation is highly flexible, and because of this virtue it makes it possible for material to be arranged in the way that suits the individual library more readily than the notation of a more rigid scheme of classification. No fixed citation order governs the facets (the Auxiliaries) within a subject field. So Librarians can orientate the scheme to their own need. For example, a library specializing in area studies, may cite the place facet first, then period, then subdivide by the whole classification, or such parts of it as are required. For example, (492)347.77 Netherlands, Patent law. Again, while the order of division in the class Literature in the DC can only be: Literature—Language—Form—Period—Author (e.g. 822.33), in the UDC it can be varied. Thus, 920-2 "1558/1625" (Shakespeare) or 820"155" (Shakespeare) or 820 (Shakespeare) or even 8-2=20 (Shakespeare).

The flexibility of the UDC notation admits of **intercalation.** In subjects like Social Sciences and Fine Arts the application of Place, Time and Race or Nationality auxiliaries (i.e. facets) is very frequent and important. It is often desirable that in these fields we have intercalation, that is, the citation of Place, Time or Race in a part of the full subject-matter other than the extreme end of it. Thus, 338 (42)5 Prices in England, instead of 338.5 (42); 785"18"7 19th century Chamber music, instead of 787.7"18".

Through intercalation, different parts of an aspect of a place or period or nationality can be brought together. The following will exemplify the process.

The main schedule of 33 gives:

338 Economic situation.
338.4 Forms of production.
338.5 Price and value.
338.51 Demand and supply.
338.6 Corporative organization.
338.7 Industrial federation.
338.8 Monopolies.

Now if we want to have together the various aspects of the Economic situation in England, we make it possible through intercalation of the place auxiliary between 338 and its subdivisions. Thus,

338 (42) Economic situation in England
338 (42)4 Economic situation in forms of production
338 (42)5 Economic situation in prices
338(42)51 Economic situation in demand and supply
338(42)6 Economic situation in corporative organization
338(42)7 Economic situation in industrial federation
338(42)8 Economic situation in monopolies.

Mnemonics

Besides the mnemonics obtained as a legacy of the DC, the number-building devices of the UDC have afforded further mnemonics on a large scale. Common Auxiliary divisions form mnemonic schedules for the whole of the main classification, and the Special Auxiliary divisions are mnemonic within the sections to which they apply.

Index

The abridged English edition of the UDC, which is the basis of our discussion, contains an index to the terms used in the schedules. The index is relative, but constructed with much economy, which is not a feature of the DC's index. The following is an instance in point:

Acoustics 534 cf. Vibrations

Architectural	534.84
Physiological	534.7, 612.85
Technical	681.8 cf. Broadcasting

Use and Revision

The UDC is widely used throughout the countries of western hemisphere and is very popular in eastern Europe. In India it is used in quite a number of libraries.

The authority on general UDC policy and development is the International Committee on Universal Classification, of which the Central Classification Committee is a part responsible for day-to-day control and supervision. Revision is based on a policy of compromise: to make the classification better for established users and more attractive to non-users, to reduce confusions and shortcomings and to incorporate new concepts without greatly disturbing the schedules.

A recent proposal for revision is to make compulsory the combination of Class 4 Linguistics with Class 8 literature (by the use of the special auxiliary .07, as shown earlier). The vacated Class 4 is to be used to accommodate the comprehensive subject fields which have grown lately and have a bearing upon science and technology.

6

Decimal Classification

Overview

The Decimal Classification scheme was first published in 1876. It was devised by Melvi Dewey (1851-1931) who was then Assistant College Librarian in Amherst College, New York, and was aged only twenty-five years.

Dewey (full name: Melville Louis Kossuth Dewey) is famous not only as the father of modern library classification, but also as the father of the library movement in the USA. He was a wonderful personality of his days. He founded in 1876 the Spelling Reform Association, the Metric Bureau, the American Library Association, and the Library Journal. He was one of the leaders in starting the Library Association, London (1877), the Readers and Writers Company (1879) and the Library Bureau (1882).

The first edition of the DC was a slim volume of 42 pages, consisting of 12 pages of introductory matter, 12 pages of tables and 18 pages of index. The tables enumerate 1000 subjects. The index contained 2600 entries.

Subsequent editions have been the product of constant revision and expansion. The 14th edition, published in 1942, was the 'fullest'. The 15th edition (1951) was a drastic revision and virtually an abridged edition. In the drastic revision and virtually an abridged edition. In the 16th and 17th editions (1958 and 1965 respectively) expansion was effected, though both the editions have been still shorter than the 14th edition. Both the editions are in two volumes, one containing the main schedules, the other containing the index and some auxiliary tables.

Principles

The DC is enumerative in character. It is based on the principle of hierarchy, on the relationship between the general and the specific. As Dewey has said, the Tables of Classification have been "so mapped out as to show in 4 ways—i.e. by size of type, face of type, indention, and number of figures prefixed—each subject's rank in the Classification."

Though Dewey has propped his hierarchical scheme on the traditional philosophic system, his aim has been to make it practical and never rigidly theoretical. "Everywhere philosophic theory and accuracy have yielded to practical usefulness. The impossibility of making a satisfactory classification of knowledge as preserved in books, has been appreciated from the first, and theoretic harmony and exactness have been repeatedly sacrificed to practical requirements."

For practical usefulness what Dewey has sought is "to find a method that would class, arrange and index books and pamphlets on shelves, cards of a catalogue, clippings and notes in scrapbooks and index rerums, references to all these items, and indeed any literary material in any form, as readily as an ordinary index guides to proper page of a bound book."

Structure

Historically, the DC is based on the classification scheme devised by W. T. Harris for the Public School Library of St. Louis in 1870. The outline of Harris' scheme is:

Science

- Philosophy
- Religion
- Social and Political Science
- Natural Science and Useful Arts

Art

- Fine Arts

Poetry
Pure Fiction
Literary Miscellany

History

Geography and Travel
Civil History
Biography

Appendix

Miscellany

The DC outline is:

- General Works (Including Bibliography, Library Science, Museums, Journalism)
- Philosophy (Including Psychology)
- Social Sciences (Including Statistics and Customs)
- Philology
- Pure Science
- Applied Science (Including Medicine, Agriculture, Business and Industry)
- Fine Arts, Recreations (Including Architecture, Photography and Music)
- Literature
- History (Including Geography and Biography)

The close relationship between the outlines is evident. Harris was indebted to Francis Bacon for dividing the Universe of Knowledge into three broad classes: Science, Art and History. Bacon said, "The sense, which is the door of the intellect, is affected by individual objects only. The images of these individuals – that is, the impressions received by the sense are fixed in the memory, and pass into it, in the first instance, entire, as it were, just as they occur. These the human mind proceeds to review and ruminate on; and, thereupon, either simply rehearses them, or makes fanciful imitations of them, or analyses and classifies them. Therefore, from these three fountains – Memory, Imagination, and Reason-flow these three emanations – History, Poesy, and Philosophy, and there can be no others". Harries took this order – History, Poesy, and Philosophy.

Schedules

Our study will be limited to the 16th edition of the DC. Volume 1 contains Editor's introduction and Melvil Dewey's introduction, which should be read carefully. After these introductions the Tables or Schedules are enumerated. The basic pattern is presented in three summaries. The first summary shows the ten classes, the second one hundred divisions, and the third approximately one thousand sections. Then follows the table of Form divisions. After these are full classification tables are presented.

In Volume 2 there are, besides the Relative index with its explanation, a table of 'geographic divisions', special author table for William Shakespeare, a table for college and university publications, and finally the 'obsolescent schedules' of inorganic and organic chemistry.

Collocation of Subjects

A proper organization of knowledge entails a sounds collocations of subjects. The main classes in DC have limited collocation, that is, they are in an order in which some subjects do not have the expected relative positions. Philology and Literature should have been side by side; instead, they are widely separated. So is the case with Sociology and History, and with Philosophy and Science. Bliss has rightly said that the separation of Science from Philosophy "is neither philosophic nor scientific, nor historical nor practical. General Science as generalized, is almost indistinguishable from Philosophy, somewhat as the philosophy of society is inseparable from the science of society, for it should be based on it." (The Organisation of Knowledge in Libraries, 2nd ed., 1930, p. 203).

Collocation suffers not only in the lay-out of the main classes but also in any one class. In class 300 the order of subjects is very unsatisfactory, related topics having been separated. As for example, Sociology at 301 is cut off from Social Welfare at 360, and Social Anthropology at 390. Similarly, Economics at 330 Public Service at 380 and Business at 650,—all containing closely allied material,—are at different places. Between Private Finance at 332 and at different places. Between Private Finance at 332 and Public Finance at 336 are placed Land-economics (333) and Co-operative (334) and Economic Ideologies (335), subjects with little bearing on the practical aspects of finance. Industry at 338 is separated from Labour at 331, and from Management at 658.

Again, World Was are placed under European History. World History at 909 is separated from the history of individual countries by Geography (910) and Biography (920). Subjects related to Ancient History (930), such as Ethnology (572) and the Geography of the ancient world, including Pre-historic Archaeology (913), are scattered.

Method of Division

The universe of books, according to the DC, is divided into ten classes, each class into ten divisions, each division into ten sections, and each section into ten sub-sections, and so on. The 'tens' are represented by Arabic numbers from 0 to 9. Classes numbered 1 to 9 represent books pertaining to 9 main branches of the whole field of knowledge, as conceived by Dewey, whereas class 0 is for such books as Encylopaedias, General periodicals, etc., which are too genera to belong to any of the 9 classes. In the same way, each class will have 9 divisions, and general works of any subject class will come under the division represented by 0. In the words of Dewey, "where 0 occurs in a class number, it has its usual numerical value. Thus a book numbered 510 is class 5, division 1, but not section; i.e. treats of division 51 (Mathematics) in general, and is limited to no one section, as is Geometry, marked 513. 500 indicates a treatise on Science in general, limited to no division.

The conception of dividing every subject into 9 parts is fallacious. Dewey therefore says, "when more than 9 divisions are needed the difficulty is commonly obviated by grouping on single numbers the subjects most closely allied, or by assigning 1-8 specifically to most important subjects and grouping minor subjects on 9 as 'Other'." (op.cit., p.37). Any of these groups may be further subdivided for specific topics by the decimal device.

Re-allocation

From the 2nd to the 14th editions the DC always inserted new topics and expanded, but did not alter the places of subjects. For, such alternations would require libraries to reclassify, and reclassification is an expensive and arduous task.

However, expansion without re-allocation of classes made the scheme look antiquated and too bulky at some parts. So with the 15th (1951) and the 16th (1958) editions re-allocation of subjects became a special feature. Fifteenth edition involved major re-allocation; 45 per cent was maintained in the 16th, the balance was returned to original places.

In the 16th edition over 1600 placings have been revised according to 'literary warrant' (i.e. according to groups into which books tend to fall for use). A set of [ ] (square brackets) has been used in the schedules to distinguish numbers which are no longer in force or no longer in force with the meaning indicated; a dagger + preceding a number means that the number was used in the sense indicated in the 14th edition, while an asterisk(*) means the same for the 15th edition. For example, under 294.5 Hinduism it is indicated "[*.58] Theosophy Class in 212.5", which means Theosophy is 212.5 in the 16th edition, and it was 294.58 in the 15th.

Enumerative Feature

The DC is enumerative in character, which means that in this classification scheme there is little facet analysis and scope for combining isolate numbers belonging to different facets. In other words, the DC lists compound subjects; when compound subjects are not enumerated, it is normally not possible to build class numbers for them. As a result classification becomes partial and 'co-extensiveness' is not reached. For example, in 300 Social Sciences we have the following subjects enumerated:

330 Economics

331 Labour economic

331.4 Employed women

331.43 Employed married women

Again,

331.8 Industrial sociology

331.83 Health, welfare, recreation facilities

331.833 Housing

Now, what will be the class number for the subject 'Housing facilities for married women labourers'? It will be either 331.43 or

331.833, for the two numbers cannot be combined. To take another example, 'Cataloguing in children's libraries' will be either 025.3 Cataloguing or 027.625 children's libraries. Because of this limitation the DC often gives rise to cross-classification.

Facet Analysis and Synthesis

At the DC is basically enumerative in structure, at some places in its schedules faceted structure is visible. Classes like Language, Literature, and History show such a structure.

In 400 Philology, the method of division is first by Language, then by Problem. In 800 Literature, it is first by Language, secondly by Form, and thirdly by Period or Chronology. In 900 History, from 940 to 999, it is first by Place, then by Period.

The facet structure has made provision for synthesis of compounds, particularly in classes 400 Philology and 800 Literature. In 400 Philology, 410 is divided into the 'Problem' of the study of a language. Thus,

411	Written language
412	Etymology
413	Lexicography, dictionaries
414	Sounds of language
415	Grammar
416	Prosody
417	Inscription and paleography
418	Texts

These problems with their symbols are applicable to any language. Though unnecessarily these division have been repeated with 430 German language to 480 Greek language, the provision for synthesis is seen in the case of 490 Other language. In 420 English language, the problem facet has been elaborated, and therefore the instruction under 400 Language reads, "Divide specific language like 420". So 'Bengal grammar' will have the class number 491.445. The symbols 491.44 stand for Bengali language enumerated in the schedule, and 5 standing for Grammar has been synthesized with 491.44.

The 400 Language table provides numbers for any specific language. Thus 820 in English literature, the symbol 2 representing

'English' having come from 420 English language; 891.44 is 'Bengali' literature, the symbols 9144 representing 'Bengali' having come from 491.44 Bengali language.

The **Literary Form Divisions** have been separately tabled, and these are commonly applicable to the literature of a specific language. These Form divisions are:

1 Poetry
2 Drama
3 Fiction
4 Essays
5 Oratory
6 Letters
7 Satire and humour

Having got the divisions, we can easily build the class numbers for compounds of literary form. For example, 820 in English literature, 821 is English poetry; 891.44 is Bengali literature, 891.441 is Bengali poetry.

With regard to the Period divisions, however, the scope of synthesis is limited. There is no common table of period divisions, applicable to any specific literature. Instead, with every literature from 810 American literature to 880 Greek literature, a separate chart of period divisions has been enumerated, which divisions, however, can synthetically be used for all the literary forms of a particular literature. For example, with 820 English literature, the Period divisions are enumerated under 822 English drama:

822.1 Early English period, 1066-1400
822.2 Pre-Elizabethan period, 1400-1558
822.3 Elizabethan period, 1558-1625
822.4 Post-Elizabethan period, 1625-1702
822.5 Queen Anne period, 1702-1745
822.6 Later 18th century, 1745-1800
822.7 Early 19th century, 1800-1837
822.8 Victorian period, 1837-1900
91 20th century
912 Early 20th century, 1900-1945
913 Later 20th century, 1945

Following the above division-pattern, 821.8 is English poetry of the Victorian period; 824.8 is English essays of the Victorian period, and so on.

The Literature schedule of the DC would have become much briefer, if there were a separate chronological table out of which Period division of a particular literature could be synthesized. For want of such a table the DC has not only indulged in unnecessary enumeration, but also has engendered the limitation that except for the literatures denoted by 810 to 880, no other literature can have period divisions unless a classifier using the DC makes a table of such divisions for himself.

In the class 900 History, the Period facet again suffers from unnecessary enumeration for individual countries. A separate table of Period divisions commonly applicable to any country would have given much scope for synthesis.

However, a big significance of the class History is that the divisions 930-999 are used as symbols for Geographical divisions whenever necessary, thereby a lot of enumeration of place names against subjects is avoided and synthesis is effected. The instruction "Divide like 940-999" or "Divide like 930-999" brings about the synthesis. Thus, below 027.3 subscription libraries, the instruction is "Divide like 930-999"; so 'Subscription libraries in India' is 027.354. The symbols 54 represent the Geographical division 'India', and have come from the History schedule, where 954 is 'History of India' (9 is History, 54 represent the Geographical division 'India').

As has been shown, Dewey's instruction "Divide like" is a synthetic or number-building device. Such instruction is of three kinds. The one kind, "Divide like930 or 940-999" has been described. Another kind is, "Divide Like 000-999". This instruction forms the annotation of a number of subjects. For example, 016 Subject bibliographies contains this instruction. The reason is obvious. There may be bibliographies on any of the subjects listed in the DC schedules, from 000-999. So symbols for a specific subject can be taken from 000-999. Thus, 016-02 is Bibliographies on Library Science, 016.1 is Bibliographies on Philosophy, 016.546 is Bibliographies on Inorganic chemistry, and so on.

The third type of "Divide like" instruction is limited to a particular scheduled of subject. For example, 338.17 Economics of specific agricultural products carries the instruction "Divide like

633-638". Following this instruction we can build the class number for 'Economics of wheat products' as 338.17311, bringing 311 from 633.11 Agriculture of wheat (63 is Agriculture, 311 represent the division 'wheat'). It may be noted that the digit 7 coming after 338.1 works as a connecting link or facet indicator.

The DC also takes recourse to the alphabetic device in number-building at some places. Thus, 338.47 Economics of specific secondary industrial products bears the instruction either "Divide like 000-999" or divide alphabetically by using the 'Cutter number' for a specific industrial products. For example, 'Economics of motor vehicles industry is either 338.476292 (629.2 is Motor vehicles engineering), or 338.47M7, M7 being taken from Cutter's Table to represent 'Motor'.

With the 15th edition of the DC the scope of synthesis has been much reduced. The 13th and the 14th editions made it possible to combine any two numbers showing relation by the linking symbols 0001. Thus, 'Algebra or Engineers' would be 512.000162. Also, it was possible to represent some common points of view from which a subject may be treated. For example, 003 Economic point of view.

7

COLON CLASSIFICATION

Overview

In respect to books, classification can be all-pervasive. Certainly it can pervade storage and retrieval. It can also pervade book selection and book weeding. Classification can take advantage of open access and the reader's self-effort through browsing in the stack room. But in the case of articles, open access and browsing in the stack room become nearly imparticable. And yet, a good substitute for it is scanning through the Main Entries of the documents in the documentation list. Here, depth classification can be extremely helpful. Further, a specialist reader is often in need of micro-thought presenting any combination of any of the multiple facets and of the multiple quasi isolates (or first characteristics) likely to occur in the subjects going with the Basic Class forming the field of his specialization. Therefore, in saving the time of the reader and in helping him in finding micro-documents, the librarian has to play an important role. He must help the reader formulate, to a close approximation, the micro-thought needed at the moment. Here a guided scheme for analytico-synthetic faceted depth classification can have great potentiality.

History

The first version of the Colon Classification was only a faceted classification. It was not free from rigidity. However, it was less rigid than a non-faceted enumerative classification. Its later version has taken it to the status of a guided analytico-synthetic faceted classification. In this version of the Colon Classification there appears to be potentiality for its use in depth classification work and in the efficient retrieval of micro-thought from documents. This is seen again and again. In discovering and exploiting this potentiality many problems have been and are met with. This chapter gives a rapid survey of the genesis and development of the Colon Classification, and deals with some of the new problems met within its development, including the various steps taken in the past and those to be taken in the future.

Terminology

The terminology used in this document is the latest version of the classification terminology, as developed during the last forty years. Some of the terms are defined in this document. The full terminology has been published by the Indian Standards Institution. This standard in turn was based upon a provisional glossary published as the basis for the work of the Documentation Committee of that body. It must be stated explicitly that this terminology did not come into vogue in its entirety until recently. Its slim first version was recorded in 1937. Since then, it is being steadily added to and refined.

Predisposing Cause

While taking the course on Classification in the School of Librarianship of the University College, London, October 1924 to June 1925, some weeks were first spent in studying the schemes of classification then available in the library of that School. These were the Decimal Classification, the Expansive Classification, the Library of Congress Classification, and subject classification. The Universal Decimal Classification was not available in English. The four schemes were applied to the classification of some books which were published in that year. They did not yield coextensive classes numbers in many cases. But subject classification gave better results in this respect. The cases without coextensive class numbers were studied. Lack of coextensiveness was seen to be due to the subjects presenting two or more free facets; whereas, the schemes generally provided either for one free facet only, or for one frozen and only one free facet. Some of the books published in midnineteenth century in the United Kingdom and listed in the English Catalogue were then examined. They almost always presented only one facet. This experience led to a vague feeling that a Scheme for Classification, suited to books embodying multi-faceted subjects, should provide for two or more free facets and not merely one. This was the predisposing cause for designing a faceted Scheme for Classification.

Exciting Cause

The lecturer in classification was W.C. Berwick Sayers. The clearness of his thinking, the lucidity of his exposition, and his analytical approach created respect for library classification as an intellectual discipline. Outside the class hours, the idea of a faceted classification was discussed with Sayers. His intellectual sympathy for the idea was encouraging. Longer hours of discussion with him became possible in December 1924, while I was working as an apprentice in his library in Croydon. These discussions brought us to an even closer understanding of classification. In the first quarter of 1925, we used to sit together for long stretches of time and discuss the provisional draft of the faceted classification I was developing at that time. After a struggle of about a month, a method of keeping each facet in a class number free – free to take in additional digits – was hit upon. It was realized that to keep a facet, not occurring at the very end of a class number, free to grow on its own right and according to its own needs, a facet number should be separated from the succeeding facet number by some digit with no semantic content of a rich variety. But this digit should have an ordinal value. It was further realized that the ordinal value of this semantically poor digit should be smaller than that of any semantically rich digit used in building class numbers. The semantically rich digits used in the Colon Classification are normally a to z, 1 to 9, and A to Z. Thus the digit used to separate one facet number from the succeeding facet number should have an ordinal value less than that of one. At this juncture, the fact that zero is elliptical in shape gave a clue. According to the Geometry of Conics a point-pair may be deemed to be a degenerate form of an ellipse.

Occasionally, as in the representation of a year such as 1920, the digit 0 has also to be used as a semantically rich digit. But in no other context is the digit 0 used in this way. It is not necessary to make the digit (:) colon have an ordinal value smaller than that of 0.

Faith in Coextnesiveness

Until about May 1925 many details were worked out. The schedule of Main Classes was drafted, discussed with Sayers, and nearly completed in that period. Some of the Main Classes such as Mathematics, Physics, and Philosophy were divided in the first instance along traditional lines. These classes were called Canonical Classes. The term "Basic Class" is now used as a generic term to mean both the terms Main Class and Cononical Class. The facets likely to occur in subjects going respectively with some of the Basic Classes were conjectured in the light of the books then currently published. The schedule was drafted for each of a few of these facets. These schedules were again discussed with Sayers and made final in that period. Provisional class numbers were constructed with the aid of this Faceted Scheme for Classification for some of the books announced in 1924-25 in the Publishers' Circular. The appearance of the class numbers was different from that of the class numbers in any of the four schemes. It required some courage to reconcile oneself with their odd appearance. The courage came from the faith that, for efficiency in library service, the class number should be made coextensive with the subject of the book classified; indeed, coextensive in each of its facets.

Physical Analogue

At this juncture, another experience changed faith into conviction. This experience was gained while visiting one of the Slefridge's Department Stores in London. There I saw for the first time a Meccano set consisting of slotted strips, wheels, rods, screws, nuts, and pieces of string. By the combination of a suitable assortment of these pieces, several kinds of toys could be easily constructed. I spent an entire hour observing a demonstration of the construction of different kinds of toys with the aid of a Meccano set. It brought to my mind that the alphabet of a language was itself a formidable analogue of a Meccano set. With a few digits, called the ltters of the alphabet, an endless variety of words, phrases, sentences, paragraphs, and whole works are being produced, each totally different from every other. Viewed from one angle, the work in every book is only a combination of an assorted collection of the letters of the alphabet. These ideas gave me the courage to think that there was nothing wrong in building up class numbers as in a Meccano set, though the look of the numbers was unusual. I was encouraged to pursue the designing of the Colon Classification as a type of Faceted Scheme for Classification

Further, the earlier aversion in some persons against the structured class numbers of Colon Classification has now nearly died out. A few have even begun to welcome and to prefer structured class numbers.

Development

While sailing back home from London to Madras in July 1925, I made additions to the tentative schedules drafted in London. These were used in classifying the books (about 30,000 volumes) listed in the printed catalog of the Madras University Library and of the books in the library of the ship. The books in the catalog with obilique titles were either omitted or marked for examination after reaching Madras. This practical work gave an insight into the way in which the scheme would work. But there were no means of experiencing the effect of arranging the books in the classified sequence. For, unfortunately, cataloging slips were not brought with me for use during the voyage. This failure was no double due to lack of experience and forethought. Soon after arrival in Madras, the books in the University Library were successively sorted out into Basic Classes and classified with the help of the tentative schedules and class numbers. Then the books were arranged in a classified sequence. The sequence was found by readers to be fairly helpful. This was encouraging. The first edition of the Colon Classification was brought out in 1933.

During the next six years the reaction of the readers to the arrangement was observed in the stack room, objectively and unobtrusively. Unhelpful spots in the arrangement were discussed with the readers themselves at first and later with the experts in the subjects concerned. In many such cases, the helpfulness was traced to hindrance in the sequence of the facets. At that time there were no principles to determine the sequence of facets. These were set right, although it meant a considerable amount of revision of the routine connected therewith. Thought was given to the theory of classification implied in the design of the Decimal Classification, the Expansive Classification, the Library of Congress Classification, subject classification, and the Colon Classification. Canons for classification were formulated. This theory was published in 1937 in order to elicit help from other thinkers in the field. The Facet

Sequences and the Isolate Sequences in the different facets in the Colon Classification were critically examined in the light of the theory. The second edition of the Colon Classification (1939) incorporated all such changes. The version of the scheme embodied in the book was mainly intended for the classification of whole books. We may call it Basic version.

From 1939 to 1947 we began to develop other areas in library science such as reference service, bibliography, school and college library work, and library development plans for some university and research libraries, for some constituent states and for India as a whole. Moreover, there were managerial difficulties. These two factors stood in the way of the deep thinking needed for a conscious development of the Colon Classification. However, classificatory thinking must have been going on in the subconscious level; for, it occasionally came to the surface with some new ideas. Further, migration to the Banaras Hindu University Library in 1945 provided a supplementary experience. Unlike the carefully selected, balanced collected of the Madras University Library, the collection of the Banaras Hindu University Library was a conglomerate of many thousands of donated volumes. Some of these created new problems in classification. That library had a richer collection in the applied sciences than the one in Madras. This fact also raised new classificatory problems. But the twenty-two months spent in Banaras had to be spent largely in classifying nearly 100,000 volumes and recognizing the service on the basis of open access.

In June 1947, an invitation was received from Sir Maurice Gwyer, Vice-Chancellor, University of Delhi, to organize a Department of Library Science with postgraduate courses in three tiers awarding Diploma (now B. Lib. Sc.) course, M. Lib. Sc. Course and Ph.D. course in Library Science. This opened up a bright new opportunity. In October of the same year an invitation was received from Donker Duyvis, Secretary of the FID, to attend a meeting of the FID and to prepare a paper on classification and international documentation for discussion at the meeting. An invitation from the British Council made the travel possible. This stimulated the entry of the Colon Classification into the sphere of the depth classification needed in documentation. In April 1950 the Rockerfeller Foundation provided facilities to visit several industrial enterprises in the United States. These experiences gave rise to the question, what can a depth classification achieve. The invitation of the Graduate Library School of the University of Chicago to participate in its Fifteenth Annual Conference in July 1950 provided an opportunity to think about the rigidity in the Colon Classification. This led to the removal of some of the rigidity through the concepts of the five fundamental categories PMEST (Personality, Matter, Energy, Space, Time), Round, Level, and generalized facet formula. By the end of 1951, this led to the conviction that the Colon Classification could give coextensive class number even for micro thought. The fourth edition of the Colon Classification (1952) incorporated these ideas.

In the meantime, the invitation of FID to take charge of the FID/CA (Committee on General Theory of Classification) was accepted. Stimulating work in this Committee continued for about ten years. The potentiality of a mixed notation was explored with the aid of the Efficiency Table based on Zone Analysis. Application of the results of this work increased the capacity of Colon Classification to depth classification. By the end of 1956 an experimental schedule was constructed for the Depth classification of the Basic Class Management.

In the meantime, an International Study Conference on Classification Research was suggested at the International Congress of Libraries and Documentation Centres held in Brussels in 1955. This Conference was held at Dorking (England) in 1957 and provided an opportunity to rethink classification as a discipline. This led to the conviction that the maintenance of the Colon Classification (in fact of any scheme) so as to make it versatile enough to keep fit to organize the unending formation of myriads of new micro-thought would be possible only if it is based on a set of postulates for the analysis of any micro-subject in the Idea Plane and synthesis in the Notational Plane, and also on a set of basic principles for determining sequence among the facets of the micro-subject and among array-isolates. By 1961 such a set of postulates and principles was established.

The establishment of DRTC (Documentation Research and Training Center, Bangalore) in 1962, due to the farsightedness of Professor P.C. Mahalanobis of the Indian Statistical Institute, helped the development of team research in depth classification in general and in Colon Classification in particular. The training of documentalists who intend to work in diverse enterprises has been helping the continued refinement of the Colon Classification. In 1964 this led to the realization that the versatility of the Colon Classification, or of any scheme, for depth classification could not reach the necessary level if it be merely a faceted scheme; that is, a scheme providing a facet formula of many facets for each Basic Class. In fact, it has been brought home now, how the concept of facet formula, once helpful, proved to be an obstruction. This was due to its false suggestion that the facets belongs to a Basic Class. The fact is that the facets belongs to a subject going with a Basic Class. By 1964 it was realized that full versatility can be attained only by making the Colon Classification a scheme guided in continued design an refinement by a set of postulates and principles. Indeed, it is now further realized that any faceted scheme should not be called an analytico-synthetic scheme. A faceted scheme is an analytico-synthetic scheme if and only if the design of its schedules and their augmentation are guided by a set of postulates and principles. Some pilot projects in the working out of schedules for Depth Classification have been attempted for subjects going with a few Basic Classes.

Thus, fundamental research has now given us a methodology for the systematic design of schedules for the depth classification of subjects by the Colon Classification. From now on applied research is needed for developing further schedules in the Colon Classification along these lines. This will be a continuing process which will be best done by international teams, one for each subject area. As the development work proceeds and the development of the universe of knowledge itself proceeds, fundamental research and development will have to alternate continuously. On the basis of such team work, fascicules of volume 2 of the Colon Classification will have to be published for the respective subject areas, when the schedules for them are completed. Hundreds of such fascicules will have to be published.

Ranganathan Colon Classification Board

At the request of Peter Jayasinghe of the Asia Publishing House, a self-perpetuating Ranganathan Colon Classification Board has been formed. Its function is to stay up-to-date and bring out new editions of the Colon Classification, the Basic Version as well as the fascicules containing the Depth Versions for diverse subject areas. It will also bring out new editions of such of the other books of Ranganathan as deserve to be so treated. The Board will have a panel of probable authors from whom it will choose the editors and the revisers of the respective books. All these books will appear as volumes in the Ranganathan Series in Library Science. This series may also include books by other authors, at the discretion of the Board. The Board will be an auxiliary of the Sarada Ranganathan Endowment for Library Science (1963), whose funds are vested in the Treasurer for Charitable Endowments of the Government of India.

Extent of Use of Colon Classification

The Colon Classification is in use in the universities of ten Constituent States of India. Almost all the public libraries and the college libraries in the States of Madras and Maharashtra use it. It is also in use in some public libraries in other states. Some of the legislative libraries and libraries of government departments are also using it.

Knowledge Classification

Universe of Knowledge and Its Quality

A class in the universe of knowledge can comprehend the entire universe of knowledge – past, present, and future - - at one extreme. For Example, the vast mass of knowledge embodied in a general encyclopedia has to be recognized as a class. The mass of knowledge embodied in the respective books *Treatise on agriculture, Treatise on the agriculture* of cereals, and Treatise on the agriculture of rice is progressively smaller in size. We shall denote each of these by the term Macro-Thought. We shall call its embodiment Macro-Document. At the other extreme, the tiny mass of knowledge embodied in an article in a periodical or in a chapter or a paragraph of a book must also be recognized as a class. We shall call this Micro-Thought. We shall call its embodiment Micro-Document. A Micro-Document does not usually have an independent physical existence. It is often contained within a Macro-Document, and the latter is called its Host Document. At an even further extreme, a tiny spot of knowledge embodied in a sentence or even in a word may have to be recognized as a class. We shall call this Spot-Thought. We shall call its embodiment Spot-Document. There is a continuous spectrum of the size of a class stretching between the two extremes. This implies that the potential number of classes in the universe of knowledge is large at any moment. With time, this number tends to infinity. An implication of this is that at any moment some classes of knowledge have not emerged, though foreseen.

Array of Classes

Among the classes of the universe of knowledge can be found many sets of mutually exclusive classes. Some of these classes may be coordinate in status; that is, they may have a Common Immediate Universe. Such a set of coordinate classes is called an Array of Classes of their immediate Universe. For example, Sound, Heat, Radiation, Electricity, and Magnetism from an array of classes with Physics as their Common Immediate Universe. We may represent this as follows:

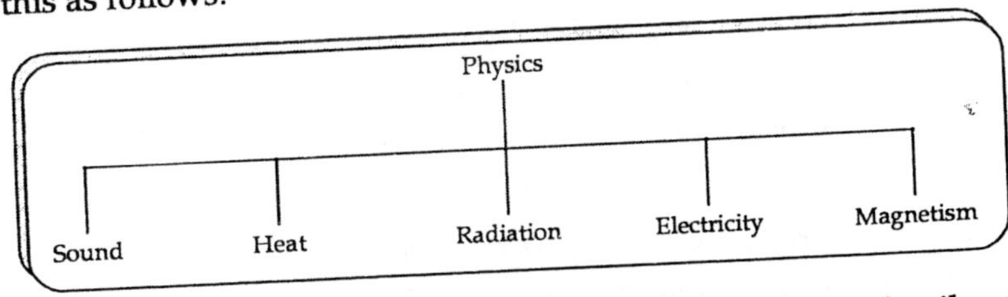

An array of classes may be taken to correspond to a family of blood brothers.

Collateral Arrays

Two arrays of classes may share in common their Immediate Universe of Remove 2. Such arrays are said to be Collateral Arrays of Remove 2. Any class of one such array is said to be collateral to any class of any other such array. For example, the array of the classes Infra Red, Visible, Ultra Violet and X and Gamma Rays and the array of the class Current and Static Electricity from collateral arrays. We may represent this as follows:

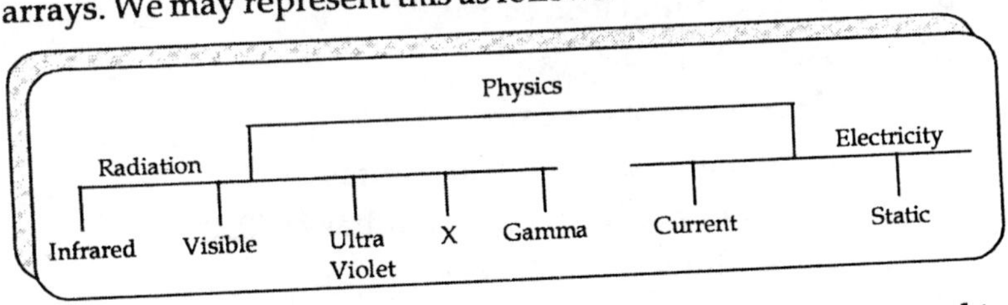

Collateral Classes of Remove 2 may be taken to correspond to Cousins of Remove 1. Similarly, we have Collateral Arrays and Classes of Removes greater than 2.

Chain of Classes

Again, among the classes of the universe of knowledge can be found many sets of classes in succession, in the relation of container and contained. Such a set of classes is called a Chain of Classes. Here are examples:

1. Agriculture
11. Agriculture in Madras
12. Agriculture in Madras in 1950's
2. Agriculture
21. Disease of crops
22. Fungus disease of crops
3. Argirulture
31. Disease of crops
32. Fungus disease of crops
33. Fungus disease of crops in Madras
34. Fungus disease of crops in Madras in 1950's
4. Agriculture
41. Agriculture of food crops
42. Agriculture of cereals
5. Agriculture
51. Agriculture of food crops
52. Agriculture of cereals
53. Agriculture of rice crop
6. Agriculture
61. Agriculture of food crops
62. Agriculture of cereals
63. Agriculture of rice crop
64. Agriculture of rice crop in Madras
65. Agriculture of rice crop in Madras in 1950's
7. Agriculture
71. Agriculture of food crops
72. Agriculture of cereals
73. Agriculture of rice

74. Stem of rice crop
75. Disease of stem of rice crop
76. Fungus disease of stem of rice crop
77. Fungus disease of stem of rice crop in Madras
78. Fungus disease of stem of rice crop in Madras in 1950's

Each class in a chain is said to be obtained by the Denudation of its immediate universe.

Order of Class and of an Array

Several chains of classes may have a common universe. To put it in a different way, any class in any array may originate several groups of chains. In particular, all the chains of classes have the Class Universe of Knowledge as the common universe. Stated differently, the Class Universe of knowledge is the origin of all the groups of chains. Each class in a chain may be called a link of it. The number of removes of a link from the Class Universe of Knowledge is the Order of the Class forming the link. The order of the Class Universe of Knowledge itself is zero. It is usual to break the Universe of Knowledge in the first instance into an array of Main Classes. The order of each Main Class is 1. The order of the array of Main Classes is also 1. In a similar way, each Main Class can give rise to an array or Order 2. Each class in it will itself be a class of Order 2. A Main Class may give rise to more than one array of Order 2, in fact, as many as the number of characteristics available for its first division. Here is an illustration.

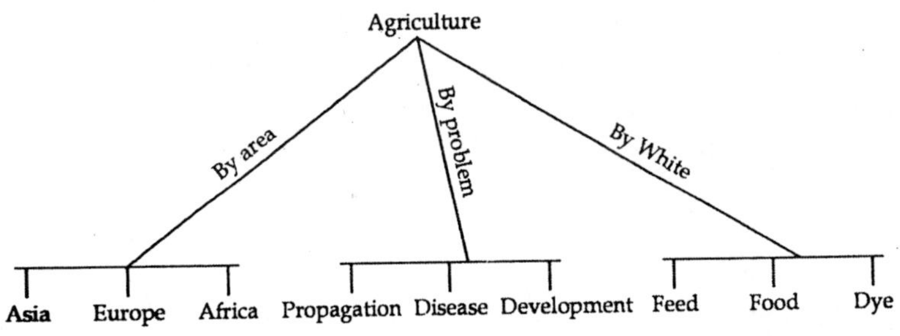

We can also have an array of Order 2 by the linkage of one Main Class with another. Here is an illustration:

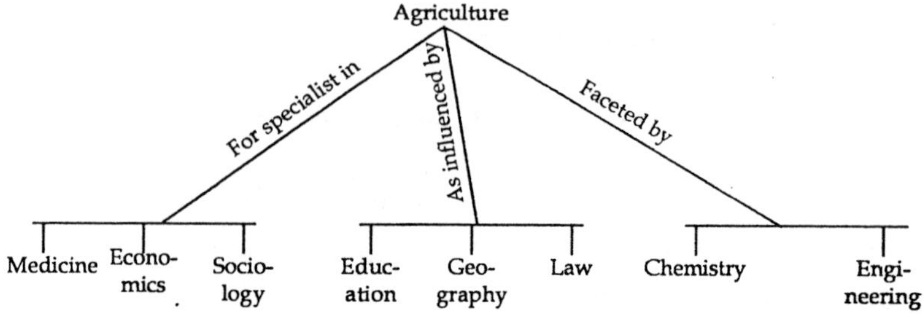

Exponential Rate of Proliferation

Similarly, a number of arrays of Order 3 can branch off from each class in each array of Order 2. So also with each array of Order 3, and so on. Thus, the rate of increase of arrays is exponential and not merely additive or multiplicative. So also with the rate of increase of classes. The proliferation of classes due to this exponential increase is intensified by another factor. Arrays of Order 3 can be formed not merely by the introduction of a train of successive characteristics of the same species down the chains of, say, Utility, Problem, and Area occurring in the first illustration given in the Sec. B4. Arrays or Order 3 can also be formed by "Hybridization of Classes," that is, by the linkage of any class of any array of Order 2 with any class of any one or more of the other arrays of Order 2. Here is an illustration.

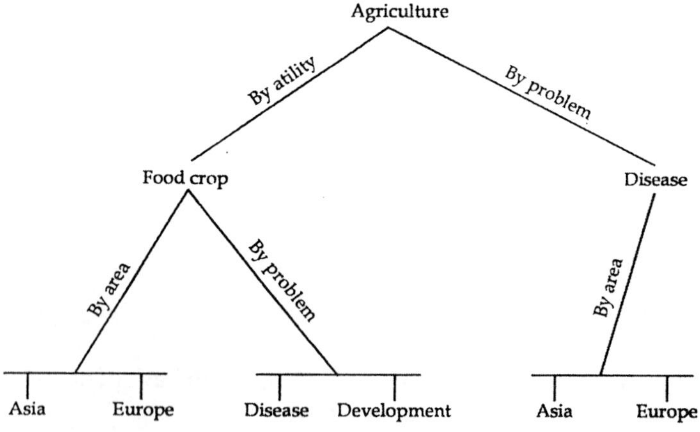

Hybridization of classes can also be done by the linkage of any of the classes of an array of any Order with any of the classes in one or more arrays of any other Order or Orders. This will further intensify the proliferation of classes.

Tree of Porphyry : First Approximation

Such possibilities for the formation of classes in the Universe of Knowledge transcend representation by the traditional.

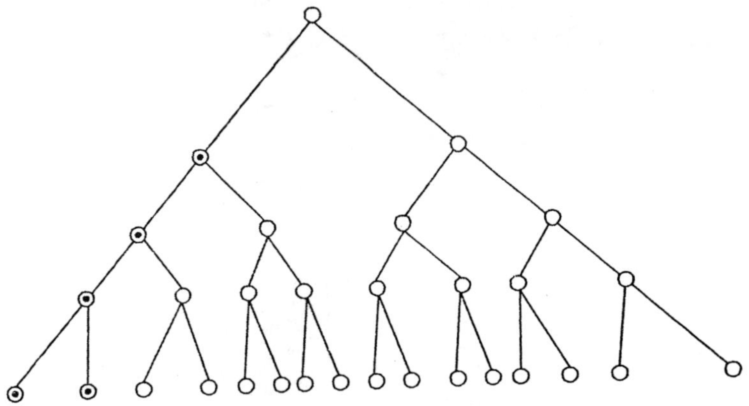

Figure 7.1. 'Tree of Porphyry.'

It is greatly oversimplified picture. If Bentham were alive today, it is doubtful that he would speak of 'the matchless beauty of the Tree of Porphyry."

Second Approximation

A slightly closer approximation would be to represent the Universe of Knowledge as a 'Tree' with enormous proliferations. To facilitate comparison with the Tree of Porphyry, this tree also should be presented upside down. Even this picture would give only a fractional view, for it would show only two or three of the chains of the branches emanating from each class.

Banyan Tree : Third Approximation

A still closer approximation is a century old Banyan Tree. Here in addition to the original trunk there are many secondary trunks. It is not easy to see to which trunk a particular branch belongs. To facilitate comparison with the Tree of Porphyry this tree should be

Schematic Diagram of The
Tree of Knowledge

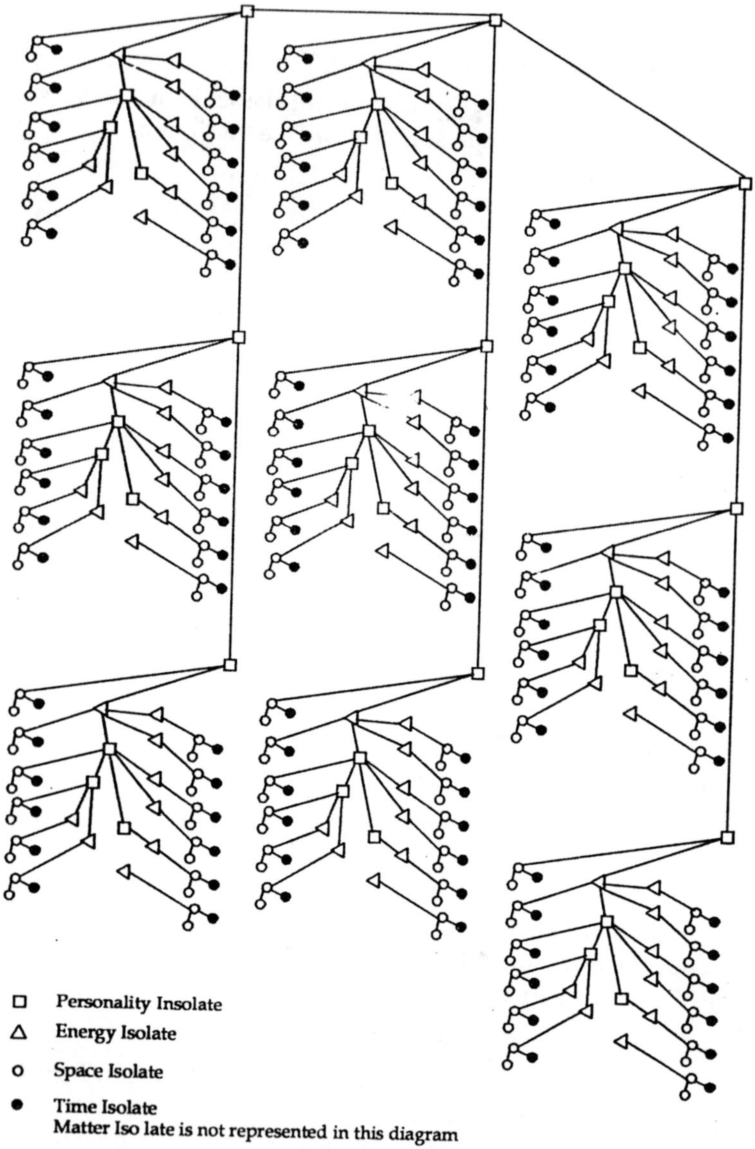

□ Personality Insolate
Δ Energy Isolate
o Space Isolate
● Time Isolate
Matter Iso late is not represented in this diagram

Figure 7.2

shown upside down. Even this is an over simplification as a picture of the Universe of Knowledge.

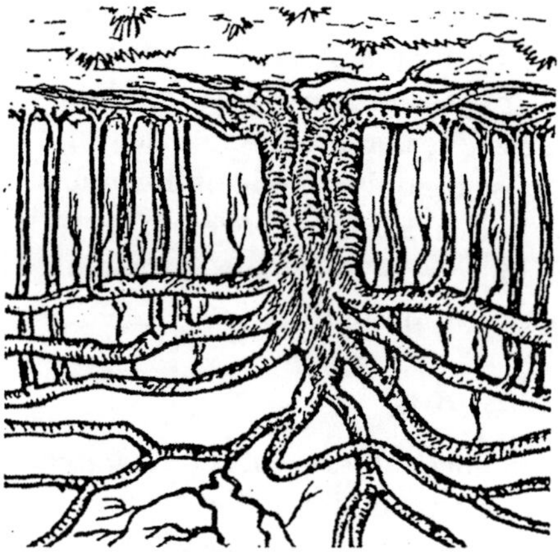

Figure 7.3. Banyan Tree

Document Arrangement and Its Problems

Such a complicated mutually linked classes of knowledge scattered in many dimensions is the domain of Knowledge Classification and Document Classification. Practical considerations demand the arrangement of documents on the shelves, or their main entries in a documents on the shelves, or their main entries in a documentation list, in a single linear sequence; that is, in one dimension. The comfort of the human mind also demands the thinking out or recalling the knowledge classes in one single sequence. Further, the associative quality of the mind would arrange and recall them in accordance with their Immediate-Neighborhood-Relation.

Mapping

To meet either of these demands, the multi-dimensional universe of knowledge has to be transformed into a one-dimensional universe. Here arises an insoluble problem. It is well known that in the transformation of an n-dimensional space into a space of smaller number of dimensions and into a one-dimensional space or line in particular - - or its equivalence. In the mapping of an n-dimensional space on a space cf smaller number of dimensions and on a line in particular -- many of the Immediate-Neighborhood-Relations among the classes are necessarily lost. For example, let us look at the first diagram in Sec. B4. The diagram shows ten classes. Let us now arrange these ten classes in a line. For simplicity, without loss of generality, let us assume that the class Agriculture is put in the first place. Then it is possible only for one of the nine remaining classes -- Asia, Europe, Africa, Disease, Development, Harvesting, Food crop, Dye crop, Oil crop -- to have Immediate-Neighborhood-Relation with the class Agriculture.

Invariant in Mapping

To use a mathematical term, of the nine possible Immediate-Neighborhood-Relations possible in the diagram of two dimensions, only one can be kept Invariant, when the two dimensions are mapped on one dimension. The problem is to decide which one of the nine Immediate Neighborhood-Relations is to be kept Invariant. This is the crucial problem in document arrangement.

The Crucial Problem and the Phenomenal Level

The crucial problem of knowledge classification is the choice of the Invariant. In the phenomenal level, all the myriads of classes stare at us. Each of the myriads of the Immediate-Neighborhood-Relations plead for its being kept Invariant in preference to all the others. Each pleads with more or less equally valid reasons. The work of judging their relative claims and making a firm decision is a maddening problem. We feel it tantalizing to make the decision even when we consider only a small assortment of closely related classes. It causes sleepless nights and nightmares in persons with an extremely scientific attitude and meticulous respect for the Law of Impartiality. A person with a less vigorous mind might assert that his decision is the best. In defence of their respective choices all such persons get into the fray and indulge in polemical attacks on one another. The myriads of Immediate-Neighborhood-Relations in the Universe of Knowledge watch these polemics, laughing up their sleeves, as it were. Such polemics serve little purpose. More light is required to by-pass such an attitude.

Approach of the Colon Classification

Seminal Level

The approach of the Colon Classification to this crucial problem is different. It acts on the assumption that thinking about the mapping of the n-dimensional space of the universe of knowledge on the one dimensional space implied by Classified Sequence should not be started at the baffling phenomenal level crowded with myriads of Immediate-Neighborhood-Relations, each claiming the status of Invariant. The more we recede from the Phenomenal Level towards the Seminal Level,

the less the number of claimants to the status of Invariant will be;

the more amenable to grading the nature of the claimants will be; and

the less complicated the problems will become.

We should go back in the direction of the Seminal Level until we reach the position where

a few Fundamental Categories appear;

most of the phenomenal elements get absorbed and appear as manifestations of one and only of one or other of the few Fundamental Categories; and, consequently

the claimants for the status Invariants become very few and their claims can be judged on the basis of some set of equitable positive principles.

Planes of Work

In working on the problem so close to the Seminal Level, the Colon Classification finds that the work gets resolved into work in three different planes: the Idea, the Notational, and the Verbal Planes. Looking back from this position into the work done before these three planes of work were clearly seen and separated, it is found that much of the difficulty arose out of frequent, listless, and unconscious change from one plane to another. Another cause of difficulty was the inhibition of work in the Idea Plane by the limitations of the Notational Plane, and by the inherent defects of the Verbal Plane.

Work in Progress

The damage done to work in the Idea Plane by the limitations in the Notational Plane is now being progressively set right. Awareness is being developed to keep clear of such damage. The limitations of the Notational Plane are also being progressively reduced by a systematic exploitation of the potentialities of the mixed notation of the Colon Classification. The policy of separating the work in the two planes and allowing each to develop independently of each other has, incidentally, sown the seeds of mutual cooperation and beneficial influence in the place of the old inhibition. Establishment of technical terminology, its continuous development, and its persistent use are minimizing the confusion usually caused by the Verbal Plane. The methodology used by the Colon Classification, in conducting the work in the three planes is described in the succeeding chapters.

Main Class

Whether document retrieval is conventional or done with the aid of electronic machinery, a preliminary break down of the Universe of Knowledge into a few regions in the first instance is a convenience. In the conventional retrieval it is a necessity. In the machine retrieval too, it is being increasingly preferred for economic reasons, by any sound management. The regions formed by such a preliminary break down may be called Main Classes. Main Classes are determined in the light of current practice in the learned world. It is possible to have several more or less equally helpful sequences of Main Classes. Main Classes are determined in the light of current practice in the learned world. It is possible to have several more or less equally helpful sequences of Main Classes. The scholarship of the Vedic period had a preferred sequence; the Greeks had another one. So did the philosophers and the scientists of the modern age. The sequence of Main Classes. The scholarship of the Vedic period had a preferred sequence; the Greeks and another one. So did the philosophers and the scientists of the modern age. The sequence of Main Classes in the Colon Classification is one alternating pure and applied disciplines. Concentrating on the pure disciplines alone, the sequence among the Natural Sciences begins with the abstract discipline of Mathematics. Then follow in succession the discipline of Physics dealing with matter qua matter and all forms of energy except chemical energy. The next is the discipline of Chemistry dealing with substances; that is, differentiated matter and chemical energy. Then follow the disciplines in which life principles are progressively intensified. In other words, the progression is from the abstract to the concrete, and from primary to integrated levels. The culmination is in the discipline of Spiritual Experience concerned with concreteness and integralness par excellence. The discipline of Spiritual Experience forms, as it were, a peak. Then follows the descent from the peak on its other side. First comes the discipline of Fine Arts, including Literature - - the Fine Arts par excellence. These disciplines are soaked in Spiritual Experience and emanate from intuition. Then comes the recession into the region of greater intellection and less intuition; that is, Religion as distinct from religious experience, and Philosophy and Psychology. All these disciplines predominantly concern the individual or emanate from them. Therefore, they are collectively called Humanities. Then follow the disciplines concerned with human groups and communities. These are collectively called Social Sciences. Life in society is very complicated. The only way of living the moment in an orderly way is to regulate life by laws. The variety of legal systems in the world - - almost contradicting one another at several points - - suggests that the artificiality or arbitrariness and deviation from naturalness culminate in the discipline of Law. The peak of naturalness is again in Spiritual Experience. As we move down from that discipline towards the disciplines of Law, there is an increasing recession from naturalness and progression towards the arbitrariness or artificiality. To highlight the peak position among the Main Classes occupied by Spiritual Experience, it is denoted in the Colon Classification by the digit. One reason for the choice of this digit is that it makes it distinctive. The second reason is that it is the international symbol for Spiritual Experience. A fuller account of the different sets of Main Classes and their different sequences in different ages is given in the *Prolegomena*.

Canonical Classes

The history of the evolution of Main Classes shows that as proliferation increases in the Universe of Knowledge, the number of Main Classes recognized in one age proves insufficient in a later age. Most of the newly emerging Main Classes have differing affiliations to the old Main Classes. On the basis of this affiliation, it is found practicable to group the new Main Classes under the respective old Main Classes as if they were sub-classes of the respective old Main Classes. At any rate, tradition groups them generally in that way. Therefore, the new Main Classes are called

Canonical Classes. The sequence among the Canonical Classes of a Main Class can be determined in a consistent way according to some helpful principle. The Colon Classification attempts to do so.

Basic Classes

We may use the generic term Basic Class to denote either Main Class or Canonical Class indifferently. At the present stage of proliferation in the Universe of Knowledge, document-search is facilitated if the primary break down of the universe of knowledge lands us in the regions of Basic Classes. At the present moment, the schedule of Colon Classification lists 330 Basic Classes. This proved adequate in literature search in the universe of books or macro-documents of the recent past. In November 1963, a methodology for the design and development of depth classification suited in micro-documents was launched. Experience gained in the exploitation of this methodology indicate that it will be a convenience to increase the number of Basic Classes not only in establishing facets of schedules for subjects failing in the respective diverse disciplines, but also in document search either by conventional or by machine methods. The basis on which the increase in the number of Basic Classes can be helpfully made is now under study. There is thus a continuing fluidity in the concept of Basic Class. Neither classification nor document search can wait until fluidity is stopped and the number of Basic Classes is frozen. Their number can never be frozen, knowing as we do the turbulently dynamic nature of the Universe of knowledge. In this condition, Colon Classification adopts the method of postulating the list of Main Classes, Canonical Classes, and other kinds of Basic Classes necessary and nearly sufficient in the light of the accumulated literary warrant at the moment. This postulational method keeps the door open for adding to the schedule of Basic Classes and even adding new kinds of Basic Classes.

Basic Class with a "Built-in" Facet

Work on the design of the depth versions of Colon Classification suited to several subjects in the field of applied sciences has been in progress since the beginning of 1964. The schedules are being published in the quarterly Library Science, with a slant to documentation, founded in 1964 and sponsored by the Sarada Ranganathan Endowment for Library Science and the Documentation Research and Training Centre (Bangalore). The experience gained in the course of this work has suggested the helpfulness of a new kind of Basic Class. It may be called a Basic Class with a Built-in Facet. Here are examples:

D9a Tool production engineering

D9i Wood cutting tool production engineering

D9d Stone cutting tool production engineering

D9e Machine tool production engineering (Metal cutting tool production eigineering).

Relative to 'D Engineering' as the universe, the first of the above classes belongs to Array of Order 1. The last three belong to Array of Order 2. In the schedule, Array of Order 2 stands telescoped into Array of Order 1. The last three classes are derived from the first class on the basis of the "Material to be cut" as the characteristic. In the Idea Plane, each of these three is derived by attaching to the class "Tool production engineering" an isolate of the Personality Facet. We say that each of the three classes is a "Basic Class with a Built-in Facet." We find that this concept is helpful.

8

MECHANICAL CLASSIFICATION METHOD

Overview

All library and information services are still largely concerned with providing the enquirer with a document which they hope will give the answer to his question. Few have yet got round to considering what must be the ultimate aim, the provision of actual items of information. This technique is known as 'data providing', as opposed to reference providing. The best discussion on data providing system is the Library of Congress, National Science Foundation and Council on Libraries Resources report Libraries and automation (Library of Congress 1964). A review of this vital document appears in Library Association record 67(1) January 1965 30-31. All librarians concerned with automated system should study this at first hand, for it cover all aspects of library automation, and also pays some attention to a frequently neglected topic-cost.

The cost of automation and mechanization should be looked at very carefully before a decision to install any particular system. A careful analysis should be carried out to determine what gain will be achieved and how it will actually help before expensive equipment is installed. It must first be ensured that all present systems are working to maximum efficiency, and this of course includes the classification system. It is often possible to increase efficiency at little extra cost by improving existing work rather than by making major changes.

The improvements which can be carried out involve firstly the use of either edge punched or center punched cards. It is important to remember that mechanical methods are not necessarily synonymous with coordinate indexing.

Purchased Card

There are three basic uses for the common seventy six hole single row edge punched card. Firstly for applications where the items of information to be coded number seventy five or less. This involves straightforward coding of single items round the edge of the card. It is generally better to sort the information into basic groups for retrieval purposes. This in itself is an elementary form of classification. A good example is for student record cards, where hole one is punched if male, holes two to seven record type of library experience, eight to ten formal education, and so on.

The second coding application, frequently described as indirect coding, occurs where there are more terms required than there are positions available on the cards. In this method meanings are assigned to certain combinations of holes, the first of which is the 'selector code' where the card is divided into a series of fields each containing four holes, each hole being given a numerical value of seven, four, two or one. A combination can be obtained of nine numbers from only two holes; 1:2:3 is a punch of both holes one and two; 5 is a combination of one and four, and so on.

Thus on a seventy six hole card we have the potentiality of nine fields each with a maximum of ninety nine positions. This raises the potentiality considerably, and allows the possibility of classification in the traditional sense.

The third application is random coding, where each previously determined class subject is given a random pair of numbers which can be punched on the edge of the cards. In the cards of a seventy six hole card the potential of such a system is some five and a half thousands positions. If this potential were used with a synthetic classification it is obvious that a classification like colon could be accommodated, although the random coding is the commonest used.

For example, if the combination 22-39 were to represent classification and 45-33 libraries, then a book on library classification would be needed in 22-39, 45-32.

Centre punched cards can be used either for traditional classification or for various forms of indexing. The basic idea of punched cards is that there are a certain number of columns, usually eighty, on a card and each column can be used to convey a prescribed piece of information.

The information which is to be given must be sorted out very carefully beforehand so that each column always contains the same information. If a document is to be recorded the first ten columns could be given to the class number, the next sixty nine to titles, with the final column indicating the form of document. In the author was also required then this could be included instead in, say, columns 12-25. This means that the first ten columns would be left for class numbers and the author starts in column twelve. These fixed areas of information are known as 'fields' and can be anything from one to eighty columns in length.

The technique can have a valid use in classification. For example one project on the punched card machinery at the College of Commerce in Birmingham was the reproduction of a completely new classification. This was done from an existing but inadequate scheme. New notation was given and the classes slightly rearranged.

Production of punched card indexes and guides using machines is the obvious next step from the edge punched card. The subsequent development is into electronics and the result is the computer.

A great deal is written about the computer and its potential applications. But before we consider computer use in relation to librarianship, it is important to see what processes are involved in the science of information retrieval.

First we have the analysis of documents to decide their meaning; then we have a translation of this analysis into terms of an index language (e.g. UDC or UNITERMSs). These terms must be linked with related terms either in a classification or a controlled thesaurus to ensure retrieval of related documents. The decisions taken must be stored in an index file together with some form of document identification. The documents themselves must be stored for easy retrieval from the document identification.

Deciding which of these process can be done by machine at the present time, which are potentially capable of mechanization and which are economically capable of mechanization, demands great care. Most writers on mechanization tend to assume that the process of the future has already arrived and is at work in libraries. This is not true. A great deal of speculative writing is being done, but at the present few libraries have their own computers, and most, when they do automate, are going to rely on buying time from other departments.

For analysis of documents there is still no machine which can read ordinary and variable forms of typescript. Optical scanning will come in the future but for the moment documents have to be translated into machine readable form before they can be analysed, and it is therefore still quicker for human beings to carry out the analysis. Translation the analysis arrived at into the system language can be done by machine, provided no uncommon terms are involved. The problem of translating new terms into the system is considering and expensive. Linking with existing terms can be rapidly achieved if notation is used. Mechanization can quite easily adapt existing notation.

Storing decisions on description, together with the document identification, is easily accomplished by machine once the decisions have been put into machine readable form. Storing the documents themselves is a task that machine system have concentrated on, and this can already be accomplished with a reasonable degree of efficiency.

Computerize Information Retrieval

The first stage in retrieval is understanding the question and translation it into machine readable form. This must be done by man, and the search programme must also be manually devised. The computer can in some cases now devise its own search programme for a given set of terms or classmarks. The actual search is done by machine, ensuring maximum coverage and the elimination of error (or at worst there is consistency of error).

At the present moment comparatively little can be done by computer. The computer is not a wonder machine which will reveal all known knowledge, but one which is capable of utilizing and processing information which it has been given to a pre-ordained pattern. The limitations of computer work are admirably described in M Taube Computers and common use sense

It is necessary to view computers in perspective. They are extremely efficient tools which will considerably improve library potential, but they are decidedly not a panacea for all information problem.

It is desirable to have direct knowledge of how computers can be used in relation to classification. The best description is by R. R. Freeman 'Computers and classification systems' in Journal of documentation 20(3) September 1964 137-143. Here the author suggests that multi language editions of UDC could be printed simultaneously, and valuable technical translating dictionaries could incidentally be provided as well.

Another speculative suggestion is that in the future computers may be used to do statistical analysis necessary for 'literary warrant's in compiling new classifications. This implies that documents will be machine translated, then scanned and significant words and phrased picked out by counting the frequency with which the occur. The technique is already available where the document is translated into machine readable form and is also the basis for the production of abstracts which can also be accomplished by computer.

Another technique closely akin to those of classification is the 'selective dissemination of information' currently being practiced by the IBM Corporation. This is very well described by Trischler in ASLIB Proceedings 14(2) December 1962 473-502. The important point to notice here is that as well as the abstracts being translated into machine readable form, a 'profile' of the readers' interests is also obtained. This profile consists of a set list of keywords which are retrieved when the frequency factor in the document is high enough to suggest that an article would be of interest. This is one of the most advanced dissemination of information techniques, yet it is interesting to note how well the classification scheme, if projected, could perform a similar task. Closely classified documents could be compared with a classified list of readers' profiles in the computer in the present manner. At any time readers' interests in a particular field could be narrowed or broadened simply by scanning a different range of the classification, which would provide a similar type of point and information.

The main consideration in reading on automation and mechanization is to distinguish clearly between what is possible at the moment and what is going to be possible in the future. Once this has been done, the next stage is to decide what kind of service should be supplied to users; then to establish where machines are needed to make the service a practical possibility and how much they will cost. But before these points are considered the question must be answered whether existing resources have been utilized to the point where change is essential.

Ideally, the posters should be designed by experts—the cooperation of the local school of art is usually freely given. Otherwise the form and method of execution are limited only by the enthusiasm and artistic ability of the staff and the material placed at their disposal. Hand-drawn designs and lettering are usually the more effective, but satisfactory posters can be made with mechanical printing sets. Dust-jackets, illustrations, and cuttings can be used with advantage for the body of the poster.

Another useful form of display is the grouping of a selection of books between suitably labelled book-ends, placed on reading tables or on the tops of low bookcases. Special shelves or cases designed for display purpose are also available; a modified form is a type of shelving barrow, which can be wheeled, if necessary, to different parts of the library according to the particular display. Many libraries have specialized in display work, even to the extent of developing a shop-window type of frontage in branch libraries.

The displays may be of a semi-permanent nature, or may consist of a temporary collection of books referring to an event, personality, item of topical interest, or any section of the stock to which the librarian wishes to draw attention. Whatever the display, the classification makes it easily practical, and, indeed, it is often possible to bring before the reader aspects of a subject which are widely separated on the shelves, e.g. a display on "The Sea" might include books from each of the divisions 359, 387, 623.8, 639.22, 797.14, 799.16, 910.4, and 920 in the Decimal Classification.

It has been said that display work tends to destroy the value of book classification, but as classification in itself has little real meaning to the majority of our readers, and as displays reveal new and often unsuspected avenues of reading to the public, the advantages outweigh the disadvantages. The specialist reader is more equipped to fend for himself, and, after all, the librarian and the staff are aware of the displacement.

The essential of display work in the modern library has been stressed by Dr. Savage who maintains that a "classed open-shelf... is nothing but an exhibition" and ask "may we not copy the methods of museums, art galleries, shops and stores to heighten its effect?"

As a development of display work, some libraries, especially in small lending centers in the dormitory areas of town, are experimenting with the arrangement of non-fiction stock into broad groups under attractive pictorial headings. The detailed classification numbers are ignored and the books grouped under some such head as "In and About the House", which might include such subjects as Cookery, Keep Fit, Needlework, Home Mechanics, Gardening, Hobbies, Pets, Do-it-Yourself, and the like. The result is perhaps a negation of classification, but readers seem to like it and reports say that more non-fiction books are issued.

Classification of Fiction

Some aspects of the classification of fiction may be considered as a development of display work. The treatment of fiction varies from library to library. Many group all novels in English, translated or otherwise, on the main fiction shelves in alphabetical order. Other consider as fiction only those novels written by English authors, placing translations with the literature of the original language. Some make a further distinction, and place on the fiction shelves post-Victorian English novels only, classifying earlier English novels with English literature.

Attempts have been made to group fiction on the shelves, according to the type of story, into such classes as "Western Stories", "Mystery Stories", and "Love Stores". In practice, this may tend to encourage the reading of "light" fiction and to strain inadequate book funds merely to ensure that these groups are always supplied with representative collections. Again it is questionable if the arrangement is worth the trouble, especially if a series of distinguishing symbols is added to books and records. An elaborate, perhaps too elaborate, system for the classification of fiction has been outlined by L. A. Burgess. Briefly, this entails the allocation of symbols to groups of fiction according to the type of story. Few libraries would willingly undertake the very considerable amount of work involved even if such a scheme were considered necessary.

Some libraries report favourably on the practice of adding a distinctive symbol to the spine of the novel but maintaining the usual alphabetical sequence; others have experimented with distinctively coloured bindings for certain groups; many more offer assistance to readers by the publication of selective lists.

It has been advocated that some novels might with advantage be spread over the main classification according to their subject interest. This arrangement, it is said, not only would be useful to students of special subjects, but also would bring the hardy fiction reader into contact with the more serious books, suggestions which are both of extremely doubtful value. The Subject Classification allows for such classifying: "Fiction may be distributed according to its ascertained subject-matter by adding the Fiction number from the Categorical Tables to any subject number thought appropriate. This classification would confuse the majority of readers, while being of little real value to students, who, in any case, are usually aware of any title likely to be of interest. Although many novels present a subject more forcibly and vividly than other more serious books, the real facts are usually distorted for the sake of the story. This splitting up of fiction is against the fundamental principles of the form class, Literature (if fiction, why not poetry, and drama?), and, moreover, would separate sequels and the work of one author. If the subject-matter of a novel is deemed of sufficient importance, the classification should be limited to an entry under the appropriate subject in the catalogue; this entry to be clearly marked as referring to a work of fiction.

The distinction is a rough one only, with no alternation of existing records or symbols. This arrangement has proved successful in a busy lending library for the following reasons: it does not separate the works of an author; it breaks up the long sequence, and collects, in the first two groups novels which have a certain individual appeal; it relieves the main fiction shelves of certain individual appeal; it relieves the main fiction shelves of long sets of less popular novels; all types of readers are catered for—those who require modern novels, those who are keen on "translation" and those who enjoy the older type of fiction; no extra burden is placed on the staff. This rough grouping, together with a number of displays labelled "Selected Novels", "Fact in Fiction", "Novels of Country Life", and the like, greatly assist the general reader.

In ideal, members of the staff should be immediately available to offer guidance in the choice of reading, but in practice these can rarely be specifically appointed, nor can existing staff be spared in sufficient numbers for this most important service. The wide use of the modern "plastic jacket" will ease this burden to some extent—the fiction stock lends itself admirably to this modern treatment. In addition to the preservation of the story synopsis printed on the dust-jacket, readers greatly appreciate the transformation of the usual somewhat drab array of novels into a colourful display.

9

Idea Plane

Universe of Subjects

The Universe of Subjects is the field of work in Library Classification. A subject is an organised or systematised account of some idea or another. Thus the basic work of Library Classification will have to he done in the Idea Plane. The efficiency of a Scheme for Library Classification will depend upon the dynamic nature of the Theory of Library Classification pertaining to the Idea Plane. To develop the Theory in the Idea Plane, we should first examine the mode of development of the Universe of Subjects itself. The first attempt at this examination was made in 1944 (24).

Overview

An opportunity to resume the work started in 1943 on the modes of formation of subjects came in the middle of 1947. At that time, Sir Maurice Gwyer, formerly Chief Justice of India, was the Vice-Chancellor of the University of Delhi. He had a great faith in the social value of Library Science and of Library Service. He established a Department of Library Science in his University for teaching and research and invited Ranganathan to take charge of that Department and spend his whole time in teaching Library Science and doing research in that subject without any distraction by administrative work. Further, Sir Maurice had regulations passed for the institution of the first post-graduate degree in Library Science, now known as B Lib Sc, and for the post-B Lib Sc degree - M Lib Sc - thereafter.

This event created a splendid opportunity to resume the development of Library Science in general and a Dynamic Theory of Library Classification in particular. This was the first time that any advanced study and research in the Theory of Library Classification was taken up anywhere in the world. The teaching of "Advanced Library Classification" in the M Lib Sc class soon led to the discovery that the roots of the Theory of Library Classification had not been fully explored. While teaching the M Lib Sc students of the first two batches, the important features in the development and structure of the Universe of Subjects came to be realised with certitude.

First Publication of the Preliminary Results

The provisional results obtained in the M Lib Sc classes were taken from time to time, to the Library Research Circle (See Sec Jh). The discussion in the Circle led to some refinement of the results.

Shera's Evaluation

According to Dr Jesse H Shera, this probe into the roots of the Universe of Subjects "is an Intellectual exercise and surely librarians need to have their intellects exercised . . . Look at these things as intellectual exercises for the light they can throw, the insight they can give us, into the problems" (43).

[Ranga.nathan] asked himself first, `How does knowledge arise?' He said, `It arises in a variety of ways, by assembling, by co-ordinating, and so on.' This itself was something to which his contemporaries had not addressed themselves. He began to think in terms of facets. This was a tremendous step forward. He broke through, literally, the crust of taxonomic rigidity into which the classification had been poured and said, `We want every little pigeon hole.

Idea Plane in USA

Dr Herald Wooster has stated that the Idea Plane gets missed in the conventional classification courses in USA, whereas in the method originated in the Universities of Madras and Delhi half of the time appears to be devoted to training the students in the work to be done in the Idea Plane (21). Actually it is not 50 per cent, but a much larger percentage of the time that is spent on the work in the Idea Plane. Some librarians of India, trained in USA, are allergic to Library Classification. Probably, one reason for this is the conventional classification courses in the United States, without even a reference to the work in the Idea Plane. But some of those who had taken the courses in Madras or Delhi, with full zeal, speak of many of the Schools in USA presenting Classification as looking up the index and hitting or missing. Or as Mr Fairthorne said, "Marking and Parking".

Absorption of Terminology into Postulates

When the investigation of a discipline is started in the Idea Plane, we cannot escape landing ourselves in the Verbal Plane. For, without the use of terms in a natural language we cannot communicate ideas either to others or even within ourselves. The Indian tradition with regard to this early stage is to start with some "Assumed Terms" (Anirvachaniya) and their respective denotations. This necessity is made explicit by Korzybsky (9). Though we do not give a formal definition of the Assumed Terms, we are obliged, at least, to explain them. Some of the terms and the ideas denoted by them get explained together by their being used in a proposition or a statement. The Prolegomena has been following this method, and it begins with a section on Terminology.

Residual Assumed Terms

It is not possible to do away with all Assumed Terms. The following are the residual assumed terms; with some explanation of them:

hl Idea. — The product of thinking, reflecting, imagining, etc got by the intellect by integrating with the aid of logic, a section from the apperception mass, and/or what is directly apprehended by intuition, and deposited in the memory.

h2 Subject. — An organised or systematised account of some idea or other whose extension and intention are likely to fall coherently within the field of interest and comfortably within the intellectual competence and the field of inevitable specialisation of a normal person.

h3 Isolate Idea. — Any idea or idea-complex fit to form a component of a subject, but not by itself fit to be deemed to be a subject.

h4 Non-Main Basic Subject. — A Main Subject taken along with any of its Basic Divisions.

h5 Facet. — A generic term used to denote any component - be it a Basic Subject or an Isolate - of a Compound Subject. Thus a Facet can be a Basic Facet or an Isolate Facet.

h6 Focus. — A generic term used to denote the Basic Subject Idea in the Basic Facet or the Isolate Idea in an Isolate Facet of a Subject, in the Idea Plane, and also the Number representing each of them in the Notational Plane, and the term representing each of them in the Verbal Plane.

Work in the Idea Plane and Postulates

This task is regulated largely by the Postulates for work in the Idea Plane. Therefore, the Postulational Procedure (33) in organising the terms in the title of a subject to the point where the Verbal Plane and the Notational Plane can take aver and complete the work of classifying. The remaining steps in classifying a subject will be taken for these fall in the Verbal and the Notational Planes.

Canon Applicable to Work in the Idea Plane

In addition to the Postulates and the Canons given in Sec Ga to Gp in connection with the descriptive theory of Library Classification which are also to be observed in doing work in the Idea Plane, there are three Canons applicable only to the Dynamic Theory of Library Classification. These are given in Sec Pb to Pe.

Paramountcy of Work in the Idea Plane

The work in the Idea Plane is Paramount in classifying a subject. The Notational Plane should implement the decisions made in the Idea Plane in classifying a subject. For this purpose, the Versatility of the Notational System should be made as rich as possible. In the past, in most of the Schemes, the Versatility of the Notational Plane has been very poor. It has been so to some extent in C C also. The inability of the Notational Plane to implement the findings in the Idea Plane has led to inhibition of the work in the Idea Plane.

Postulates as Given in the Prolegomena

No Postulates pertaining to work in the Idea Plane in respect of the design of a Scheme for Library Classification is given in the Classification, theoretical and practical, or the Manual or the Organisation o f knowledge in libraries. Indeed, these three are largely descriptive theories and are not dynamic ones. Postulates pertaining to work in the Idea Plane are given only in the Prolegomena. Those given in Ed 2 of this book do not differ in substance from those given in its Ed 3. Therefore, the version in Ed 3 is given in this Chapter. It also contains the new Postulates being experimented upon. Further, the definitions of some definable terms are also interpolated amidst the Postulates.

The Universe of Ideas consists of the following kinds of Ideas:

Note – Under each kind of Idea the definitions of the terms arising out of it are given. These definitions are given serial numbers with Roman Caps as the first digits of the numbers.

cl Main-Subject-Ideas (assumed term) ;

Definition A: A Main Subject is an organised or systematised account of one and only one Main Subject Idea (See Sec Kh4) ; Example "C Physics."

c2 Basic-Division-Ideas (assumed term), going with one or another of some Main-Subject-Ideas;

Definition B1: A Basic Subject Idea is either a Main Subject Idea taken by itself or a combination of a Main-Subject Idea and any one or more of its Basic-Division Ideas; Example, the ideas represented by the number and denoted by the terms in the following: "C Physics," "C - 5 Physics - Radiation" (=Physics of radiation).

Definition B2: The Basic Division of a Main Subject is the component of the Basic Subject got by excluding its Main Subject component; Example, in "C - 5" "5 Radiation" is a Basic Division of th'e Main Subject "C Physics."

Definition B3: A Basic Subject is an organised or systematised account of one and only one Basic Subject Idea (See Sec Kh6}; Example "C Physics," "C - 5 Physics - Radiation."

c3 Isolate Ideas, each of which is fit to form a component of a subject idea but not by itself fit to be deemed to be a Subject Idea.

Definition C1: A Simple Subject Idea is a Basic Subject Idea taken by itself without any Isolate Idea as a component; Example, the ideas represented by the numbers and denoted by the terms in the following: "C Physics" "C - 5 Physics - Radiation."

Definition C2: A Simple Subject is an organised or systematised account of a Simple Subject Idea; Example, "C Physics" "C - 5 Physics - Radiation."

Definition D1: A Compound-Subject-Idea is a Subject-Idea with a Basic Subject Idea and one or more Isolate Ideas as components; Example, the idea represented by the number and denoted by the term in "C - 5,3 Physics - Radiation, X-ray" . (= Physics of X-ray Radiation).

Definition D2: A Compound Subject is an organised or systematised account of a Compound-Subject-Idea; Example, "C - 5,3 Physics - Radiation, X-ray (= Physics of X-ray Radiation).

Definition E : An Isolate is a component of a Compound Subject, other than the Basic Subject (See Sec Kh3) ; Example, " 3 X-ray" is an Isolate of the Compound Subject "C - 5,3 Physics - Radiation, X-ray."

Definition F 1: A Common Isolate Idea is an Isolate Idea which can be a component of any Compound-Subject-Idea going with any Basic-Subject-Idea. Example,

1 The Idea represented by the number "m" and denoted by the term "Periodical" in each of the following:

C"m Physics "Periodical (= Periodical in Physics).

C - 5,3 "m Physics - Radiation, X-ray" Periodical (= Periodical in Physics of X-ray Radiation) .

Here the Common Isolate Idea is an Anteriorising Common Isolate Idea.

2 The Idea represented by the number "cF" and denoted by the term `Texture' in each of the following:

J,371; 77;cF Agriculture, Apple Crop; Apple fruit; Texture (= Texture of apple). KX,311; 713;cF Animal -husbandry, Cow Butter; Texture (= Texture of Caw butter)

Here the Common Isolate Idea is a Common Property Isolate Idea.

3 The Idea represented by the number "44" and denoted by the term `India' in each of the following:

J. 44 Agriculture. India (= Agriculture in India) KX.44 Animal husbandry. India (= Animal husbandry in India) .

Here the Common Isolate Idea is a Space Isolate Idea.

Definition F2: A Common Isolate is an Isolate which can be a component of any Compound Subject going with any Basic Subject; Examples are similar to those given above.

Definition G1: A Special Isolate Idea is an Isolate Idea which can be a component of a Compound Subject Idea going with a specific Basic-Subject-Idea, or with a few but not all, Basic-Subject-Ideas;

Definition G2: A Special Isolate is an Isolate which can be a component of a Compound Subject going with a specific Basic Subject, or with a few, but not all, Basic-Subjects.

Examples of Schedules of Special Isolates occur in C C, in the chapters devoted to the different Main Subjects.

Definition H1: A Complex-Subject Idea is a Subject-Idea which contains two or more Compound or Basic Subject Ideas.

Definition H2: A Complex-Subject is an organised account of a Complex Subject Idea.

Similarly we can have Complex Isolates and Complex Array Isolates.

For examples See Sec Mf.

Postulates for Modes of Formation of Subjects and Isolates

Note – The statement of each Postulate automatically contains also a definition of the kind of subject formed by the Mode Postulated.

Postulate of Distillation

A Distilled Main Subject may be formed as a pure discipline by distillation from the experiences with its appearance-in-action in diverse Compound Subjects going with different Basic Subjects.

Note – Distill = To get an extract.

Example, "8 Management Theory."

Postulate of Fusion

A Fused Main Subject may be formed by the Fusion of two or more Main Subjects in such a way that each of them loses its individuality in respect of the schedules of special isolates for farming Compound Subjects going with it. But the Fused Main Subject may have its own distinct schedule of special isolates for forming Compound Subjects going with it.

Note – Fusion - Merging of diverse elements into a unified whole.

Examples,

1. EX Chemical Engineering

2. GX Biochemistry

3. LYX Medical Jurisprudence.

Postulate of Loose Assemblage

A Complex Mean Subject (or a Complex Isolate or a Complex Array Isolate) may be formed by the loose assemblage of two or more subjects (Isolates or Array Isolates } whose mutual relation - such as Bias, Comparison, Difference, Application, and Influence-forms the subject of study.

Examples,

1. B&bX Mathematics for economists (Inter Subject Bias)

2. L; 4&r3 Influence of human physiology on disease (Intra-facet influence)

3. 2,5N3&wM9 Difference between C C and D C (Intra-array differ nce).

Postulate of Lamination

A Compound Subject may be formed by the Lamination of one or more Isolate Facets over a Basic Facet.

Note – Lamination = Structure made by uniting superposed layers of one or more materials.

Examples,

1. T,4 University education (one Isolate Facet)

2. T,4; 2 Curriculum for University education (Two Isolate Facets)

3. T,4; 2.44`N7 Curriculum for university education in India in the 1970s (Four Isolate Facets).

Postulate of Fission

A fissioned isolate or a fissioned Basic Division of a Main Subject may be formed by Fission.

Note

1. Fission = The process of splitting; or breaking up into parts.

2. The mode of formation of Fission had been denoted by the term `Dissection' till now. Dissecting is the act of separating into parts, or cutting into pieces, and exposing the several parts and their locations and connections, especially with precision and skill, for scientific examination. This implies work by an outside agency. But a Fissianed Isolate or a Fissioned Basic Division is found formed without any outside agency. This is better denoted by the term `Fission'.

Example,

6 Indian philosophy

61 Hindu philosophy

693 Jain philosophy,

among the Basic Divisions going with the Main Subject "R Philosophy."

3 Circulatory system

32 Heart

34 Aorta,

among the Schedule of (1 P 1) isolates going with the Main Subject "L Medicine."

2 Executive

21 First minister

22 Deputy minister, among the Schedule of (1 P2) isolates going with the Main Subject "V History."

Postulate of Fundamental Categories

There are five and only five Fundamental Categories; namely Time, Space, Energy, Matter, and Personality (PMEST).

j 1 Some persons relate these Fundamental Categories to the Categories of Aristotle. But, there is no such relation.

j2 The Fundamental Categories (T) and (S) are self-explanatory.

j3 The Fundamental Category (E) denotes Action. In the earlier years it was also taken to denote certain Isolate Ideas, such as Morphology, Physiology, and Disease, wrongly listed as, Energy Isolates. It has been later realised that these do not denote "Action." Therefore they are no longer taken to be manifestations of the Fundamental Category (E).

j 4 The Fundamental Category (M) is now taken to comprehend,

j41 Property, represented by the abbreviation (MP);

j42 Method, represented by the abbreviation (MM); and

j43 Material, represented by the abbreviation (MMt).

The first two were formerly wrongly deemed to be manifestations of (E).

It is worth considering whether we may not regard each of Property, Method, and Material as a Fundamental Category on its own right, and thus bring the number of Fundamental Categories to seven:

j5 The Fundamental Category (P) is elusive and ineffable. One way of recognising (P) is that of the Method of Residues. Anything which is not a manifestation of (T), (S), (E), (MMt), (MM) or. (MP) is taken to be a manifestation of (P).

Postulate of Officiation

One Fundamental Category may officiate for another. For example,

K1 In "History of India," "India" may be hastily taken to be a manifestation of (S). But, it is only "officiating" for the (P) -- the "Community living in India."

k2 In the Main Subject "O Literature," C C uses the year of birth of an author to represent him.

For example, "Shakespeare" is represented by "1564." The year "1564" may be hastily taken to be a manifestation of (T), but it is only officiating for the (P) — "Shakespeare."

Postulate of Isolate Facet

Each isolate facet of a Compound Subject can by deemed to be a manifestation of one and only one of the fundamental categories.

Postulates for Rounds of Facets Postulate of Rounds for Energy

The fundamental category "Energy" may manifest itself in one and the same subject more than once. The first manifestation is taken to end Round 1 of the manifestation of the three fundamental categories "Personality," "Matter," and "Energy." The second manifestation is taken to end Round 2 and so on.

Example, In "L; 4 : 6,2 5 ; 4 : 3 Medicine;

Disease: Treatment, Radiation; Side effect: Diagnosis," the (E) isolate "6 Treatment" ends Round one; and the (E) isolate " 3 Diagnosis" ends Round two.

Postulate of Rounds for Personality and Matter

Each of the Fundamental Categories "Personality" and "Matter," may manifest itself in Round 1, Round 2, and so an.

Example, In "L,32;4:6,25 Medicine, Heart; Disease: Treatment, Radiation," the (P) isolate " 32 Heart" is manifestation of (P) in Round one; and the (P) isolate "25 Radiation" is manifestation of (P) in Round two.

In the example given in Sec Mn, the (MP) isolate "4 Disease" is manifestation of (MP) in Round one; and the (MP) isolate "4 Side effect" is manifestation of (MP) in Round two.

Postulate of Level

Any of the Fundamental Categories "Personality" and "Matter" may manifest itself more than once in one and the same Round within a Subject. The first manifestation of a Fundamental Category within a Round will be said to be its Level 1 Facet in that Round. Its Second manifestation within that Round will he said to be its Level 2 Facet in that Round, and so on.

Example, In "KX,311,32;4 Animal husbandry, Cow, Heart; Disease," the (P) isolate "311 Cow" is the manifestation of (P) in Level one; and the (P) isolate " 32 Heart" is the manifestation of (P) in Level two.

In "L,32; 4; 3 Medicine, Heart; Disease; Symptom," the (MP) isolate "4 Disease" is the manifestation of (MP) in Level one; and the (MP) isolate " 3 Symptom" is the manifestation of (MP) in Level two.

Postulates for Facet Sequence Postulate of Concreteness

The five Fundamental Categories fall into the following sequence when arranged according to their decreasing concreteness: P, M, E, S, T.

Postulate of Facet Sequence within a Round

In any Round of Facets of a Compound Subject in which each of any of the Fundamental Categories - Personality, Matter, and Energy - occurs only once, their sequence should be: Personality Facet, Matter Facet and Energy Facet.

Postulate of Facet Sequence within Last Round

In the last Round of Facets of a Compound Subject in which each of the Fundamental Categories other than Energy may occur and occurs only once, the sequence of the facets should be Personality Facet, Matter Facet, Space Facet, and Time Facet.

Postulates for Level Postulate of whole and Organ

The Organs of successive removes of the whole are deemed to be Level 2, Level 3 etc. the whole itself forming Level 1. In a subject with a, concrete correlate in the phenomenal world, Organs of successive removes are recognisable with the primary senses: In other subjects also, Organs can be recognised with the intellect.

10

Facet for Rounds

Example from Medicine

Subject 48 is "X-ray treatment to tuberculosis of the lungs". We shall decrease its extension by the addition of a [S] and a [T]. Let us take the resulting subject to be "X-ray treatment of tuberculosis of the lungs in India brought up to the 1950s". We shall now pursue systematically the process of classifying the above subject, demonstrating the work to be done in each of the three planes-idea, verbal, and notational. We shall call the above name of the subject "Raw Title".

Filling Up Ellipsis

The (BC) is not stated explicitly in the above name of the subject. But though implicit only, the (BC) is obviously Medicine. This happens quite often. The first step in the Idea plane is to supply the name of the (BC), in the appropriate place among the words in the name of the subject. So also any other word implied in the expressed words in the name of the subject must be made explicit in the first step.

Full Name of the Subject

As a result of the above two steps, the name of the subject becomes "X-ray treatment of the disease of lungs caused by tubercular bacillus, in Medicine, in India brought up to the 1950s". We shall call this the Fully Expressed Name of the Subject, or Full Title of Expressed Titte.

Analysis into Facets

A systematic procedure in the analysis of a subject into its facets is to identify in its fully Expressed Name the word-groups which are manifestations of the successive fundamental categories. We have already stated that the fundamental category Personality is the most elusive one, and that it is helpful to catch it as the residual facet, after all the other facets have been separated out. We have also seen that, arranged according to the decreasing ease of recognition, the remaining four fundamental categories fall into the sequence: Time, Space, Energy, and Matter. It is wide to begin with the easiest.

Time and Space Manifestations

The two following results are obvious:

Focus in [T] i e, Time Isolate = "Brought up to 1950s".

Focus in [S] i e, Space Isolate = "India".

Energy Manifestation

Let us remove these two word-groups mentally and concentrate on the remaining ones. We must now pick out the manifestations of Energy. We find there are two of them.

Foci in [E] i e, Energy Isolates are 1 "Treatment"; and 2 "Disease".

Matter Manifestation

Examining the remaining word-group for any manifestation of Matter, we find none.

Personality Manifestation

The word-group still left are 1 X-ray; 2 Lungs; 3 Tubercular bacillus; and 4 Medicine. Of these, Medicine is the (BC). We have thus only three word-groups still defying assessment. We are satisfied that none of them is a manifestation of Time or Space, of Energy, or Matter. Therefore by Postulate 1, they must be taken to be manifestations of personality.

Result of Facet Analysis

As a result of the above steps, we are now able to give the result of the Facet Analysis by writing out the full name of the subject as follows:

"X-ray [P] treatment [E] of the disease [E] of lungs [P] caused by tubercular bacillus [P] in Medicine (BC), in India [S] brought up to 1950s [T]."

New Phenomenon

This subject presents a new phenomenon, not found in the agricultural subjects considered earlier. [P] as well as [E] occurs more than once. In arranging them, we should be guided by our common method of thinking of them. With regard to[T] and [S], however, we shall be guided by the following postulate:

Postulate for Space and Time Facets

Ordinarily,[S] and [T] should be put last and in the sequence in which they are mentioned here.

Arrangement of Facets

We shall now go through the thought processes of arranging the various [E] and [P] in a more or less helpful sequence. We know that "Treatment" cannot arise unless there is "Disease". Therefore, we can agree to arrange the two [E] in the sequence "Disease" and "Treatment". We next seek to place the three [P] in relation to these two [E]. We can say that "say that "X-ray" will not be thought of unless we think of "Treatment". Therefore, we can agree that the [P] "X-ray" should succeed the [E] "Treatment". We may then say that "Tubercular bacillus" is not likely to be thought of unless we think first of "Disease". Thus the [P] "Tubercular bacillus", should succeed the [E] "Disease". Again "Treatment" cannot begin until the cause of the disease is determined. This makes us say that the [P] "Tubercular bacillus" should precede the [E] "Treatment". This fixes the position of the[P] "Tubercular bacillus" just between the two[E] "Disease" and "Treatment". This leaves us with only "Lungs" to be placed. We know that the disease in question is affecting the lungs. We therefore feel that the [P] "Lungs" should come before the [E] "Disease". Thus, the transformation in the verbal plane is:

Rounds among Facets

In the above table of Facet Analysis, we find that [E] occurs more than once. We also find that each [P] succeeding it. Since we have postulated that the normal sequence is [P], [M], and [E], we presume that [M] too can come more than once and that if it does, it may occur after the successive [E], even as [P] does. The subject we have used as the sample does not present any [M]. It can only be said here that the conjecture we have made is found to be true in subjects having [M].

Postulate of Rounds for Energy in Succession

Energy may manifest itself n one and the same subject more than once-that is, in more than one Round.

We now introduce some new terms and the symbols to represent them. The second, third, etc, Manifestations of Energy in one and the same subject will be respectively called Second Round Energy Facet, Third Round Energy Facet etc. These will be represented by the respective symbols [2E], [3E], etc. Analogously, the first manifestation of energy may be called First Round Energy Facet and be represented by [1E], if we so desire.

Postulate of Rounds for Personality and Matter

It is possible for a manifestation of Personality and Matter to occur after [1E], again after [2E], again after [3E], and so on-that is, in any Round.

These manifestations will be called respectively, Second Round Personality Facet, Second Round Matter Facet, Third Round Personality Facet, Third Round Matter Facet, etc. These will be represented by the respective symbols [2P], [2M], [3P], {3M], etc. Analogously, the first manifestations of Personality and Matter may be said to belong to the First Round, and may be represented by [1P] and [1M] respectively, if we so desire.

Postulate of Sequence Within a Round

The sequence of the isolate facets within a round should be the same as given by the Postulate for Sequence.

Restatement of The Transformation

In the light of these postulates and the associated symbols, we may rewrite the transformation of the subject under consideration in the following form:

(BC)	[P]	[E]	[2P]	[2E]	[3P]	[S]	[T]
Medicine	Lungs	Disease	Tubercular bacillus	Treatment	X-ray	India	1950s

Translation from the Verbal to the Notational Plane

The result of translating the (BC) and the Isolate Terms into the (BC) and Isolate Numbers is as follows, if we use the Colon Classification:

(BC)	[P]	[E]	[2P]	[2E]	[3P]	[S]	[T]
L	45	4	21	6	253	44	N5

Synthesis in the Notational Plane

To do the synthesis in the notational plane, we shall use the additional postulate stated below:

Postulate 2 of Omission of Connecting Symbol

In Colon Classification, the connecting symbol need not be inserted before [2P], [3P], etc, if these follow immediately after [E], [2E], etc.

Colon Classification

In the light of the postulates, we get the following Colon Number for the subject under consideration: L45:421:6253.44'N5.

Universal Decimal Classification

The Universal Decimal Number is 616.24-002.5:615.849, where

61 =Medicine (MC)
6 = Disease [E]
24 = Lungs [P]
02.5 = Tubercular bacillus [2P]
61 = Medicine (MC)
5 = Therapeutics [E2]
849 = X-ray [P3]

Facet for Levels: Example from Literature

Its name is given as "Criticism of Hamlet". This name is extremely elliptical. In the first instance, we have to supply the word "Literature" as the name of the (BC). We have next to recall that "Hamlet" implies that it is a work of Shakespeare, the English dramatist. If we fill up the ellipsis fully, the Full Name of the Subject becomes "Criticism of the Hamlet of Shakespeare, the dramatist, in the literature of the English Language."

Analysis in the Idea Plane

Obviously there is no [T] or [S] or [M]. "Criticism" [E]. The Isolate Idea denoted by the respective residual word-groups has to be taken as a manifestation of Personality. This is indicated by the method of residues. Thus, the facet analysis of the Full Name of the Subject gives the result:

"Criticism" is [E] of the Hamlet [P] of Shakespeare [P] the dramatist [P] in the literature (BC) of the English language [P]."

Transformation in the Verbal Plane

Our thinking in arranging the five facets will run along the following lines:

"Criticism" presupposes the work criticized. Therefore, we agree that the [E] "Criticism" should some only after the [P] "Hamlet". Similarly, "Hamlet" presupposes "Shakespeare"; "Shakespeare" presupposes "Drama"; and "Drama" presupposes "English Language." Thus the transformation in the verbal plane will give the result shown in the following table:

(BC)	(P)	[P]	[P]	[P]	[E]
Literature	English	Drama	Shakespeare	Hamlet	Criticism

Levels among Facets

In the above table, [P] occurs four times in the first round itself. Subjects such as this give rise to the postulate stated below.

Postulate of Level

Personality may manifest itself in one and the same round in a subject, more than once-that is, in two or more Levels.

So also in the case of Matter, Space, and Time.

We now introduce some new terms and the symbols to represent them. The Second, Third, etc. Manifestation of Personality in one and the same round of a subject shall be respectively called the Second Level Personality Facet, the Third Level Personality Facet, etc. These will be represented respectively by [P2], [P3], etc. So also with manifestations of Matter, of a similar nature.

A little consideration will show that the second and later levels of [P] in the second round should be represented by [2P2], [2P3], etc. Analogously the first level of [P] in the second round may be represented by [2P1], if so desired.

Analogously, the levels of [P] in the first round may be represented by [1P1], [1P2], [1P3], etc, if so desired.

So also with manifestations of Matter, Space, and Time, of a similar nature.

Postulate of Level Cluster

Facets of different levels of the same Fundamental Category within a round should be kept together.

Restatement of the Transformation

As a result of these postulates and the associated symbols, the statement of facet analysis will take the following form:

(BC)	(P)	[P2]	[P3]	[P4]	[1E]
Literature	English	Drama	Shakespeare	Hamlet	Criticism

Synthesis

As a result f the translation of the (BC) and Isolate Terms into the respective (BC) and Isolate Numbers, and of their synthesis, we get the following Colon Number for the subject:

O111,2J64,51:g

The omission of the connecting symbol (which in this case is a comma) between the Isolate Number 2 and J64 is due to the postulate stated below.

Postulate 3 For Omission of Connecting Symbol

In Colon Classification, of two consecutive facets, if all the isolate numbers in the earlier facet are known to consist of the same number of digits, the connecting symbol between the two facets may be omitted.

Postulation Approach

This postulation approach to classification helps to see the discipline objectively and provides a safeguard against loose or hazy yhniking. It makes each subject brings its own facet formula in its pocket, so as to speak. One must have much drill in the recognition of the fundmaental categories, and of rounds and levels of facets, in teh formation of the full name of a subject and of its transformation according to the postulates, in the separation of the work in teh idea, verbal and the notational planes, in the translation of the (BC) and the Isolate terms into numbers, and in synthesising the (BC) and teh Isolate Numbers into the Class Numbers. Then classification will become an interesting piece of work. The Colon Classification gives a facet formula for most of the (BC) in part 2, and names those facets in colourful significant terms in part 1, just to help beginners to get familiar with the procedure of classifying set out in the next chapter. After some experience, student otgrow the need for such props. They become able to analyse the name of any subject into its facet straight away, and to arrange those facets in proper sequence with teh aid of the concept of fundamental categories, the postulates, and the principles for sequence of facet given section N3.

Analytico-Synthetic Classification

It may be further stated that a scheme of classification which admits of facet analysis, provides rule for the arrangement of facets, provides for teh schedules for teh different kinds of facet needed in diverse subjects, provides connecting symbols, and admits of eth synthesis of the (BC) and teh Isolate Numbers of a subject into its Class Number, is called an Analytico-synthetic Scheme of Classification. The Colon Classification and the Universal Decimal Classification are Analytico-synthetic schemes.

Enumerative Classification

On the other hand, and Enumerative Scheme does not rest on facet analysis. It does not, in general, give a multiplicity of schedules for (BC) and the different kinds of Isolates. Generally speaking, it gives only a single schedule which enumerates full0fleged classes with their ready-made class numbers.

11

Canons in Idea Plane

Canons for Filiatory Sequence

In a coalesced array, if A_1, A_2, A_3, etc are subordinate subjects of any order whatever of subject A, originated in one or another of the chains originating from the subject A, the subjects A_1, A_2, A_3, etc should immediately follow the Subject A in succession, without being separated from it or among themselves by any other subject. [Far the significance of this new Canon see Prolegomena Ed 3, Sec EU1.]

Canon of Coordinate Subjects

In a coalesced array, if Subject A and Subject B had originated in one and the same array and had been consecutive in it, they should not be separated from each other by any subject other than the subjects A_1, A_2, A_3, etc, having A as their common immediate universe.

Concept of Level Cluster

The Dynamic Theory of Library Classification includes the concept of Levels of manifestation of one and the same Fundamental Category in one and the same Round (See Sec Mv). Further, Sec Mw gives the Postulate of Level Cluster and Sec Mx gives the Postulate of Sequence of the Levels in a Level Cluster of one and the same Fundamental Category within one and the same Round. This last mentioned Postulate calls for a Canon in respect of Levels, similar to the Canon of Modulation f or Chain (See Gp). The next section formulates the necessary new Canon for work in the Idea Plane.

Canon of Modulation of Levels of Facets

A Level Cluster should comprise one Level, of each and every Remove lying between the Manifestation of the Whole and the last Level in the Level Cluster.

Principles for Facet Sequence / Wall-Picture Principle

If two facets A and B of a subject are such that the concept behind B will not be operative unless the concept behind A is conceded, even as a mural picture is not possible unless the wall exists to draw upon, then the facet A should precede the facet B.

For example, in "Prevention of Disease" the concept behind the term `Prevention' is not operative unless the concept behind the term `Disease' is conceded. Therefore the sequence of the two facets should be "Disease" and "Prevention."

The Postulate, prescribing the sequence of the manifestations of the five fundamental categories in any Subject or in any Round to be PMEST (See Sec Ms), can be seen to be a corollary of the Wall-Picture Principle. If the Facets are arranged according to the Wall-Picture Principle, on applying the Principle of Inversion (8) , on the shelf the documents will get arranged according to Increasing Concreteness.

Corollaries of Wall-Picture Principle / Whole Organ Principle

If, in a subject, facet "B" is an organ of facet "A," then A should precede B.

For example, in "Mouth of Cow," the facet "Mouth" is the organ of the facet "Cow." Therefore, the sequence of the two facets should be "Cow" and "Mouth."

Cow-Calf Principle

If a facet A and another facet B belonging to the same subject are not to be separated though they are distinct from each other and thus separable, A and B should be kept together in the same Round, even as a milch cow and its unweaned calf are not separately sold out though they are distinct entities and thus separable, but are kept together in possession of the same owner.

For example, in "President of India," the facets "President" and "India" should not be separated and put into different Rounds, although they are separable. Both of the facets should be kept together in one and the same Round. The determination of the sequence of these two facets will have to be done with the help of the Wall-Picture Principle; it will be "India" and "President."

Commodity or Result-Actand-Action-Actor-Tool Principle

If in a subject, facet C denotes Action on facet B which is Actand by facet D as Actor with facet E as the tool, and facet A is the Commodity or Result of the Action, then the five facets should be arranged in the sequence A, B, C, D, and E.

For example, in the "Spinning of Cotton with Charkha by Girls, thus producing the Commodity Yarn" the Action is "Spinning," the Actand is "Cotton," the Actor is "Girls," the Tool is "Charkha," and the Commodity or Result is "Yarn." Therefore, the sequence of the facets will be "Yarn," "Cotton," "Spinning," "Girls," and "Charkha."

This Principle also can be seen to be a corollary of the Wall-Picture Principle. For, unless the concept behind "Yarn" is conceded, the concept behind "Cotton" will not be operative. Again unless the concept behind "Cotton" is conceded, the concept behind "Spinning" will not be operative. Further, unless the concept behind "Spinning" is conceded, the concept behind "Girls" will not be operative. So also, unless the concept behind "Girls" is conceded, the concept behind "Charkha" will not be operative.

Principles for Chronology and Evolution Principle of Later-in-Time

If the isolates in a schedule have originated in different times, they should be arranged in a parallel progressive time sequence, except when any other overwhelming consideration rules it out.

For example, in C C in the Schedule of Religions, the Religions are arranged in the sequence: Vedic, Post-Vedic, Jainism, Buddhism,

Judaism, Christianity, and Islam. On the other hand the sequence given in D C and U D C is unhelpful, as the Principle, of Later-in-Time is violated. They arrange the Religions in the sequence Christianity, Vedic, Post-Vedic, Buddhism, Jainism, Judaism, and Islam. Obviously, Christianity and Jainism are in wrong places.

Principles Involving "Bottom" and "Top" Principle of Bottom-Upwards

If the isolates in a schedule can be conveniently taken to occur along a vertical line, they may be arranged from Bottom-upwards, if it is helpful. For example, the Organs of a Plant should be arranged in the sequence Root, Stem, Branch etc. C C and U D C give this sequence. Further, one set of the organs of a cycle will stand arranged in C C in the sequence, Wheel, Driving mechanism, Frame, and Steering, mechanism.

Principle of Top-Downwards

If the isolates in a schedule can be conveniently taken, to occur along a vertical line, they may be arranged from Top-downwards, if it is helpful.

For example, the helpful sequence of the sub-organs of the Root of a plant will be to start from Root-stem and follow its successive branchings.

Principles Involving "Left" and "Right" / Principle of Left-to-Right

If the isolates in a schedule can be conveniently taken to occur along a horizontal line, they may be arranged from Left-to-Right, if it is helpful.

Principle of Right-to-Left

If the isolates in a schedule can be conveniently taken to occur along a horizontal line, they may be arranged Right-to-Left, if it is helpful.

For example, the following is a helpful sequence of the lanes and other items on a highway: Crown, Motor cars way, Heavy motors vehicles way, Bicycle way, Cart way, Pedestrian way, and

Kerb. Since the "Crown" is in the centre, if the sequence on one side of the Crown is taken to be from Left-to-Right, the sequence on the other side will have to be taken to be from Right-to-Left. It is helpful to begin with the Crown of the road, because the lanes in the road stand arranged symmetrically on both sides of the Crown.

Principles Involving "Front" and "Back" / Principle of Front-to-Back

If the isolates in a schedule can be conveniently taken to occur from "Front" to "Back" they may be arranged Front-to-Back, if it is helpful.

For example, in a Railway train the helpful arrangement of its components will be, Locomotive, Parcel van, Passenger vans, and Guard van.

Principles Involving "Clockwise Direction" and "Counter-Clockwise Direction" / Principle of Clockwise Direction

If the isolates in a schedule can be conveniently taken to occur along a circular line, they may be arranged in the clockwise direction, if it is helpful.

For example,

1 In C C the Zodiacal divisions are arranged in the Clockwise direction.

World library, National library, Regional library, State library, District library, and City library. Here the quantity is the area or the size of population served.

Principle of Increasing Complexity

If the isolates in a schedule show different degrees of complexity, they should be arranged parallel to the sequence of increasing complexity, except when any other overwhelming consideration rules it out.

For example, in C C the "Elements" in Linguistics are arranged in the sequence: Isolated sound, Syllable, Word, Phrase, Clause, Sentence, and Piece of composition.

Principle of Canonical Sequence

If the isolates in a schedule are traditionally referred to in a specific sequence, although no underlying principle is discoverable, it will be convenient to conform to this traditional sequence.

For example,

1. In C C the Basic Divisions of Mathematics are arranged in the sequence: Arithmetic, Algebra, Analysis, Calculus, Trigonometry, Geometry, and Mechanics.

2. In D C the fruits in "Agriculture" are arranged in the sequence:Pome fruits, Stone fruits, Citrus fruits, Minor fruits, Nut fruits, Palmaceous fruits, and Small fruits.

Principle of Literary Warrant

The isolates in a schedule may be arranged in the sequence of the decreasing quantity of the documents published or anticipated to be published on them, except when any other overwhelming consideration rules it out.

For example, C C arranges the agricultural crops in the sequence: Rice, Wheat, Oat, Rye, Corn, Barley, and Millet. D C and U D C have put "Rice" at the end.

12

Postulational Procedure

The Pastulational Procedure in Classifying is in nine steps. The results at the end of each step are given below:

b0 Raw title. – The title found on the title page or the one provided by a classifier in the case of a fanciful title;

b1 Expressive title. -Title derived from the Raw title by:

b11 Filling up the ellipses, if any, in the Raw title, be they names of isolates or of Basic Subjects; and

b12 Breaking composite terms, if any, into their fundamental constituent terms.

b2 Title in Kernel Terms. – Title derived from the Expressive Title by:

b21 Removing all the apparatus wards, if any;

b22 Bringing each Kernel term (= remaining substantive term) to its nominative singular farm; except that the qualifier terms. if any, may have to be kept in the adjectival form;

b3 Analysed Title. – The title derived from the Title in Kernel Terms by:

b31 Finding out the Fundamental Category of which the idea denoted by each Kernel term may be deemed to be a manifestation (See Sec Mj) ;

b32 Determining the Round to which each Kernel Term should be assigned (See Sec Mn/q) ;

b33 Determining the Level of each Kernel Term within each Round (See Sec Mr);

b34 Putting, after the Kernel Term denoting the Basic Subject, the symbol (BF) (See Sec My);

b35 Putting, after each of the other Kernel Terms, the symbol for the Fundamental Category of which it is deemed to be a manifestation;

b36 Putting, before the digit of each Fundamental Category, the digit showing the round of the manifestation of the Fundamental Category; or

b37 Putting, after the digit of each Fundamental Category, the digit showing the Level of the Manifestation of the Fundamental Category;

b4 Transformed Title. —Title derived from the Analysed Title by:

b41 Rearranging the Kernel Terms along with their respective Symbols and Digits given after them within brackets, in accordance with their respective Fundamental Categories, Rounds, and Levels.

b5 Title in Standard Terms. —Title derived from the Transformed Title by:

b51 Replacing each of the Kernel Terms by its equivalent Standard Term, given, if any, in the schedule of the Scheme for Library Classification.

b7 Class Number of the Subject. — Derived from the Title in Focal Numbers by:

b71 Replacing the symbol and the digit within brackets, by the Indicator Digit appropriate to the succeeding Focal Number, as prescribed by the Scheme for Library Classification.

b8 Verification. — Translating the Facet Numbers into, Facet Terms, transforming the sequence of the Facet Terms according to the Syntax of the Natural Language and checking up if the result got is equivalent to the Title classified.

Nine Steps of the Postulational Procedure

Steps in the Idea Plane

Steps b0 to b3 belong to the Idea Plane. Steps b0 to b2 may appear to belong to the Verbal Plane. But it is not so in reality. A Little thought will show this. The purpose of these steps is merely to lay bare the idea in the raw title in its pure form by removing all the verbal elements hiding it.

Steps in the Verbal Plane

Steps b4 and b5 belong to the Verbal Plane. Step b4 is only changing over the sequence of the words in the natural language - that is, from the syntax of the natural language - to the sequence of the words as they should be in the classificatory language - that is, into the syntax of the classificatory language - even as it is done in translation from one natural language to another. Step b5 is only changing over from the non-technical terms of the natural language into technical ones, so as to make translation into Focal Numbers easy and unerring.

Steps in the Notational Plane

Steps b6 and b7 belong to the Notational Plane. In fact step b5 marks the entry into Notational Place. Step b7 introduces the punctuation marks (Indicator Digits) necessary to make a Class Number meaningful. A Class Number in a classificatory language corresponds to a sentence in a natural language. A classificatory language is agglutinative; but natural language is not. In a classificatory language the syntax depends on the relative position of the facet numbers, which corresponds to words in a natural language; the Focal Numbers correspond to noun farms in nominative singular as they are given in the Title in Kernal Terms. The relative position of the Focal Numbers in the classificatory language is indicated by Indicator Digits. But in a natural language the syntax does not depend on the relative position of the words.

Step of Verification

Step b8 is only by way of abundant caution as is usually done when the translation is from one natural language to another.

Long-Winded Nature of the Procedure

The several steps indicated in Sec Nb do imply the long-winded nature of the Postulational Procedure in Classifying. This slowing dawn of the process of classifying is necessary in drilling a beginner in ,the work of classifying. But a veteran will go through most of these steps in his mind almost in a few minutes, if not seconds.

Example 1 of Postulational Procedure in Classifying

Only the results in the successive steps 0 to 5 in the Procedure in classifying are given here. The results in steps 6 and 7 will be given in Chap W.

Step 0 Raw Title. – Essentials of Cardiology

Step 1 Expressive Title. – Disease of heart, in medicine

Step 2 Title in Kernel Terms. – Disease [1MP1]. Heart [1P1]. Medicine (BF).

Step 3 Analysed Title. – Disease [1 MP1] . Heart [1P1]. Medicine (BF).

Step 4 Transformed Title. – Medicine (BF') Heart [1P1]. Disease [1P1].

Step 5 Title in Standard Terms. – Medicine (BF). Heart [1P1]. Disease [1MP1].

Example 2 of Postulational Procedure in Classifying

In this example the results in Steps 0 and 5 only are given

Step 0 Raw Title. – Cardiac diagnosis.

Step 5 Title in Standard Terms. - Medicine (BF). Heart [1P1]. Disease [1MP1]. Diagnosis [lE].

Example 3 of Postulational Procedure in Classifying

Here also, the results in Steps 0 and 5 only are given

Step 0 Raw Title. – Cardiac radiology.

Step 5 Title in Standard Terms. – Medicine (BF). Heart [1P1]. Disease [1MP1]. Diagnosis [lE]. Radiation [2P1].

Example 4 of the Postulational Procedure for Classifying

Here, the results in Steps 0 and 5 only are given

Step 0 Raw Title. – Diseases of the Chest.

Step 5 Title in Standard Terms. - Medicine (BF). Thorax [1P1]. Disease [1MP1].

13

Fundamental Categories, Arrays and Chains

FUNDAMENTALS OF KNOWLEDGE CLASSIFICATION

Structure of Knowledge Classification: The whole universe of knowledge is divided into three areas—Natural Sciences, Humanities and Social Sciences. This is the first step in the process of the division of knowledge. From these three areas, the main classes are derived. Main classes have been established by tradition. They are the areas under which study and research have been conducted in the past. The academicians have contributed sufficient literature on them. They are the organizational units for teaching, particularly in the Universities, all over the world. The specialists and professions exist in each of these classes. For example, Chemists for the main class Medicine; Botanists, specializing in main class Botany; Economists, dealing with the main class Economics, and so on.

Main class as a term in classification has been defined in various ways by different authors. Ranganathan has defined main class as "the fairly homogeneous, conventional regions of knowledge, which together form the first order array of classes which are mutually exclusive and totally exhaustive of the field of knowledge". In *Prolegomena* he mentions:

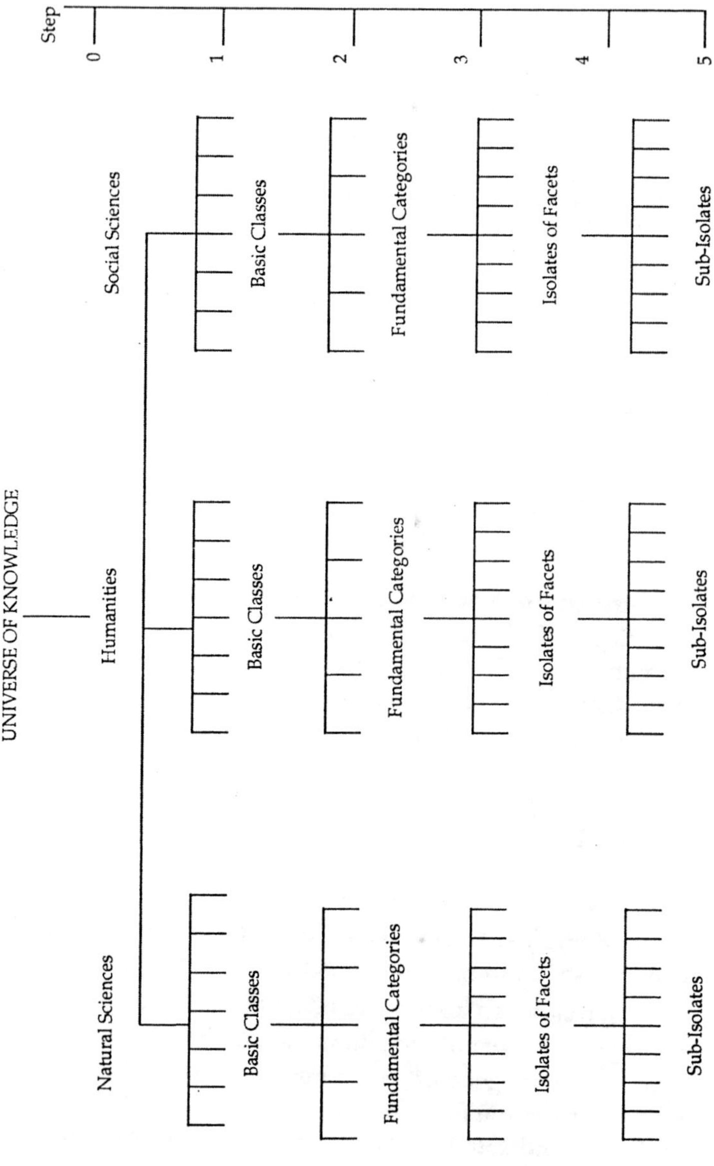

Chart Showing Division of Knowledge

Main class: Any class enumerated in the first order array of a scheme of classification of the Universe of Knowledge. This definition is valid only for the scheme concerned.

This means that the main classes in all the schemes of classification may not be the same. But the classes which appear as the major divisions of the Universe of Knowledge, are the main classes in that scheme. This also means that Main class is not a very precise term. But the determination of correct main classes is a vital point in knowledge classification, because the success of further division with the help of the fundamental categories would rest on the right connotation of each main class under which an effective facet formula can be worked out.

Once the Knowledge is organized into a number of main classes, the next step is to mark out for each main class the facets which are likely to be presented by subjects falling within it. Most of the main classes admit of this being done. Recognition of the possible facets of subjects in a main class and relating each such facet to its fundamental category is the third step in the division of the Universe of Knowledge. The concept of fundamental categories will be taken up separately. After the application of the idea of categories to enumerate the facets, the isolates which make up each facet are sorted out and arranged in a helpful sequence. The enumeration of the isolates corresponding to each fundamental category is the fourth step in the process of the division of the Universe of Knowledge. When the need arises, the isolates are further sub-divided into sub-isolates; and if the need continues, the sub-isolates are further sub-divided. These may be termed fifth or sixth step, as the case may be, in the process of division.

The table given in the beginning shows the various steps in the division of knowledge classification. In this table, we find that at very step a group of co-ordinate isolates arises. They are derived from the isolate of an earlier sequence. These isolates are said to be isolates in an ARRAY. When divisions continue further, the isolates from the first chain to the last chain are said to be isolates in a CHAIN.

So far, the following important concepts have been named here:

1. Main classes.
2. Facets under a subject.

3. Isolates in facets and their sub-isolates.
4. Classes in an array.
5. Classes in a chain.

The fundamentals of knowledge classification are the principles associated with these concepts and the implications arising therefrom.

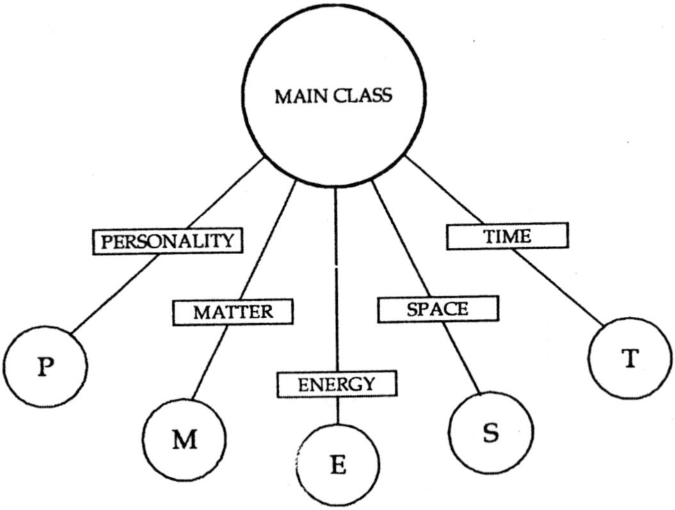

Figure 13.1. Chart Showing Five Fundamental Categories

Facets of a Main Class:

(i) **Where applicable?** The term 'facet' is used at a particular stage in the process of the division of the Universe of Knowledge. When we divide the Universe of Knowledge upto the stage of Main classes, facets do not appear. But when we have to divide a main class, the concept of facets appears in the case of some main classes.

(ii) **Purpose.** The purpose of facets is to divide a main class into its possible aspects. As a Main class, contains a number of smaller units of ideas or entities within it, one method of their division is to group all of them only in one line. Suppose, a main class has a total of one hundred entities, according to one method, they can be enumerated as below:

Main Class

1
2
3
4
5
.
.
72
73
.
85
.
93
.
.
.
100

All the hundred entities that arise in a main class, can be arranged in a column. This placement may still be helpful. This type of division of main classes is said to be the arrangement in one direction. It starts fromitem 1 and goes to the last item. Here decimal fraction notation has not been followed. This method can be named as direct division of the entities of a subject in one column.

(iii) **How applicable?** Another possible method for the division of a main class is to divide it first into its possible facets. The process can be termed as recognizing categories under a class. Thereafter the entities under each sub-group are individualized. This method can be named as indirect individualization of entities under different aspect-heads (facets), of a subject, in many columns. This concept of facets can be further explained thus : Suppose the main class is Psychology. It will obviously contain certain entities. In the circle below we get a total of only nine entities. They have to be arranged and individualized.

The direct method of their arrangement will be as follows:-

Psychology

1. Sensation.
2. Sex.
3. Cognition.
4. Adolescence.

5. Personality.
6. Abnormals.
7. Nervous System.
8. Emotion.
9. Child.

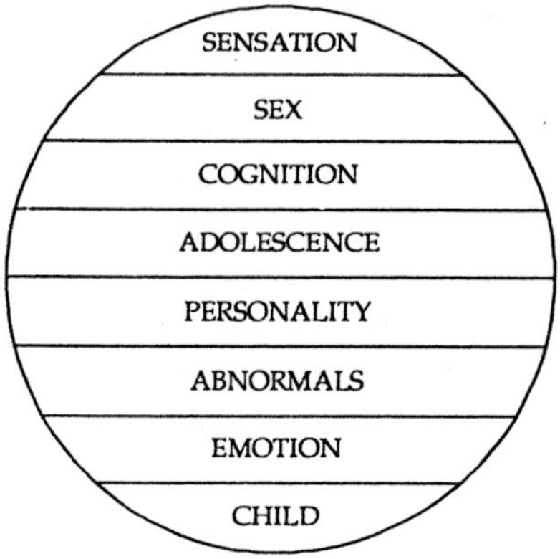

Figure 13.2. Method of individualization

The following is the method of individualization through facets. An examination of the nature of the contents of the circle will show that there are two types of facets into which these nine entities can be grouped.

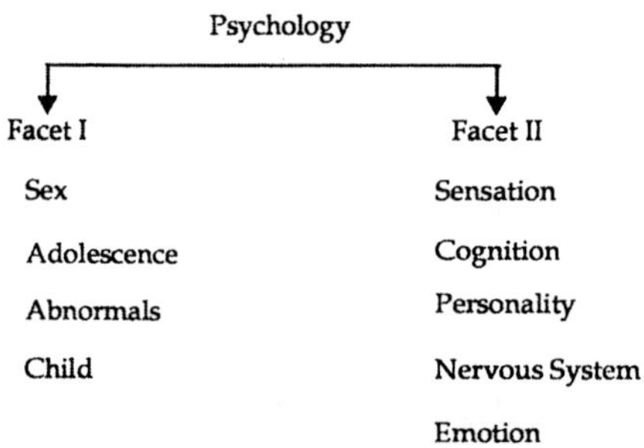

Figure 13.3. Division of Facets

(iv) **Definition.** So, facets are divisions of a main class through which all the entities of a class are first grouped under each possible category and then individualized. The facets of a class are determined with the help of a certain train of characteristics which are applied to the subject for its division. These are many trains of characteristics each of which divides a subject. A certain number of trains of characteristics will yield an equal number of facets of a class.

But the question of facets is not a simple affair. It is certain that the concept is the best find of the 20th Century of knowledge classification, and it is universally accepted that credit for it goes to Ranganathan. All modern researches in documentation, coding and classification, have been influenced by the concept of facet analysis. Various attempts have been made to define the term. They are as follows:

Metcalfe: "Facet analysis seems to mean either what has been called subject analysis of particular documents, as a step to their synthetic representation by so called class or code numbers, or it means the analysis of a subject field to discover a basis for its classification, whether enumerative or analytico-synthetic."

Here the author himself is not sure.

Palmer and Wells: "..... facet analysis, which simply means the analysis of a specific subject into the facets produced by the application of different characteristics."

Ranganathan: "The totality of the isolates formed on the basis of a single train of characteristics is a facet, in the idea and verbal planes. The isolate number belonging to a facet is a facet of the class number, in the notational plane."

Wildback: He considers it as a synonym of 'point of view' according to which a subject can be divided.

Foskett: He believes that facet analysis consists in an analysis of a subject in its entirety into a certain number of facets or categories of things; within each category, the subject headings, enumerated all possess the same relationship vis-à-vis subject in its entirety.

"Glossary and Subject Index": "A concept of high generality and wide application which can be used to group other concepts."

A comparative examination of the above statements is bound to lead to an advanced treatment of the topic which is not the purpose of this book. Here it will be sufficient if the concept of facets is understood in the following words:

> *Facets or categories are the sub-major groups of a subject dealing with fundamental aspects into which a main class is divisible. They are derived with the help of different trains of characteristics.*

(v) Facet Analysis. The entire process of determining the facets of a subject is known as Facet Analysis. Once, while dividing a subject we break it into different facets and mention therein all possible entities. Secondly, when we have to classify a document, we examine the entities it contains and the facets to which these entities belongs to in knowledge classification. Atonce we notice the real value of breaking a subject into its facets and that is, when we find that one isolate is in relation with an isolate of a different facet of the same subject. The relation between one whole of a facet with an isolate of a second facet, an isolate of a still other facet and so on, is commonly found in many documents. When we have to individualise this type of relationship, the concept of Facet Analysis comes to our help. Let us take an example.

There are three documents:

a. On flowering plants;
b. On ecology of plants; and
c. On ecology of flowering plants.

These three documents belong to the main class Botany. Document (a) belongs to one facet of the main class based on the family of plant. Document (b) belongs to another facet of the main class based on the problems of study in Botany. These two documents can be classified under two separate facets. But when we take the third document, we find that it deals with the relationship or contact between two units, i.e., ecology and flowering plants. How can we classify this book? If we put it in either of the categories or facets, it is not a proper classification. The solution to this problem comes from the concept of Facet Analysis which will classify the three documents in the following manner:

(vi) **Major issues regarding Facets:** Now we have to decide the following important questions: (a) How many facets or categories are possible in a subject? (b) Do all the subjects possess different types of facets; or is there similarity between the facets of different subjects? (c) Will all the subjects be divisible into facets or some will not lend themselves to division? (d) What should be the sequence between different facets? (e) What shall be the structure and process of division of facets? (f) How to indicate different types of relations between the units of facets? And so on.

Before we take up these major issues, it will be necessary to mention that Ranganathan has expounded certain theoretical principles to deal with these issues. What others have contributed on these issues is not comprehensive. If their contribution is significant, then we have to admit that their starting points had been the formulations by Ranganathan. This argument, however, in no way means that all what Ranganathan has contributed to this topic is the final word.

Facets or Categories in Main Classes: Ranganathan has postulated five fundamental categories, namely:

1. Time
2. Space
3. Energy
4. Matter
5. Personality.

According to him most of the subjects are divisible in these five categories (aspects or points of views). That is, a subject may have a Personality aspect, a Matter aspect, an Energy aspect, a Space aspect, and a Time aspect. The isolates of PMEST under different subjects may be different in idea plane but the types of characteristics which will yield them will be more or less the same, and if different, they will be relevant to the subject concerned and its particular facet.

Time

Time is a simple concept. It indicates that the entities under different subjects must go on changing in its structure, meaning, history, development, etc., with the progress of time. Subjects get expounded differently with the progress of time. Suppose it is the question of science in the 20th Century. It differs in its structure, and development, etc., from the science of the 19th Century or the 18th Century. Like this, time occurs under every main class. So all possible divisions of time including century, decade, year, month, day, hour, etc., together may form a facet of a subject. In CC, we find a "Chronological Table" and this can be applied to any subject requiring time facet. In DC, we find that Time as a facet of a subject has been used under the classes History, Literature and at other places. The Need for this facet is due to the necessity of distinguishing between the documents on a subject differing only from the point of view of time. Further, the following examples will justify the need for Time facet under a subject:

a. International Organisations in 1925.
b. International Organisations in 1963.

In the above specific subjects the isolate of International Organisations is common, i.e., the same. So these two subjects should go together, but the time isolate concerning them differs. In one subject it is 1925 and in the other it is 1963.

Space

Space is no less important than time in its being a facet of a subject. Most of the subjects, if not all, get manifested, in relation with continents, countries and their sub-divisions. Music in Europe is different from that in Africa. Painting in India is of different style then in Japan. Economics of Soviet Union is different from that of the United States. History of different countries will often vary. You will always find difference, a vast one, in the scope of subjects if they are related with Congo on the one hand and New York on the other. Space matters in the manifestation of a subject, and because the approach by people to a subject is often in accordance with its scope prevalent in a particular geographical area, individualization through space becomes a great necessity. Ranganathan considers the surface of the earth as manifestation of the fundamental category space and it is required under every subject for indicating local description (variation) or local history, as he puts it.

In CC, we find a schedule of Geographical Divisions which can be attached to a subject. In DC, we find the space facet applicable under the class History and throughout the scheme the facet is available under the direction divide like 940-999. At places where the above instructions are not given and the division is found necessary according to countries, etc., one can get it as a division of '094-099' under from divisions. DC has fully provided for the space facet in its divisions. Palmer and Wells feel that it is an intuitive recognition by DC.

Energy

The fundamental category Energy covers the problems, actions including methods, functioning, etc., aspects of a main class. Palmer and Wells further qualify it as a mode of work or approach. Mills feels that Energy is a category of facet which characterizes the exercise of energy, i.e., activities, operations, processes problems, etc. Many main classes will have certain units which deal with the problems in the subject. These problems are generally applicable to all the organs of the class. In class Agriculture we find certain processes and actions like sowing and harvesting. In Botany, Zoology and Medicine we find units like Physiology and Pathology which deal with functioning. Isolates which make the category Energy are generally the important problems of the subject and command a greater influence on the subject from two directions. One is, when they are in general reference to the class and the second when they refer to the organs of the subject individually. For example, Morphology, Physiology and Pathology are at one hand the general disciplines in Biological Sciences and Medicine, and are referred to as abstract techniques in relation with respective main classes. But when they are connected with a particular family of animals or plants and are in relation with various organs of human body, they deal with concrete entities in their context.

A further clarification of Energy is given by Ranganathan when he deals with common energy isolates, viz., Intellectual activities, Industrial activities and Institutional activities. He Identifies Energy with activities. When they are common to all they become common isolates and when they are special to a class, they make its fundamental category Energy.

Both CC and DC incorporate fundamental category Energy in their main Classes as illustrated below:

Main Class	DC No.	Energy Facet	CC No.
Botany	581.1	Plant Physiology	I:3
Botany	581.2	Plant Pathology	I:4
Botany	581.4	Plant Morphology	I:2
Botany	581.5	Plant Ecology	I:5
Education	375	Curriculum	T:2
History	327	Foreign Relations	V:19
Economics	337	Tariff Policy	X:53
Chemistry	543	Analytical Chemistry	E:3

The above topics are the Energy aspects in different main classes in DC and CC.

Ranganathan postulates that the energy aspect in a main class may manifest itself in different rounds of energy. 2E = second round of energy after IE; 3E = third round of energy after 2E, and so on. In a subject like the main class medicine, pathology or disease is a problem and therefore it is [1E] of the subject. Treatment and surgery, etc., are for actions on diseases themselves and therefore they are the [2E] of the subject. A particular subsequent round of energy facet may be further subdivided by its own Personality, Matter and energy facets.

In *Classification and Communication,* Ranganathan says that Energy is perhaps the most ubiquitous of all the fundamental categories and he expects that there can be no basic class whose subjects do not present an energy facet. On the potency of this facet Ranganathan says, "The efficiency of a scheme of classification and its expectation of life will be determined largely by its capacity to isolate, handle and organize energy facets in different subjects. It is only when energy facet develops that personality gets differentiated and becomes comprehensible. Such is the potency of energy facets."

Matter

The fundamental category matter has been defined by a number of thinkers.

To Mills: Matter is the category of facets which reflect substances, materials, etc; it is manifested clearly in most technologies, and in many of natural sciences; it is generally absent from theoretical disciplines like Law, Economics, Literature.

To Vickery: Matter comprises constituent materials of all kinds.

To Palmer and Wells: This is another fairly simple concept to visualize in the forms it takes in various subjects. If we were classifying books on the manufacturing of paper we should want some divisions based on the raw materials; this would relate to the concept matter. The first characteristic of division (in DC) for 691, building materials, is based on Matter.

Matter facet is inherent in many subjects falling within main classes. But those in which it is enumerated in CC are : Library-Science, Engineering, Sculpture, Painting and Music. The main classes Economics, Sociology and Anthropology, have now sufficient literary warrant calling for a schedule of matter isolates for use in classifying the subjects belonging to them. There can be different levels in the manifestation of matter in a main class, like M_1, M_2, M_3, M_4, etc.

Personallity

The fundamental category Personality is most concrete and the category Time is the most abstract. Mills thinks that Personality does not correspond to yet recognizable and consistent characteristic. Yet, Personality facet is the category of first importance in many of the subjects belonging to any class, and while being so, it is the most recognizable facet at least to the specialists of a class. Mills himself says: "The term personality is used to describe those facets of any subject which are generally unique to that subject and which give it its essential character or personality." Palmer and Wells rightly feel that it is not really difficult to recognize the Personality facet of a class. They consider it the wholeness of any subject.

Personality is the first facet in many subjects and it is often experienced that the other facets work as attributes of personality for its further sub-division. Matter, Energy, Space and Time are often required in relation with personality facet, and it is comparatively in lesser degree that they are required in direct relation with the main class, as a whole, wherein Personality also remains diffused. Such important Personality isolates in subjects belonging to different Main Classes are, for example, crops in Agriculture; human body in Medicine; educands in Education; substances in Chemistry; business in Economics; groups in Psychology and Sociology; families of plants and animals in Botany and Zoology, respectively, communities according to Geographical areas in History and Law; and name of the language in Linguistics and Literature, etc. these isolates (Personality) are vital and can thus be termed as first among the equals, or the Prime Facet, etc. in short, the personality of a subject will be a vital area which forms the body of the subject or makes its basic structure. Without personality there can be no organ, constituent, attribute, action, etc. any main class, where categories are applicable, may have the personality facet. They were almost first to develop under each main class and it was only later on that other aspects of a main class came into importance for study and research, etc.

Within the Personality facet, we find a number of levels into which the whole personality is spread. These are known as levels of

Personality facet. P1, P2, P3, Pr and so on. The different levels are arranged with the help of the principles of helpful sequence. Examples:

Main Class	DC No.	Personality facets	CC No.
Psychology	132	Abnormal Psychology	S 6
Economics	336	Public Finance	X 7
Chemistry	546	Inorganic Chemistry	E 1
Chemistry	547	Organic Chemistry	E 5
Botany	586	Cryptogamia	I1
Zoology	596	Vertebrates	K 9
Engineering	621	Mechanical Engineering	D 6

Levels of Personality

Illustration A	Personality Facets			
Main Class	P1	P2	P3	P4
Literature	Language	Form	Author	His Work

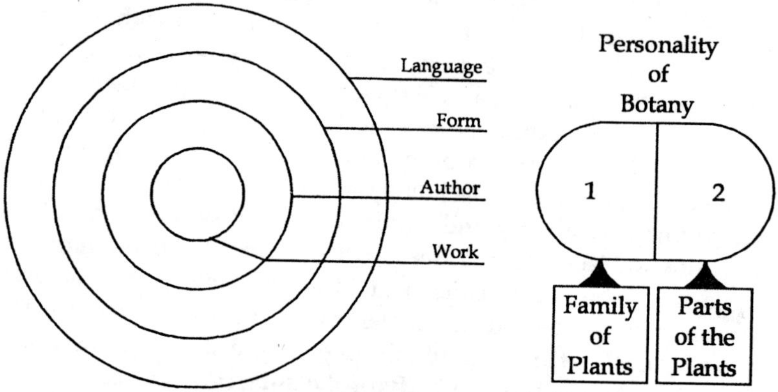

Figure 13.4. Levels of Pesonality

The above illustrations indicate the existence of levels in Personality. The characteristics have been named and with their help isolates are enumerated.

2. Facets of Main Classes: Personality, Matter, Energy, Space and Time are five general fundamental categories under different subjects. These concepts have similar meanings whatever the class be. But as these categories are optional and not compulsory, all may not be present in all the subjects or documents on a subject.

3. Subjects divisible into Facets. The concept of categories should be applicable in all subjects. Its application only under certain subjects shall not be a sound principle. It is not impossible to divide all subjects in their respective categories, but due to the traditional practice, certain subjects should not be divided into its facets. Such subjects are known as Canonical Classes. Probably, their divisions in traditional manner is still more helpful than the helpfulness, our attempt to categories them would yield as in the case of Mathematics, Philosophy, etc. Ranganathan calls them the Canonical Classes because they are divided on canonical lines.

In order to distinguish between them in notation, different connecting symbols have been prescribed by Ranganathan:

, Comma for Personality Facet.

; Semi-colon for Matter Facet.

: Colon for Energy Facet.

. Point for Space Facet.

' Single inverted comma for Time Facet.

4. Process of Divisions of Facets. Facets are divided into their isolates. They are generally enumerated in the schedules of a scheme of classification. The personality facet in main class Education comprises the type of educands. They are enumerated in CC Schedule:

Isolates under [P]:

1. Pre-secondary.
2. Secondary.
3. Adult.
4. University.
5. Sex.
6. Abnormal.
7. Backward.
8. Other classes.

The energy facet in main class Education comprises the various problems. They are enumerated in CC as follows:

Isolates under [E]:

1. Nomenclatures, etc.
2. Curriculum.
3. Teaching technique.
4. Students' work.
5. Educational measurement.
6. Physical education.
7. Student life.
8. Management.

The isolates mentioned under [P] and [E] categories are further sub-divided into sub-isolates if the need arises.

5. Relations between the Different Units of Facets. The analysis of a specific subject, having an isolate each from five or less number of categories, into its constituents is facet analysis. Suppose the specific subject is curriculum for secondary education in India in 1963.

Notation in CC Synthesis

Main class	Personality	Energy	Space	Time
Education	Secondary	Curriculum	India	1963
T	2	2	44	N63

T 2 : 2. 44r 'N63.

This type of relation between different facets of a subject is known as facet relation.

When one isolate of a facet is in relation with another isolate within the same facet, for example, relation between Secondary and University education, this type of relation is known as intra-facet phase relation.

T 2 O j 4

There is still a third type of relation possible within a facet. When two sub-isolates of an isolate are in relation with each other, this is known as intra-array (Sub-isolates in a facet) phase relation, for example, influence of man on woman.

Y 15 O y 16

Here woman and man are the sub-isolates under the isolate 'group determined by age and sex'. The relation exits between the two sub-isolates.

Conclusion. To sum up, the fundamental categories is a unique concept. It is extremely useful. Its influence has been far and wide. It is mainly because of this concept that Sayers said that if there was an age of Melvil Dewey, this (modern) is certainly an age of Ranganathan. de Grolier says, "CC is the first basically multidimensional bibliographic classification which has ever been conceived. Ranganathan has played a pioneering role; without his work a great part of the movement of ideas, which has manifested itself in recent years in the field of bibliographical classification would probably not have taken place." The postulate of fundamental categories has shown a new path. It matters little whether the categories are five in number or seven or still more. One will agree with the views of Prof. S. Das Gupta who asserted (in one of my discussion with him) that it may be too much to start and too less to end with five fundamental categories. The phenomenon of dynamic universe is, however, very much under control because of the postulates regarding rounds and levels. The fact is that in this field a better alternative to Ranganathan's principles is yet to be expounded. It is not impossible to expound them. But when will they be expounded? The gap will probably be the same as between Newton and Einstien or may be lesser due to Space Age. If the 19 th Century witnessed the exposition of one aspect in a document, many of the 20th Century documents comprise many facets. It is to suit the later mode of exposition that the concept of five fundamental categories works for solution of individualization.

In the course of my teaching, I have been explaining to my students the concept of PMEST with the help of an analogy. Think yourself for a moment equal to a subject. Your body is the Personality; the substances etc. that make your body are Matter; your power, problems and movements etc. are Energy; your presence in India, U.K. or U.S.A. is Space; and your relations with 1955, 1960 and 19621 etc., are the manifestations of time.

Principles for Arrays

An array is a group of coordinate classes. At every stage in the process of division arrays are formed. There is an array of co-ordinate classes at the level of the three areas—Natural Sciences, Humanities and Social Sciences. After this, we find an array of Main classes. PMEST are really in an array as subdivisions of a subject. These facets are further divided into isolates, which form separate arrays. Each isolate is further sub-divided and their divisions form an array of sub-isolates. These levels of arrays are distinguished as first order array, second order array, third order array and so on.

Arrays are formed at every stage in the process of division of knowledge and every order of an array is derived from some bigger whole with the help of a train of characteristic. It is certain that arrays cannot be formed at random or in a 'as you please manner'. There are four requisites, which an array should satisfy. The (1) requisite of an array is that it should accommodate in it all that is available in the upper class (immediate universe) which is under division. The (2) requirement of an array is that the isolates in it should not overlap one another. The (3) quality needed for it is that the classes in an array should be arranged in a helpful sequence. The (4) feature of it is that whenever similar things are repeated and required to be arranged in a sequence, they should be in the same helpful sequence as at the place of their occurrence.

i. Canon of Exhaustiveness;
ii. Canon of Exclusiveness;
iii. Canon of Helpful Sequence; and
iv. Canon of Consistent Sequence.

(i) Exhaustiveness: This canon demands that while sub-dividing a class of any extension it should be seen that all its entities find a place in one of the sub-classes, in the array derived from it, meaning thereby that nothing which is available in the common immediate universe under division should be left out of the classes in an array Suppose that the fundamental category [P] of the main class Geography is to be divided. The divisions of this class will form an array. The demands of this canon are shown in the following illustration:

Array of the divisions of (P) of main class Geography

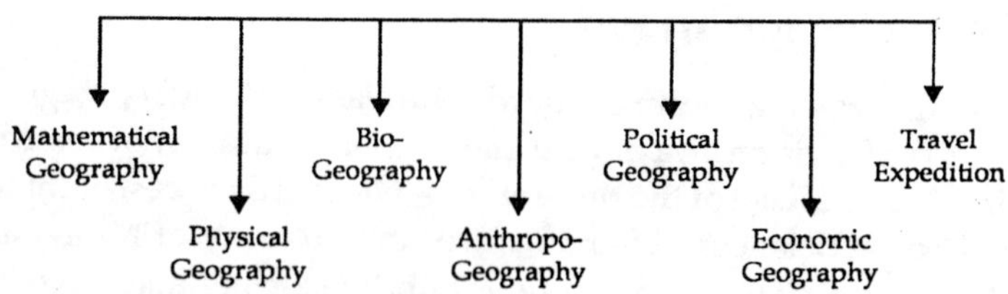

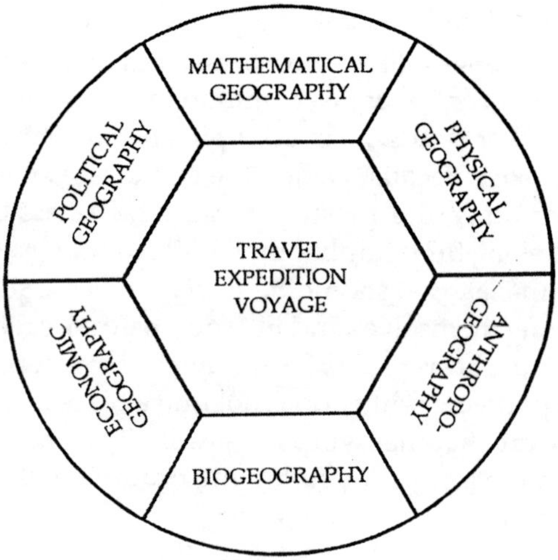

Figure 13.5. Universe [P] of Main Class Geography

These seven classes are co-ordinate among themselves and are derived from one universe. Exhaustiveness means that none of these seven classes should be omitted. Suppose the class number two, i.e., Physical Geography fails to find a place in the array. This will mean that the division is incomplete and all things that are available in the circle have not been accounted for. This absence of a sub-class is the violation of the canon of exhaustiveness. Really speaking, no scheme of classification can afford to miss a sub-class in the array. But it may happen that one may not know of all the possible sub-classes of a subject.

In that case, the best method is to leave gaps, so that whenever, in future a sub-class is fully recognized it is duly accounted for. This problem will arise in case of notation of a scheme of classification. Regarding the already existing sub-classes, the classificationist is bound to provide for all. Mills has found fault in the verdict of this rule when he argues that a class can be perfectly exhausted with the help of dichotomy (i.e., reorganizing only two sub-classes at one stage). But this is a poor way of doing the job, where one is no doubt, technically free from committing a mistake but the results got by dichotomy will be of no use. Therefore, one should exhaust the immediate universe by giving allocation in detail, the range of which may vary from one scheme of another, and from one point of time to another point of time.

(ii) Exclusiveness: The canon prescribes that the isolates in an array should not contain items common to two or more isolates in that array. In other words, no overlapping between the classes in an array should exist. Because, when the two classes will coincide in part with each other, the question arises which class that common part should belong to? It implies that while dividing a class into the array of its sub-classes it should be seen that all the sub-classes are different among themselves and in order to do so, each will have to be derived on the basis of a different single characteristic. This will assure that a particular entity does not find a place in more than one class in the array. In other words, there shall be only one place for each entity in the array. The following example will illustrate the implications of this canon:

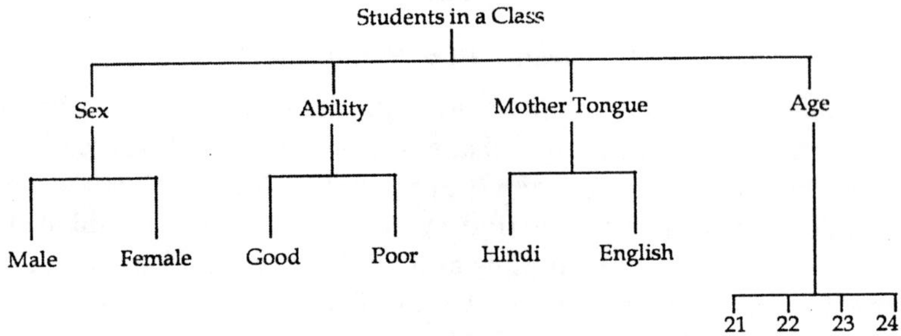

There are four classes in the array derived from the universe of students in a class. Suppose you want to classify Mr. David, an able person of 21 years of age. Under which class should he be placed? According to sex or ability or mother tongue or age, he will fall under all the four classes in the array.

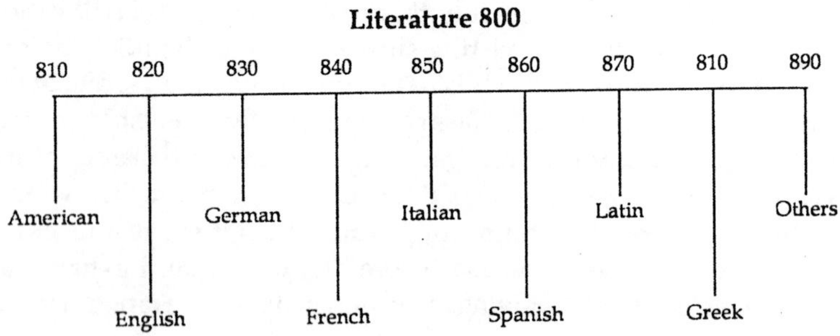

All these classes in an array comprise poetry, drama, fiction, essays, oratory, letters, etc. To arrive at German Poetry one will go to the class German and then to its Poetry. Therefore, the classes in the array are mutually exclusive.

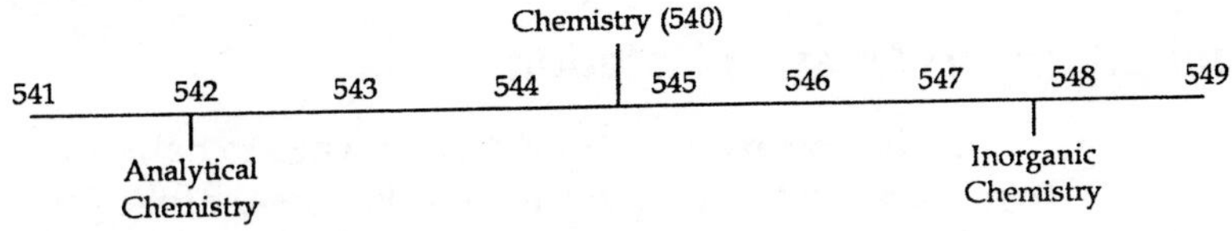

Suppose, the specific subject for classification is analytical chemistry of inorganic substances. To which class (543 or 546) this subject should go? The situation here is not as it was in the case of German Poetry. While both the classes have their claims for the specific subject, we have to select one and reject the other. This is a very difficult situation which is beyond the control of Merill and the 'Guide to Dewey Decimal Classification', where satisfactory solutions are not available.

(iii) Helpful Sequence: The canon of Helpful sequence demands that classes in an array should be arranged in a helpful manner. If there are four classes in an array, there will be $1 \times 2 \times 3 \times 4 = 24$ possible sequences. How to determine that one particular sequence is most helpful than the remaining 23 sequences? This problem has been attended to by a number of thinkers including Bliss, Richardson, Sayers, Ranganathan, etc. If we have to organize the subjects of different extensions in a helpful sequence there is not much difficulty. The principle of decreasing extension will help us. But how to decide the sequence between the co-ordinate classes which make an array? Bliss uses the term 'Collection of co-ordinate classes' and says that they should be arranged or collocated with regard to their characteristics, and relations and the interest and purpose. Sayers has summarized the following principles formulated by Richardson:

1. Logical—from complex to the simplest.
2. Geometrical—position of items in space.
3. Chronological - position according to time.
4. Genetic - per likeness in origin.
5. Historical - combination of preceding characteristics.

6. Evolutionary – from simple to complex.
7. Dynamic – sequence of power.
8. Alphabetical
9. Mathematical

Hospitality in Array in Notation

Ranganathan has been able to find certain ways to help solve this crisis. To make a notation hospital in array, he uses the following devices:

a. Interpolation Device;
b. Sector Device and Group Notation;

a. Interpolation Device: It looks after the cause of hospitality in array mostly at the level of main classes. A digit of almost similar meaning in another language is inserted between the two digits of a particular species already used in notation. In CC we find the use of bita, Lambda, mu, etc., of Greek alphabet used after B, before L and after M, respectively. The notational value of new digits is fixed at the relevant position. It is in this manner that more places are created in a notation to accommodate newly developed subjects at relevant places.

b. Sector Device and Group Notation: Confronted with a situation where the number of classes in an array is more than nine while digits are limited to nine, Ranganathan decided to sacrifice one out of nine digits (i.e., digit 9) believing in the dictum 'Sacrifice begets plenty' and he actually got plenty. When he decided not to use digit 9 in the concept of decimal fraction notation, the division of 9, i.e., 91, 92, 93, 94, etc., will not be used as subdivision of 9. Therefore, they can be brought on a par with digits 1 to 8. If the number of entities is more than 16, he will again not use 99 leaving its divisions 991, 992, 993, 994, 995, etc., unused and they too will be brought on a par with 1 to 8 and 91 to 98.

Example:

1, 2, 3, 4, 5, 6, 7, 8, 91, 92, 93, 94, 95, 96, 97, 98, 991, 992,, 993, 994, 995, 996, 997, 998, 9991, 9992, 9993, 9994, 9995, 9996, 9997, 9998 and so on.

There will thus be different sectors in an array. For example:

1st Sector	2nd Sector	3rd Sector	4th Sector	5th Sector	6th Sector
1	91	991	9991	99991	999991
2	92	992	9992	99992	999992
3	93	993	9993	99993	999993
4	94	994	9994	99994	999994
5	95	995	9995	99995	999995
6	96	996	9996	99996	999996
7	97	997	9997	99997	999997
8	98	998	9998	99998	999998

In this way the notational status of 1, 97, 994, 9996, 99992, 999993 (belonging to different sectors) will be the same. It is through this simple but useful technique that Ranganathan suggested hospitality in array, when an array is required to accommodate more than 9 classes. Later on, the concept of sector was extended to species of digits other than Arabic numerals. Capital and lower case Roman alphabets used in CC also follow the principle of sector device. One can understand the notational burden if five nines 99999 are used to accommodate 41st of 48th classes. More number of nines will be required if isolates are more than 48, 64, 72, etc. To reduce the burden on notation Ranganathan expounded the concept of Group Notation for providing hospitality in an array if the isolates are in great number. The thesis of group notation is, sacrifice the use of one digited numbers. To individualise the first entity use two or more digits at a time. This means sacrifice of one digited numbers and if need be, sacrifice of even two digited numbers. But the hospitality which this sacrifice provides for is much greater than what sector device can ever afford. Group notation is adopted by grouping the characteristics. In CC, for example, the main class J Agriculture incorporates it. Here we have utility array, and part (useful) array and with the help of these two groups, species of plants are arrived at in the third array.

This leds to the provisions for accommodating any isolate in an array. The situation is more dominant in the documents. The notation should be equipped to translate it whenever the need arises. This has been done in DC with the help of the instruction 'Divide like 000-999' at number of places CC has also provided for it. The method in CC is to put the number of the isolate required (along with its main class number) in a bracket and attach it to the main class where it occurs.

For example

1. Psychology of University Teachers S4 (T4)
2. Hindu Ethics R4 (Q2)
3. Industrial Microbiology F : (G91)

This device also provides for plenty of hospitality in an array. It is generally seen that the order of such arrays where temporary occurrence takes place is mostly in lower order of arrays.

Principles for Chain

The term chain in the classification of knowledge stands for a sequence of classes, not co-ordinate among themselves, where the second class in the chain is derived from the first class, the third class is derived from the second and the fourth class is derived from the third class in the chain, and so on. In the end, we find that the last class has been derived from the penultimate class in the chain. In a chain of classes the preceding class is the immediate universe from which the successive class is taken out. For example:

	DC		CC
3	Social Sciences	B	Mathematics
33	Economics	B2	Algebra
331	Labour	B28	Statistics
331.1	Industrial Relations	B281	Probability
331.11	Employment	B2813	Normal equation
331.114	Qualifications for Workers		

The classes mentioned under DC and CC are in a chain. Ranganathan defines a chain as a "Sequence of classes made up of any given class, its immediate Universe, and its Universe of the second remove, third remove, and so on. A chain may be arrested at any state short of the original Universe." Mills gives a short but exact definition of chain. According to him, "A chain is a series of classes in successive sub-ordination, each one being subordinate to the preceding one."

The chains in the schedules have to be worked out in a disciplined manner and not as one wishes. There are certain rules for it which should be observed in a scheme of knowledge classification. Ranganathan has expounded two canons:

(a) Canon of Decreasing Extension.

(b) Canon of Modulation

(a) Canon of Decreasing Extension: It is an important principle of helpful sequence. A wider class should come before a narrower class. In case of a chain, this canon demands that the succeeding classes should always be smaller in extension to the preceding classes. Ranganathan has defined this canon this : "While moving down a chain from its first link to its last link, the intension of the classes should increase, and the extension of the classes should decrease. This is the canon of decreasing extension." The concept of decreasing extension has been equated with the principle of general before special. But the general before special is the result of the application of this principle, which simply means that major should come before the minor; or that a smaller unit should come after the bigger unit, whose part it is. The diagrams given on the opposite page represent this concept:

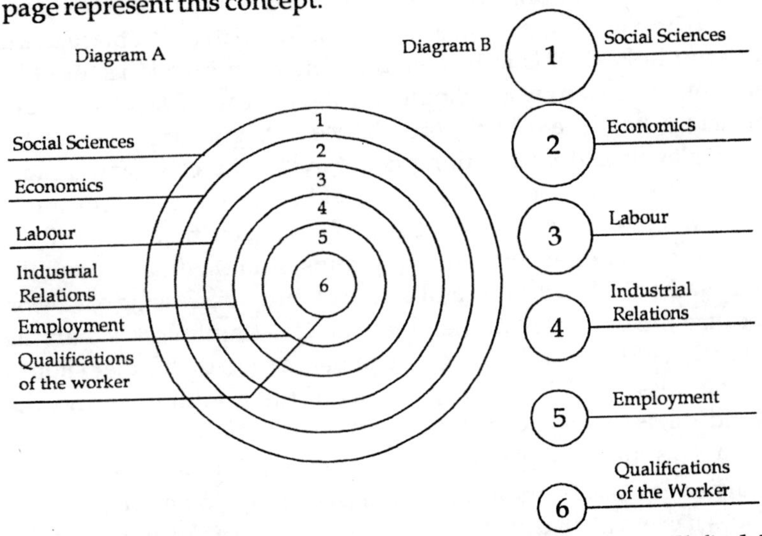

If we take out these circles from diagram A, we will find in diagram B that their extension is going on reducing from the first link to the last link. Circle 2 representing economics is lesser in extension than circle 1, but bigger in extension than circles 3, 4, 5, and 6; circle 3 labour is lesser than 1 and 2 but bigger than 4, 5, and 6. Circle 4 is lesser than 1, 2 and 3. Circle 5 is smaller than 4, but bigger than circle 6, and circle 6 is the smallest of all. In diagram A, we find that circle 6 is within circle 5; circle 5 is within circle 4; circle 4 is within circle 3; circle 3 is within circle 2; and circle 2 is within circle 1.

The canon of decreasing extension has been observed by DC and CC. The concept of decimal fraction notation of Melvil Dewey is to meet the primary need for indicating decreasing extension of the classes in a chain. Ranganathan has also adopted the decimal fraction notation in CC.

(b) Canon of Modulation : If the canon of decreasing extension prescribes as how to derive a chain, the purpose of the canon of modulation is to specify as what to include in the various links of a chain. In other words, what should comprise a chain from its first link to the last link? Ranganathan suggests that "A chain of classes should comprise one class of each and every order that lies between the orders of the first link and the last link of the chain. This is the canon of modulation." The term 'each and every order' indicates that no important isolate in a chain should fail to find a place in the relevant link. To this mills mentions "steps of division should be proximate—that division should not make a leap." The value of this principle lies in avoiding the chances of ignoring a class at a particular link. If such a thing is not avoided a class will remain hidden. It shall not be possible to individualise it. A simple example of it is when we give a place to a grandfather at the first link; omit the place for the father and put the grandson immediately after the grandfather. This will be alright for the canon of decreasing extension because the extension of the grandson is certainly lesser than the extension of the grandfather. The phenomenon that father should not be missing in between the links of the grandfather and the grandson, is the purpose of the canon of modulation.

An application of this canon in the making of schedules for knowledge classification is not a simple affair. No doubt at certain places it is not at all difficult to modulate all the links. For example, if the first link is the World and the last link is Paris; one knows for certain that the sequence in chain will be World-Europe-France-Paris. But there are many places where the canon of modulation requires special care in selecting or rejecting a class at possible links. For example:

DC	Links in Chain	CC
33=Economics	1st link	X=Economics
336=Public Finance	2nd Link	X7=Public Finance
336.2=Taxation	3rd link	X72=Taxes
336.27=Other Taxes	4th link	X729=Indirect Taxes
336.271=Indirect Taxes		
336.272=Stamp Taxes	5th link	X7299=Stamp Duty

We find that the first three links are common in both the schemes. The fifth link is also the same in the two schemes. The difference arises in the fourth link. Stamp Duty is an indirect tax and its upper link finds a place in CC, but no in DC, where we find that Indirect taxes are co-ordinate to Stamp taxes, and their common upper link is 'Other Taxes 336.27'. Here we find that the canon of modulation has been violated. The classificationists; knowledge of the class under division and of the literature available on the classes, determines the number of steps of divisions needed between a class from its first link to its last link. Ranganathan feels that the canon of Modulation requires further investigation.

Hospitality in Chain in Notation: It is not sufficient that a notation should be hospitable only in its array. In order to deal with the dynamic growth of knowledge and its manifestations in various dimensions, particularly as embodied in documents, it is necessary that the notation by extremely hospitable also in its chain. A feature of knowledge is that the classes of greater intension crop up every now and then. This is an endless process. A subject of specialization generally covers minor areas. For a long time atom was considered indivisible. But it is now established that it can be divided. In the same manner, previously an isolate was considered indivisible. But it can further be divided is now proved due to the growth of isolates. In a chain, one finds one facets of the same class. This created the need for providing for them in notation so that documents of this type could be individualized. Another feature demanding for hospitality in chain in when two or more basic classes with or without their facets, make a peculiar specific subject as often revealed in many documents. Such documents depend on the notation for their individualization. When such a relation exists at the level of main classes, with or without their facets, a miniature of it is noticeable when two isolates of the same facet or two sub-isolates of an isolate together produce a new specific subject. In order to handle such situations in the field of knowledge classification in notational plane, various devices have been invented by the profession. They are:

(a) Gap Device;
(b) Decimal Fraction Device;
(c) Facet Device;
(d) Inter-subject Phase Relation Device;
(e) Intra-facet Phase Relation Device;
(f) Intra-array Phase Relation Device; and
(g) Superimposition Device.

(a) Gap Device: This gap device means leaving a limited number of gaps in the notation at various levels. This is a method generally adopted in notations which adopt integral (non-decimal fraction) numbers. Number of gaps that can be provided will be meager in comparison to the number of new isolates that a scheme will be required to accommodate. This means that the scope of hospitality in chain is not much possible through this device. Two major schemes, i.e., Library of Congress and Brown's Subject Classification adopted this device in a prominent manner to accommodate new classes.

(b) Decimal Fraction Device: This is a wonderful device which came from the pride of the library profession, Melvil Dewey. It is such a powerful device that for about 80 years it fought almost single-handed with the idiosyncracies of the universe of knowledge. About it Ranganathan says, "The most potent and everlasting contribution of the Decimal Classification (Therefore, of Melvil Dewey) to the Philosophy of Library classification is the demonstration of the particability of securing hospitality in notation by the simple device of Decimal Fraction Notation." Due to this device every number is notation is considered as a pure decimal fraction. In knowledge classification for documents, we are forced to translate a class into an artificial language of ordinal numbers. Just as a class is divisible into various subclasses, in the same manner the translated ordinal number should also be sub-divisible. This can conveniently be done with the help of decimal fraction notation. For example:

Natural Sciences have been translated into digit 5 in DC.

Science=6

500	510	520	530	540	550	560	570	580	590
Pure Science	Maths	Astro- nomy	Physics	Chemistry	Earth Science	Paleon- tology	Anthro- pology	Botany	Zoology

Digit 5 is for Science. To accommodate the divisions of Science, we will have to adopt the decimal fraction notation. This gives hospitality. This device has been adopted by DC, UDC, CC and BC. It would have been impossible for Colon to cut new grounds, if it had not adopted the concept of decimal fraction notation.

(c) Facet Device: If the decimal fraction notation gave hospitality at one point, the concept of facet device provided for hospitality at many points. The versatility of facet device is $1 \times 2 \times 3 \times 4 \times 5 = 120$, when the versatility of decimal fraction is 1. The ratio between the two is 120 : 1. Such a remarkable difference was introduced by this concept. The following example will show the potency of facet device for hospitality:

Illustration A DC Notation	Illustration B Facet Device in CC Notation						
5	MC	P	M	E	S	T	
↓	2	3	1	5	4	N	**Step 1**
54							
↓							
546							
↓							
546.3	2	36	1511	55	421	N63	**Step 2**
↓							
546.34							
↓							
546.342							

In illustration A, we find that at each step only one digit representing a class has been added. In DC it is not possible to have simultaneously another point for expansion. In illustration B, we find that five points can expand simultaneously, as happened at step 2 in illustration B. CC has demonstrated that hospitality in chain resides not only at the end (as in DC notation) but at each of the junctions between trains of characteristics. The device is implemented by applying certain connecting symbols which are prescribed and are of lesser ordinal value than other digits. This device secures 'manifold infinite hospitality in chain'. The manner in the same way the facet device alone or even along with decimal fraction device, is also inadequate.

(d) Inter-subject Phase Relation Device: This phase device is required in a notation to meet a particular feature of mutual relations between the main classes, with or without their facets and isolates. Such mutual relations give birth of complex specific subjects, which throw a challenge to the notation of a scheme of classification. Following are the examples of such specific subjects:

Specific Subjects	Type of Inter-subject Phase relation
(i) Psychology for Teachers	Biased
(ii) Influence of Production on Culture	Influence
(iii) Comparison of Religion and Philosophy	Comparison
(iv) Difference between Engineering and Technology	Difference
(v) Relation between Physics and Chemistry	General

These are the five types of relations existing between two or more main classes. There may be many more types of relations. If a document appears with such specific subjects, a scheme of classification should not feel any difficulty in individualizing it. This demands securing addition single fold infinity for hospitality in chains. Ranganathan has expounded the following types of inter-subject phase relations and has provided for them in CC notation, with the help of a different set of connection symbols:

Type of Inter-Subject Phase Relation	Connection Symbol Used in CC
General Relation Phase	O a
Bias Phase	O b
Comparison Phase	O c
Difference Phase	O d
Influence Phase	O g

The relation phase in DC up to the 14th edition was indicated through the symbols 00 and 0001. But its editors decided to eliminate these provisions, in 15th and 16th editions. By dropping out this provision the DC editors have deprived its notation of hospitality in chain. In DC certain persons feel that the symbol 09 which says 'we will now divide geographically' and 0 which stands for 'the division by form' is identical to inter-subject phase relation. But 09 is Geography facet (not a phase) and 0 is for the common isolates under classes and thus be considered under one Basic class. Therefore, they do not deal with a complex class for which this phase relation is needed.

UDC also provides for phase relation in its notation but facet and phase do not have separate existence there. They have been put together. Vickery has examined the question of various types of phase relations. DC files such classes under the class of its utility. As the concept of the utility of a complex specific subject, as against the subject matter of it, is a vague statement, one may expect that the future editions of DC may reintroduce the concept of Phase Relation in its notation.

(e) Intra-Facet Phase Relation Device: Inter-relation between the isolates of a facet a in main class is known as intra-facet-phase relation. The types of relations are the same as in case of Inter-subject Phases. Examples are given below:

Specific subject	Type of infrafacet phase relation
Influence of Morphology on Physiology	Influence
Ecology compared to Genetics	Comparison
Relation between Secondary and University Education.	General
Difference between Physical and Mathematical Geography	Difference
Physiological anatomy	Bias

Documents on above types of relations are not difficult to be found in any library. The practice is that they are classified in a 'somehow manner'. Because many schemes of classification have not provided for the individualization of this phenomenon of the universe of knowledge in their notation. CC is the only scheme which provides for the individualization of such relations in its notation.

(f) Intra-Array Phase Relation Device: Intra-array phase relation means relation between the sub-isolates in an array. This array is not the array of the main classes for which inter-subject phase relation has been prescribed; nor it is the array of PMEST where facet analysis is valid. It is also not the relation between the isolates of a facet (e.g. E of Biology will have 1 2 3 4 5 6 7 8 isolates) because here the intra-facet phase relation has been recognized. Then, where are the intra-array phase relations applicable? They are applicable at the level of the array of sub-isolates which are the divisions of one isolate of a facet in a main class; for example:

(i) Sociology is a Main Class;

(ii) Group is personality facet in the main class;

(iii) Group got by residence is an isolate in the personality facet;

(iv) Sub-isolates like rural, urban and city groups, etc., are the divisions of the isolate by 'residence' which is a part of [P] of the Main class.

So, intra array-phase relation means relation between the sub-isolates; which occur under the isolates of a facet. Example for colon number:

Y31 Ow5 –	Difference between the rural folk and city folk.
Y	Main class=Sociology
	Personality=Group
Y3	An isolate of [P] by residence
Y31	a sub-isolate of 'by residence' of [P] of Y standing for Rural folk.
Y53	a sub-isolate of 'by residence of [P] of Y standing for City folk.

CC has provided for this type of relation in its 6th edition. But a very wide term, i.e., 'Intra-array phase relation' is used for it; because the arrays of different orders have their own types of phrase relations. The possibility of giving a specific term to this phenomenon may, therefore, be investigated. It is possible that the term 'Intra-isolate phase relation' be a better term. If so, it may replace the term 'intra-array phase relation'.

Super-Imposition Device: when two separately scheduled isolates enumerated in an array appear in a specific subject, one subordinate to another, it is said to be a superimposed situation. This happens when there is a mutual denudation between two isolates in a facet. Suppose a specific subject like 'History of Portuguese Africa' is to be individualized. The position will be as follows:

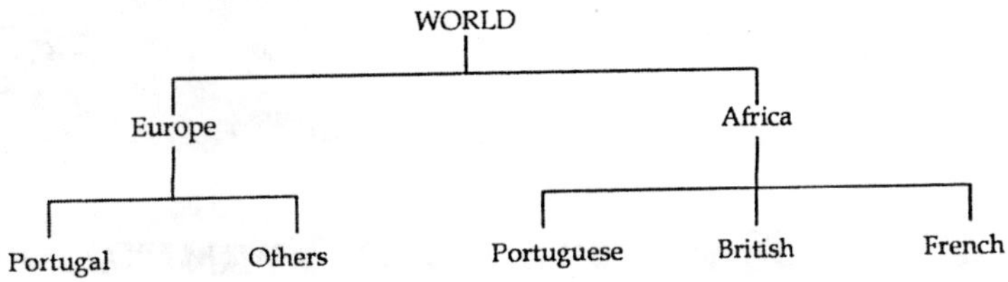

When we say 'Portuguese Africa', we mean the class Africa to be sub-divided by Portugal, an isolate under Europe. Therefore, such situations can be controlled in the following manner so long the colonies exist:

Specific Subjects	**Translation in Colon**
History ÷ Africa ÷ Portugal	V6-542
History ÷ Africa ÷ Britain	V6-56
History ÷ Africa ÷ France	V6-53

A scheme of classification should be able to translate such specific subjects through its notation. CC has examined the question in detail and has worked out certain rules for it. The connecting symbol used for it is '-' hypen. An intelligible sequence between the isolates should be maintained. Suppose we use the sequence V542-6 (because value of digit 5 is lesser than the value of digit 6) it will mean 'History of African Portugal' – a thing which does not exist; hence it is unintelligible. This device is of great help for these specific subjects in an enumerative way, under 966.57, 967.3 and 967.9 for Portuguese Guinea, Angola and Mozambique, respectively. A number for Portuguese Africa is however, not available in DC.

The concept of hospitality had always been dear for the leaders in Library Classification. Melvil Dewey insisted on it and introduced the Decimal Fraction. Bliss cried for 'Expansibility and adjustable co-relation in notation'. Cutter also coined the slogan 'Expansibility'. Richardson demanded 'indefinite expansion'. Sayers told each of his students, "Hospitality of a notation is its essential feature for without it a scheme is soon exhausted."

14

Notation with Terminology

Rules of Terminology

If one person wants to tell another person something about the sun, he may either point out his finger towards the sun during the day time and make the other man see it or he should use his tongue to pronounce the name given to the sun in a language which both know. The sun (which is an English word for the entity concerned) is known to non-English speaking world through different words. In Japanese, Chinese, Indian and other languages, the words to represent the entity sun will be different. In the same manner the wooden structure over which we sit, and where the seating space is often about one and a half feet above the surface of the floor, is known by the name of 'chair' in English language. Different languages will have different names for the entity which is known as chair in English. The classes which are known by the terms Chemistry, Sociology, etc., in English are known by different terms in other languages; for example, in Hindi language their names are Rasayan Shastra and Samaj Shastra, respectively. Whatever terms in different languages may be used to denote a particular entity, the entity will be the same in the idea plane. To make an entity understandable to another man, words of a language are used. Similarly, in the field of classification of knowledge embodied in documents, all entities must be translated into a language, which may be English, French,

German or any other. This means that the entities are represented by the words of a language. In the schedules of a classification words and terms are used to denote the respective entities. The languages used by men all the world over are not perfect. Some vagaries are associated with each language. There is no at-onement between one entity and its translation into only one word. The result is that for one thing there may be two or more words in a language; or one word may represent two or more entities. Besides this difficulty, we often come across cases of suitable words not existing in a language to represent a particular entity, for which new words are to be coined. We are concerned with these phenomena of a language, because while making a schedule we must assign a word or term to one and all the entities; and we should see with great care that the term which we assign to one entity does not have two or more meanings. Ranganathan uses the term language plane for the problems of this area.

In short, terms in schedules of a classification, are the names given by the classificationist to denote the main classes, facets, isolates and sub-isolates etc. The purpose of giving names is that they should properly represent current meanings of different orders of classes. There are five principles to guide us in the selection of terms to be used in schedules:

(i) Canon of Currency;
(ii) Canon of Reticence;
(iii) Canon of Enumeration;
(iv) Canon of Context; and
(v) Canon of Consistent use of terms.

(i) Canon of Currency: Terms used in a scheme of classification should be in current use among the specialists of that area. This is the Canon of Currency. Terms used in a class often change. An old term may become obsolete and is thus replaced by a new one. In order to cope with this phenomenon, a scheme should see that it only adopts those terms which are current at the time of the construction of the scheme. As there is no certainty that a term once adopted will not become obsolete, terms in a scheme should be replaced in its subsequent editions if the need be. Once upon a time, the term Natural Philosophy was used to denote what we now understand by the term Science.

In DC, we find that the terms used are often unsuitable. So is the case with CC. In the present day world new terms are coined. In DC the scope notes often explain the terms used and in addition to it, the relative index of about 2500 pages also helps. In CC, one finds only basic terms enumerated under facets and their fusion depends on the classifier. In DC the use of terms is often confusing. For example, Religion and Theology are two different terms. In schedule, 200 has been assigned to Religion. In the index, Theology has been referred to 200. Again, 200 as Religion stands for a main class covering all religions, but in index the Christian religion is given 200. In the index Christian Theology is given 241. the loose use of terms in this manner creates a doubtful situation for classifiers. The practice in CC, to use only basic terms is often troublesome to the classifier in making out a new term. This indicates that if DC suffers from over explanation of the terms in its schedules and in its index, CC has the drawback of under explanation of terms in its schedules and in its index. Here one should agree with Palmer and Wells, when they say that all classificationists have great difficulty in finding unambiguous terms. This also means that the decision of what is the most current term among the specialists is not always a simple affair. Two terms meaning the same idea may be equally current with the specialists. Whatever be the difficulties in the selection of current terms, the value of the canon is indisputable.

(ii) Canon of Reticence: This canon meets the requirements of a gentleman. It says that the terms used in a scheme of classification should not be critical and indecent. All schemes of classification should observe this canon. This canon can best be observed if the classificationist prefers to use only descriptive terms and not the ratiocinative terms.

Ranganathan feels that the use of the term Minor Authors in DC is against the canon of Reticence. It is true that the valuation of authors changes, yet distinction exists between the major and minor authors. The classificationist need not apply his judgment in deciding about an author as a major or minor one. The society and the circle of academicians in a subject decide the status of an author. If such a term is used by the classificationist for less known authors, it is not to be taken as the violation of this canon.

Still there is a justification when Ranganathan says that the use of the term minor authors in DC is a violation of the Canon of

Reticence. It is so, because the method used in CC to individualise authors is not at all ratiocinative nor does it require any application on classificationists' part, of his judgment on the authors' status. In CC, authors are individualized in a purely descriptive manner with the help of the year of the birth of the author (chronological device).

(iii) Canon of Enumeration: The canon of Enumeration means that scope, meaning and denotation of each term used (in higher orders) in the schedule should be determined by examining the sub-terms used under it at its different chains (in lower orders). For example, we take the term Philosophy used in CC and DC. The meaning, scope and denotation of the term Philosophy in CC and DC depends on what on what classes are included under it in the respective schemes. In DC, Philosophy also includes Psychology, but in CC we do not find Psychology under the head Philosophy. So, the denotation of the term Philosophy in DC includes, in addition to other classes, Psychology; and the denotation of the same term, Philosophy, in CC does not include Psychology.

The implication of this canon is that no uniformity be expected by the use of a term in different schemes, because the scope of the term may have been viewed differently by different schemes. Therefore, while deciding the denotation of a term, the lower links of that term should be examined. Hence, the traditional question of the observation or violation of this canon, like other canons, does not generally arise. But in one respect where it imposes a kind of control on the classificationist, is that while enumerating the lower links of a term it should be seen that no unconnected sub-terms are used under it. The above explanation can be summed up in the following two points:

1. The denotation of the term Philosophy in DC, in addition to Logic, Ethics, Metaphysics, etc., covers Psychology; in CC it excludes Psychology. The canon guides us in interpreting the scope of the term Philosophy in a scheme by examining the sub-terms used. There is no question of the observation or violation of this canon.
2. As the denotation of the term Philosophy will be understood by examining the sub-terms used under it, this canon demands that the classificationist should not use a sub-term, which does not fall under a class. This means that DC should not have put the term Psychology under Philosophy. It is

only in this respect that the practice followed in DC violates the canon.

(iv) Canon of Context. What the Canon of Enumeration demands about the meaning of the terms of higher order, the Canon of Context prescribes the same for the meaning of the terms (or sub-terms will be better) of the lower order. The need for this canon arises because one sub-term is found under a number of classes. Whenever such a term finds a place in a document, the question arises as to under which of the many classes where it is enumerated (or available), it should go. For example, the term 'Metal' is common to Building Engineering, Money in Economics, Economic Geology, and Inorganic Chemistry etc. A document on metals can go to any of these classes. But its place will be decided by examining the context in which it is used. If it has been used in the context of Building it will go there; if it is used in the context of Inorganic Chemistry, it should be placed under Chemistry. This is the way to apply this canon in practical classification. Nevertheless the canon is of equal importance in the use of terms to be assigned to entities in schedule making by the classificationist. Here, it means that while assigning terms to entities and while interpreting them, the terms used for entities at upper links should be borne in mine. Suppose the class Biology is to be assigned its sub-terms. In DC and in CC the following terms have been used:

DC	Biology	CC
574		G
Bio-Physiology		Physiology
Bio-morphology		Morphology
Bio-Ecology		Ecology

The terms Physiology, Morphology and Ecology etc. under the class Biology, will always be taken as the divisions under Biology. No chances exist for these to be taken as the divisions of Medicine or Zoology, etc. Hence, it is not necessary for DC to add the term 'Bio' to these sub-classes..

(v) Canon of Consistent use of terms: This canon means that for similar entities same terms should be assigned, if such entities occur at more than one place in a scheme of classification. To this Sayers says, "Terms in a classification, must be used consistently." For example, the ideas implied by the term Pathology occur at a number of places—animal pathology, plant pathology, social pathology, etc. The canon demands that under all such classes the term Pathology should be used in the schedule and no other term having the same meaning should be used. If different terms giving the same meaning are used at different places, it will violate the canon of consistent use of Terms. CC and DC both observe this canon, for example, by using the term Pathology under many classes. Like this, many examples will be found in DC and in CC.

Notation

Definition: Notation is a system of signs or symbols coined for a specific purpose. For classification of knowledge embodied in documents, we have already discussed that the entities in knowledge are given names or assigned terms in a natural language. But this is only the half way. The second half involves the translation of terms into a notation. If the entities are translated into the terms of a natural language; the terms are translated into a notation, which is an artificial language. Ranganathan defines notation as a system of ordinal numbers used to represent the classes in a scheme of classification. Bliss defined notation as "a system of marks or symbols in some order denoting terms or members of a series or system of things". Mann gives a very short definition : "The symbol which stands for the classes and their sub-divisions is called the notation of that scheme." She soon banks upon Sayers and quotes him, "A book notation... is a short-hand sign standing for the name of a term and forming a convenient means of reference to the arrangement of our classification."

On the role of Notation, Mann agrees that it is an important addition to any classification schedule but at the same time she feels that the notation should in no manner determine the logic, scope or development of classification. Mann underestimated the value of notation. The notation must be able to maintain the logic of classification if not to determine it; it must also be able to represent the scope of classification; and be in a position to develop at par with the development of classification. Sayers has defined, "A notation is a series of symbols, or short-hand signs-perhaps 'short signs' would be more accurate—for the terms in classification... and which in their arrangement show the arrangement of classification". Here Sayers rightly demands that the structure of a notation should be able to reveal the arrangement of classification. Palmer and Wells define it in following words: "Notation is a device for mechanizing arrangement and must be composed of written symbols whose order is defined." Their expectation that the notation should mechanise the arrangement is the proper duty that they assign to it. To Phillips, a notation is a series of symbols which stand for the names of a class or any division or sub-division of a class and forms a convenient means of reference to the arrangement of a classification.

(b) Need for and functions of Notation: The very fact that the terms used in the classification of knowledge are to be translated into ordinal numbers, reveals the basic need for notation. In addition, the following are other reasons for which notation is needed:

1. Notation is required to replace the terms. It becomes a permanent symbol through which the terms of classification are referred to.
2. It is a medium of and guide to the sequence of terms and fixes their relative position.
3. Alphabetical index is possible only through notation.
4. It is written on various parts of documents and cards etc.
5. It helps in the arrangement of documents on the shelves and the entries in the catalogue.
6. Efficient working of the catalogue is dependent on notation.
7. It figures among the guides used in a library.
8. It shows the sequence and the subordination and coordination of classes.
9. It shows various types of phase relations between classes, facets, isolates, etc., and differentiates between the facets of a class and between the types of relations.
10. It arranges entries in bibliographies and lists, etc.
11. It restores the sequence of documents, if they are pulled out from their respective places.
12. One can determine the specific subject through notation without reading the text.
13. Facilitates the use of mnemonics.
14. It is used for author marks, book numbers and sequence numbers, etc.
15. It is used for charging and discharging of documents, etc.

(c) Types of Notation: Broadly speaking, the notation is of two types: (1) Pure Notation, and (2) Mixed Notation. It is pure notation if only one kind of symbol is used. If more than one kind of symbols are used, it is known as a mixed notation.

Examples:

1. Pure Notation: (a) 1 2 3 4 5 6 7 8 9
   Or
   (b) A B C D E F G H I
   J K L M N O P Q R
   S T U V W X Y Z

2. Mixed Notation: (Two of more than two of these species of digits). 1 2 3 4 5 6 7 8 9 *and* A B C D E F G H I J K L M N O P Q R S T U V W X Y Z *and* , ; : . ' – *and* a b c d e f g h I j k l m n o p q r s t u v w x y z and others.

There was a time when pure notation was very popular. Melvil Dewey used it in his Decimal Classification wherein he adopted only the figures. Cutters used it in his Expansive Classification by adopting only the letters. Sayers went to the extent of prescribing a canon of Pure Notation which all schemes must adopt. However, it was soon realized that pure notation fails to work. Richardson was one of the leaders to raise an objection to pure notation. His ideal was the mixed notation, using both the figures and the letters. Bliss also suggested that the notation should combine letters and figures as simply as is compatible with the requisites. It is because of the demands made by Richardson and Bliss that the reasonable Sayers gave up the cause of pure notation and became an advocate of the mixed notation. Richardson went to the extent of prognosticating that every practical system sooner or later will have to adopt a mixed notation.

When the time came for Ranganathan, he used various types of digits in his Colon and included a canon of Mixed Notation in his Prolegomena. Really speaking, the mixed notation became a necessity due to the dynamic growth in the field of knowledge and its complex formations in documents. To some extent the mixed notation deprived a scheme of its simplicity. As choice was between the workability and simplicity, it was obvious that workability be preferred. The advantage was the flexibility of notation. Today, even the DC, the chief supporter of pure notation has adopted mixed notation by including capital letters. Therefore, the concept of pure notation has only a historical value, where it remains a stage of development and the predecessor of mixed notation.

(d) Qualities of Notation: The question of qualities of notation arises only in the event of a comparison between good and bad notations; and it means those features which make a good scheme of classification. This leads to the determination of what services a notation should perform in order to become a good classification. If we examine the above in another way, we find that a good classification scheme is one in which it is possible to individualise each document. This is possible when the notation is versatile enough to have an equal for each feature of knowledge and its various types of formations and expositions. Features which go to make a notation versatile should, therefore, be taken as the qualities of notation. All of us will agree that the notation 301 (three hundred and one) is simpler than 0.301 (decimal three zero one). Melvil Dewey was forced to reject the simpler number and to adopt the less simple (but more versatile) one in his Decimal Classification. Why was he forced to do so? The answer is that it was impossible for integral notation (the simpler one) to deliver the goods in the classification of documents.

To Sayers, the qualities of a notation are : (i) brevity; (ii) simplicity; (iii) flexibility; and (iv) mnemonic. Bliss prescribed that the notation be expansive with adjustable correlation as short as is feasible; mnemonics should be casual and systematic and it should be as simple as is feasible. These are perhaps the first set of qualities demanded of notation. The second set of qualities are:

1. It should be easy to write.
2. It should be easy to remember.
3. It should be more commonly used.
4. It should be easy to communicate.

A notation should have all these qualities but not at the cost of its basic quality, i.e., capacity to reveal the features, formations and expositions of knowledge. This means that notation should be versatile as against being rigid. This is the primary quality and whatever else is possible should be maintained. Ranganathan demands the following qualities in a notation:

1. It should be hospitable to new topics in its arrays and chains;
2. Synthesis should be possible in it;
3. Its expressiveness be maintained;
4. Its length should be relative to the depth of the class it represents; and
5. It should be mnemonic in its structure.

(e) Structure of Notation: Notation is made up of digits. A digits is a single symbol in a notation. The total number of digits in a notation is its base. The mode of arrangement of digits according to Ranganathan is possible in the following ways:

1. The digits can be arranged in a straight line, it is known as the Linear structure of notation.
2. The digits can be arranged in a horizontal straight line; it is known as Horizontal structure of notation. It can be of two types:
   (a) The digits can be arranged from left to right in a horizontal line, it is known as the Right handed notation.
   (b) The digits can be arranged from right to left in a horizontal
3. The digits can be arranged in a vertical straight line; it is known as the Vertical notation. This can be of two types:
   (a) Downward vertical line notation.
   (b) Upward vertical line notation.
4. When the digits are arranged along a curve, it is known as the Curved notation.
5. When the digits are arranged in two dimensions, it is known as Plane notation.

The structure of notation used in classification of knowledge embodied in documents is often the Right Handed Linear Notation. There are two types of notations for place values:

1. Integral notation.
2. Decimal fraction notation.

(f) Canons for Notation: Besides the canon of mnemonics, ranganatham has suggested three canons which a notation should observe. If we include the canon of mnemonics for notation it will make the follwoing four canons:

1. Canon of Relativity;
2. Canon of expressiveness;
3. Canon of Mixed Notation; and
4. Canon of mnemonics.

(i) Canons of Relativity: It demands that the length of notation in a scheme should be according to the size of a specific subject which is to be translated in the notation. This means that a class of greater extension should be individualized by lesser number of digits, and a class of lesser extension should be individualized by greater number of digits. The number of digits should be in relation with the size of the class. Because the process of division in classification is from the higher class to a lower class. It is obvious that the higher classes will require less number of digits and the lower classes will require greater number of digits:

Example

DC No	No. of Digits	Class Order	No. of Subject	CC No.	Digits
100	3	0	Philosophy	R	1
160	3	1	Logic	R1	2
161	3	2	Inductive Logic	R11	3

We find that 3 digits have been used for orders 0, 1 and 2 in DC. In CC the number of digits used for order 0 is 1, for order 1 is 2 and for order 2 is 3. Here CC observes the canon while DC violates it.

(ii) Canon of Expressiveness: It means that each digit in a class number should express the characteristic it represents. Its applications are that no digit should be without a meaning and that each characteristic in the line of division should be represented by a digit of its own in successive sequences. Let us examine the following class numbers in DC and CC:

(a) 621:433

6	– Technology
62	– Engineering
621	– Mechanical Engineering
621.4	– Prime Movers

621.43 – Internal Combustion Engine
621.433 – Gas Turbine Engine

Here each digit in DC expresses one characteristic in the hierarchy from technology to gas turbine engine.

(b) L21431

L – Medicine
L2 – Digestive System
L21 – Mouth
L214 – Tooth
L2143 – Kinds of Teeth
L21431 – Milk Teeth

(iii) Canon of Mixed Notation: This canon demands that the notation of a scheme should always be a mixed notation. We have already discussed the advantages of mixed notation under 'types of notation'. Here it may be stated that no scheme will be efficient. if it fails to adopt the mixed notation.

(iv) Canon of Mnemonics: There is another canon which falls under the area of notation. It is the canon of Mnemonics. Because it has a bearing on the entire scheme of classification, Ranganathan has discussed it under the general canons. We may take up this canon under notation itself.

The canon of Mnemonics demands that a particular digit should represent the same or similar ideas under different main classes where they occur. Bliss says on the value of mnemonics, "Notation as a kind of symbolical language depends extensively on memory of meaning." The term mnemonics means an aid to memory. The notation should be used in such a manner that similar idea gets the similar number. This will be an aid to memory.

For mnemonic qualities of notation, Ranganathan has expounded three canons:

(i) Verbal Mnemonics;
(ii) Scheduled Mnemonics; and
(iii) Seminal Mnemonics.

(i) Verbal Mnemonics means that the alphabets used in a notation may also be taken to represent the words. The first alphabet of the word will stand for the entire word. Suppose U stands for

Useful Arts in a scheme of classification or C stands for Chemistry, these are the verbal mnemonics. Bliss gave the name 'literal mnemonics' to this principle. Knowing the phenomenon of its rare occurrence, he said that literal mnemonics be casual.

(ii) Scheduled Mnemonics: Scheduled mnemonics demand that similar digits should be assigned to similar classes and terms, if they occur under more than one class. What the Canon of Consistency demands in case of an arrangement of entities in an array, and what the Canon of Consistent use of the terms demands in case of assignment of terms of entities; the same is demanded by the Canon of Scheduled Mnemonics in the allotment of digits, in notation, to similar terms. For example, in DC and CC the same digits are assigned to terms Poetry, Prose, Drama, etc., in all literature. In DC the same form division numbers are used irrespective of the class. In Colon the Common Isolate numbers get the same digits in different classes. In addition to these, in CC, we find that the use of instructions "same as in class so and so" fulfils the canon of scheduled mnemonics to some extent. Following are the examples of scheduled mnemonics in CC and DC:

DC No.	Class	CC No.
574.5	Ecology	G : 5
598.5	Animal Ecology	K : 5
598.25	Birds Ecology	K 96 : 5
581.5	Plant Ecology	I : 5

The following examples show the violation of this canon in DC:

DC No.	Class	CC No.
574.1	Physiology	G : 3
591.1	Animal Physiology	K : 3
598.21	Bird Physiology	K96 : 3
574.876	Cell Physiology	G11 : 3
612	Human Physiology	L : 3

In DC we find that in the first three classes, digit 1 has been used for Physiology; in the fourth class digit 6 has been used to represent Physiology and in case of the last class, digit 2 has been used. In CC we find that under all places digit 3 has been used. CC is able to satisfy this canon because of the Facet Device, Common Isolate Device, Geographical Device, Chronological Device, and Subject and Phase Relations Devices. In DC, instructions like 'divided like' and 'form division' help in observing this canon.

(iii) Seminal Mnemonics: Previously Ranganathan used to denote this concept by the term Unscheduled Mnemonics. On the suggestion of A J Wells he changed over to Seminal Mnemonics. This canon demands that the seminally equivalent entities be allotted the same digit in the subjects where they occur. The question arises as what are the seminally equivalent entities? It is often difficult for a common man to identify seminal equivalence between various ideas in subjects. But at the same time it is not impossible. There is a lot of unity found in various basic classes in the universe of knowledge. This can be termed as unity in knowledge. This means that there are basically identical ideas, but they do not possess the same terms in different main classes.

Function in Political Science; Physiology in Biological Sciences; Syntax in Linguistics; and Social activities in Sociology—all represent the ideas which are seminally identical, though they mean different things in different classes. In Colon Ranganathan has enumerated the seminal meanings of different digits. To digit 5 he assigns following sub-groups of ideas:

The digit 5 is used as mnemonic for:

(a) Energy, light, radiation, organic, liquid, water, ocean;
(b) Foreign land, alien, external;
(c) Environment, ecology;
(d) Emotion, foliage, aesthetics, woman, sex, crime, etc.

Let us examine the above from two angles. One, as far as the isolates within one sub-group are concerned, it is certain that they have seminal equivalence with each other. Light is energy, radiation is also connected with light and is energy, water is liquid and both are energy and ocean contain water etc., etc.

Second, but how far Energy isolates—alien and women belonging to different sub-groups are connected with each other? It is often difficult to find seminal equivalence between the isolates of these different sub-groups, but as already mentioned, it is not impossible. For example, woman is energy, she keeps the world going, generation after generation, she is also alien in the sense that after marriage she goes to the so-called foreign place, and until she is married, she remains external to the family where she is to live. Well, such arguments may appeal but one cannot deny the fact that it is difficult to recognize seminal equivalence between the various isolates unless a man is much enlightened. At the same time, it does not mean that what a common man does not know, does not exit.

Development of Notation: Present day classification and its notation has plunged into the areas where classificationists like Melvil Dewey, Bliss and Sayers would have feared to tread. The question arises how did it get this way? Let us peep into its lineage and heritage, perhaps we may find some clue. This much is sure that modern classification did not conjure fourth itself phoenix like, nor has it sprung like Athena full grown out of the writing of Ranganathan, Vickery, etc. its birth originated in the scholars' desire to classify and identify. Its development is parallel to the proliferation of knowledge. Its versatility is, no doubt, a result of Ranganathan's single-minded devotion, scientific thinking and analysis. The classifiers all over the world have given thought to the present structure of notation. Appreciations and rejections have been the obvious results.

1. Classification without Notation: Before the dawn of the 18th Century, there was no notation, worth is name, attached to the library classification. The reasons were:

(i) Extension of the specific subjects was still at the broader level.

(ii) Clientele of the library was limited to a selected few, and they were the cream of the intellectual community. They never required any mechanization and could have their way through their encyclopaedic knowledge.

(iii) Libraries and librarians were not feeling the pressure of full grown democracy which gave birth to the concept, Books for all.

2. Classification with Rigid and Semi-flexible Notation: The 19th Century brought in its wake many new philosophies. Concept of democracy had already established its roots and slogans for universal education were shouted with great zeal by the utilitarian school and by others. Industrialization had started paying dividends. The learned bodies which had originated in the 16th Century in the Renaissance Italy and has spread across Europe in the 16th and 18th Centuries has established homes in the American and Asian continents in the 19th and 20th Centuries. These learned bodies were engaged in the diffusion of knowledge. The population pressure was being felt and fears, multiplication of human resources was necessary. Opportunities of self-government, development of industries and many other factors made it necessary for a man to learn and known his rights and duties. It was at this stage that Melvil Dewey who had felt the necessity of the organization of documents in a library in a helpful sequence, liberated library classification from the clutches of alphabetization. His logic was : Why should we not make use of the Decimal Notation for enumerating the branches of knowledge and their sub-divisions and thus give a helpful organization to the documents in a library.

Dewey's Contribution: Dewey was ridiculed for his invention. Albiet, the librarians all over the world adopted the decimal classification and those who had not adopted it by the end of the 19th Century had to bear the curse of Lord Rayleigh who said in 1884, "In science by a fiction as remarkable as any to be found in law, what had been published, even thought it be in the Russian language, is spoken of as known, and it is too often forgotten that the rediscovery in the library may be a more difficult and uncertain process than the first discovery in the laboratory." This was a challenge to the library profession, denouncing the very existence of the creatures known as librarians. If we examine the state of knowledge in the last quarter of the 19th Century, we find that the proliferation of knowledge had started although not with a dynamic speed.

But the dynamic growth of knowledge was not going to stop, it progressed towards a greater intensiveness and documents dealing with the subjects of lesser and lesser extension had started coming up. The most powerful and ever alive gift of Melvil Dewey to the science of classification in securing hospitality of notation by decimal device had started feeling its inability against the dynamic growth of knowledge and its tactics. By the end of the 19th Century the librarians had almost lost their faith in the utility of classification in general and Decimal Classification in particular, as far as the individualization of the documents was concerned.

Emergence of UDC Notation: The urge of helpful organization of documents and articles in periodicals and their rapid increase every year and the desire to keep track of this flood, made Henri La

Fontaine and Paul Otlet to convene and International Bibliographical Conference in Brussels in 1895. This conference gave birth to International Institute of Bibliography (I I B) which sponsored the Universal Decimal Classification. This new scheme of classification primarily based on the structure of Decimal Classification had certain new features. Loyalties towards the concept of pure notation had to be given up in order to represent the exposition of intensified knowledge in documents which were coming up at that time.

The inter-relation between the various sub-divisions of a specific field of study had already become the focus of the academicians in the various branches of knowledge. In order to individualise several types of relations and manifestations of subjects, UDC did not hesitate in providing for a number of connecting symbols and several auxiliary tables. The mixed notation became a must and necessary amendments had to be made in the classificatory thought which was favouring pure notation. However, one would agree with Ranganathan that the greatest weakness of UDC was the adoption of the rigid DC core which has not only clipped the wings of the UDC in the design of its numbers but has also prevented it from providing for techniques like unscheduled mnemonics, etc. it has also fallen a prey to synonyms. Its extravagant use of numbers in representing various relations made it very expensive in its notation. But nobody can deny that UDC's associations with Decimal Classification showed a new way of representing the relations between the various units of thought without any limitation to the occurrence of an isolate idea under a different field of study.

3. Classification with Flexible and Versatile Notation: At a time when DC and UDC, separately as well as jointly, were struggling to win over the peculiarities in the trend of the universe of knowledge, which was proceeding towards greater minute specialization, along with multiplication and inter-relatedness of various subjects of different orders, their rigid core was disappointing so far as the individualization of such subjects was concerned.

By this time Library Classification has undergone a scientific treatment at the hands of Bliss, Richardson, Hulme and Sayers, etc. Sayers had worked out certain principles for the construction of the schedules of library classification. It was with this background that Ranganathan entered into the field of Library Classification and gave a scientific shape to the discipline. His first and the greatest contribution was the invention of the categories under many fields of study. However, it was not the last contribution. He provided for different connecting symbols. Provision in Notation to indicate inter-subject, intra-facet, and intra-array phase relations, and super-imposed situations, etc., made the notation richer. Enormous hospitality in Arrays and Chains of the notation was introduced.

Versatile Notation: The importance of notation in a scheme of classification was very much established even before Ranganathan. The mixed notation was the only alternative to strengthen the hands of a classificationist. The number of species in a mixed notation developed gradually. Ranganathan had started with three species, but Colon Classification has four at present. Mixed notation has served well to the requirements of the translation of ideas into numbers. Gradually, the numbers developed into the shape of a semi-language which has been called the 'artificial language of ordinal numbers' by Ranganathan.

Apart from many contributions of the mixed notation the most important one is the concept of Zone Analysis. One can safely say that it is a by-product of mixed notation. The peculiarity of the zone analysis is the provision of hospitality in an array of any order. This peculiarity has made knowledge classification a living force and is one of the greatest counter-tactics at the command of a classificationist in his struggle with the tactics of the universe of knowledge. The justification of Zone Analysis is found in the idea plane and the different species in the notation simply meet the requirements of idea plane. The emergence of the tool of efficiency table is due to Zone Analysis.

Principle of Inversion

The principle of inversion deals with the application of opposite sequence employed in classifying the documents, and their filing or arrangement on the shelves. In Colon we find that this principle has been developed. The following sequences have been adopted between facets:

While Classifying Documents	**While Arranging Documents**
BC [P]	BC [T]
BC [M]	BC [S]

BC [E]	BC [E]
BC [S]	BC [M]
BC [T]	BC [P]

While discussing the facet-analysis, we recognized that Personality is the most concrete and Time is the least concrete. In other words, in the sequence P M E S T we find that the concreteness gradually diminishes from P to T via M, E and S. Under the principles of helpful sequence we find the utility of the principle of decreasing concreteness of the principle of increasing abstractness. On the basis of these, we find in the CC schedules that the facet formula runs like P M E S T everywhere. In other words, with the help of the succeeding facet the extension of class under the preceding facet is narrowed. For example:

X	=	Economics
X 61	=	Money
X 61; 4	=	Paper Money
X 61; 4 : 6	=	Value of Paper Money
X 61; 4 : 6.44	=	Value of Paper Money in India
X 61; 4 : 6.44 'N	=	Value of Paper Money in India in 20th Century

Here we find that X 61 is Money, it has been divided by matter 4, i.e., the paper money. X 61; 4 is paper money, it has been divided by Energy 6, i.e., value. X 61; 4 : 6 is value of paper money, it has been divided by space 44, i.e., India. X 61; 4 : 6.44 is value of paper money in India, it has been further sub-divided by time N, i.e., the 20th Century. The number X 61; 4 : 6.44 'N means the value of paper money in India in the 20th Century. The other method of dividing it, i.e., T S E M P will give absurd meaning because here the division of the preceding facet will not be meaningful if sub-divided by the succeeding facets.

But what is the justification of arranging documents in the following manner on the shelves?

X 'N

X .44

X .44 'N

X : 6

X : 6.44

X : 6.44 'N

X 61

X 61 ; 4

X 61 ; R : 6

X 61 ; 4 : 6.44

X 61 ; 4 : 6.44 'N

Here we find that sequence is from most general to most specific. X 'N = 20th Century Economics is more general class than X.44 Indian Economics, which is less general. X.44 ' N 20th Century Indian Economics is a sub-division of Indian Economics. X : 6 is more specific than X.44. It is divided by space and time. In the same manner X 61 ; 4 : 6.44 'N is the most specific, here the succeeding facets narrow the extension of the preceding facets. As such we find that the nature of arrangement of the documents in this manner is from general to special.

Colon is able to maintain this sequence, by its rule number 025. This is the most important rule of Colon Classification. It fixes the ordinal value of the digits. Rule 0252 deals with the ordinal value of the connecting symbols, which is as follows:

← → O ' . : ; , —

This sequence is in ascending order (i.e., the value of the succeeding digits is higher than the value of the preceding digits). It is with the help of this rule that

X ' N comes before X : 6 because the value of ' is lower than:

To sum up, while classifying we see than concrete comes before abstract. Secondly, we notice that for narrowing the extension of a class the style is to sub-divide the concrete by abstract. The process of sub-dividing abstract by concrete is meaningless. While arranging documents we put the abstract class = general class first; and concrete = special class afterwards.

15

Mechanical Indexing and Retrieval

Overview

Mechanical indexes differ in operating principle from the conventional manual indexes commonly found in libraries. Their development began in a modest way with the edge punched cards from which relevant items were extracted by means of rods or knitting needles, and has proceeded until now the most advanced computers using magnetised tape are being studied and tested for information retrieval. In the USA the research is mainly; carried out by two agencies: the firms that make computers, and universities or private firms of documentalists who have won awards of financial grants from a trust or from the US Government Defense budget. All three Defense Services and the Atomic Energy Commission have shown sufficient awareness of the value of information service to make large sums available for research, and nearly all of those are directed towards mechanical systems. In the USSR the government acts indirectly through VINITI, the national information centre which publishes bulletins of abstracts, supplies translations and photocopies, and makes searches for information in answer, to enquiries received from all over the world. VINITI also has a'research department which investigates problems of documentation, among them the use of machines for literature searching. In France, through the Centre National de la Recherche Scientifique, in Germany at the Gmeiin Institute, in Poland at the Central Institute for Scientific and

Technical Information in Warsaw, studies are being carried out along similar lines, if not on quite such a grandiose scale.

All this effort can hardly be said to have had quite the effect one might have expected. Dozens of machines have been tested, but so far no single one has caused the world to beat a path to the inventor's door. Only the volume of publications about mechanical retrieval has been maintained at a high level, and it is sometimes unkindly remarked that one field in which there is a notable lack of information retrieval is information retrieval itself.

In a letter to the *Times Literary Supplement* of 27/4/62 Ralph Shaw, the pioneer of investigation into the use of machines for literature searching, reported that a group of General Electric Company engineers in the USA had completed a study comparing manual and machine performance. This showed conclusively that, even using an inexpensive computer, straightforward searching of an existing index (in this case the *Reader's Guide to Periodical Literature)* was many times more costly by machine than by hand. 'We cannot assume that just because it is possible to do indexing via computer it is always efficient to do so ... I have examined a large number of mechanized indexes and have yet to see one using punched cards or computers that does the job as economically or as efficiently or as fast as it can be done by hand.' More recently, similar caution has been expressed by Herbert Coblans, in the face of the great extension of services commercially available: 'Actually the extraordinary progress in hardware, as manifest in more efficient storage and accessibility, and falling costs have aggravated both the intellectual and organizational problems involved in mechanization. Subject control is increasingly frustrated by linguistic variability and semantic ambiguity as the subject coverage is widened and the bulk of entries becomes very large.

Without doubt, computers have an important part to play in research itself, and we are only at the beginning of our exploitation of their usefulness; they are valuable in the compilation of data banks such as the census, and many universities have established such repositories, as well as larger organisations such as the special agencies of the United Nations. The UK Social Science Research Council supports a data bank of the University of Essex, and the University of Pittsburgh has begun a compilation of data banks at its Social Science Information Utilization Laboratory. The

International Social Science Journal devoted a whole issue in 1971 to the use of computers and documentation. What these are able to do is to examine large numbers of marks in a very short time and indicate which of the marks correspond to a particular pattern. Thus, if we mark all our documents with a suitable code and enter the same marks on punched cards, or punched tape, or magnetised tape, according to the type of machine we are using, the machine will then be able to identify for us those documents whose marks correspond to the marks put on enquiries made by readers. This is the same operation as that performed by a conventional library index, except that the scanning is mechanical and not visual.

Because of its ability to perform a very large number of operations in a very short time, the machine can pick out similarities between great quantities of data that were originally assembled without reference to one another. This faculty puts a very powerful tool into the social scientist's hands, because one of the difficulties he has to face is that of putting the available data into some sort of order-an immensely time-consuming task if done by an individual. If we consider one set of data, the census, we can see how great a task it is to re-order all the information collected on one basis—addresses, or location in space—on to another basis—of professions, nationalities or whatever may be required. By attaching to every individual marks designating himself and all his characteristics, we collect a series of codes; feeding the series through a machine that has been instructed to watch for marks indicating one or a set of characteristics brings out in a very short time all those individuals who have that characteristic or combination of characteristics, regardless of their addresses.

These machines are already widely known and used for certain social purposes in addition to census analysis. In commerce, for example, they have been used for some years for hire-purchase records and similar accounting operations, such as insurance; they can maintain clerical records such as the membership rolls of organisations, and carry out the analysis of examination results. Sociological surveys, ethnography, archaeology, experimental psychology and even the analysis of myths are mentioned in the *International Social Science Journal* symposium. The accuracy of results based on statistical sampling improves with the size of sample, but only a machine can give the speed of operation that will enable very large samples to be used in social science research. Machines must be brought into this research on a far greater scale than at present if we are to make the most of our opportunities for extending the use of scientific method in formulating and testing hypotheses.

But the correlation of data does not constitute the whole of the information retrieval process. We are not by any means limited to enquiries of the type 'Does the combination A + B + C + D + X exist in the literature?' or 'How many Xs with A + B are also Y?', which may appear in any field of knowledge and are ideal subjects for machine searching. We have to deal also with enquirers wanting information about some subject, who are not able to give a precise specification of this type. To take a simple example, a reader who asks for information on Methodological Individualism could be helped by a machine which had in its store of codes some with marks that meant Methodological Individualism; but the same reader would also be helped by documents dealing with Holism, which would, in a machine system based on random coding (as most are), receive a totally different set of marks and would not, therefore, be retrieved. In a classified index, on the other hand, these references would be found near together because they would both be classified as theories of society, and nearby one would also find references to terms that indicated other theories; and so the index itself would help the reader by suggesting lines of enquiry that he had not perhaps thought of.

It is of considerable significance that the use of machine retrieval began in the USA, where knowledge of classification is virtually confined to DC and LC, and where the machine stands high in public estimation. Classification stood in low repute even for shelf arrangement and was hardly known for indexes, which were usually alphabetical, when the original punched card machines came to offer what seemed a brilliant solution to the growing problem of retrieval by means of concept co-ordination. It was pointed out that both alphabetical and classified indexes required time to be spent on filing cards for new documents into the existing file in prearranged places —a tedious operation giving ample opportunity for error; whereas the machine could pick out the required co-ordinates no-matter where they were, and was much less susceptible to error, being immune to boredom and fatigue.

Most of the work has been done in science and technology, and many systems using different types of machine have been described, A prototype machine constructed at Western Reserve University (now Case Western Reserve University) had one advantage over all the others in that it was specifically constructed for literature searching and not mere data correlation. It is therefore able not only to detect combinations of code marks, but also to relate individual marks, meanirig specific names, to other marks that mean more general classes of names, and thus to achieve the object of the classified index in displaying generic relationships. It does this, in fact, by using a system of code marks in which the marks for a specific topic include those for its general field–in other words, a classified notation. It is actually an alphabetico-classified notation, called a 'semantic code', with symbols such as C – PR for 'chemical property', M – LC for molecule', P– PH for 'particle of physics'. These 'semantic factors' are 'the basic building blocks for constructing semantic codes', and are generalised root concepts which may be used alone or in combination. The gaps at the second place are filled with other letters, designated 'infixes', which express the type of relationship between the semantic factor and the specific topic coded. A semantic code may also have numerical 'suffixes' to show a specific example of the class shown by the root concept itself: thus, P – PHA is Atom. This is straightforward, even primitive notation, and it is evident that it still fails to answer the key question: at what point should class terms begin? Nevertheless, the WRU project has great interest because it illustrates a return to classification (even if dignified with the impressive name of 'semantic factoring') which has been found necessary in a machine specifically designed for information retrieval.

The first searching system adopted was the 'Dequeker' system, in which cards with rows of holes punched in the body of the card are filed in a cabinet, rods are inserted through holes corresponding to the codes for the subject of an enquiry, and a half-turn of a handle operates a mechanism to raise slightly those cards bearing all the codes sought, which thus appear above the level of the rest of the pack. They can then be lifted out for consultation. An enquiry is analysed into terms corresponding to those in the system and these cards are removed from the pack. They are placed together in front of a bright light, which then will shine through those holes which are punched out of all the cards, but not through those punched out of only some of the cards. The illuminated holes give the numbers of documents referring to all the sought terms. This system requires very little in the way of equipment and could therefore be reproduced and distributed to field workers, who would then be able to have an index of their own. It is admirable for small numbers of documents, but is limited by the number of positions that can be punched on one card. A Dutch plastics card can hold up to 20000 numbers, but requires a special tool for drilling the holes.

The introduction of computers has posed problems for archaeologists, in particular those of sampling and description, but the possibilities for statistical analysis opened up should recommend themselves: 'Professional methods and habits will both have to be radically changed before computer science can be fully exploited so as to relieve archaeologists of the endlessly repetitive drudgery of compilation, which at present takes up most of their time.'

Gardin's work deserves close study, not only because it shows an interesting development and an extensive effort to apply systematic coding to new types of concept–add to our knowledge of the theory of information retrieval. He emphasises that subject or concept analysis must be the basis for all forms of retrieval, and problems of subject analysis are not simply removed by the introduction of machines; what is absolutely necessary is that librarians and those expert in machines should forget their illusory points of difference and cooperate in the basic task of concept analysis and the design of codes.

Another early use was in the analysis of legal documents, and several studies of this aspect are already in process. General appreciations of the situation have been given by Andreyev in the USSR and by Andrews in the USA. Andrews, who presented a paper to the 1960 meeting of the American Bar Association, has carried out extensive studies on retrieval of highly specific ideas for the US Patent Office, and shows how legal enquiries have obvious resemblances to the type of search that is carried out by Patents Examiners in order to establish originality. Case law and precedent, in fact, are precisely the type of data correlation problem that can easily be handled by machines. The full extent of work in Law can be seen from the review by John Myres, who has a useful discussion of full-text indexing-that is, using all significant words in a piece of text rather than assigning descriptors from a thesaurus. He concludes that here, as in some other exercises with machines, 'practitioners see clearly the gap between the demonstration of research findings and their application to reallife situations', and there is still some way to go before a computer-based searching service for law texts would be a commercial proposition.

A study begun by Colin Tapper at the London School of Economics was later transferred to Magdalen College, Oxford, and funded by an OSTI grant. Several volumes of the All England Reports and the Industrial Injuries Commissioners Decisions were processed on tape at the Atomic Energy Research Establishment at Harwell. Natural language was used, the words being taken from the reports themselves, and a number of lawyers were invited to participate by compiling sample searches. In general, the computer tended to retrieve a high proportion of the available relevant documents, but many others as well; comparisons with conventional search methods showed them to be superior, but a combination of both, as might be expected, was better than either method alone.

Early in 1959 a joint study began at the University of Pittsburgh between the Health Law Center and the Computation and Data Processing Center. The 'experimental library' consists of the complete statues of the state of Pennsylvania and those statutes of 13 other states that relate to health. As the director, John F. Horty, writes: 'Law in general furnishes an excellent initial vehicle for the development and testing of an operational retrieval system because precision of expression is sought and frequently achieved by legislators and judges. Statutes are particularly suited because each statutory section (considered a separate document) is of relatively short length, ordinarily deals with one specific concept and is carefully framed in words chosen for clarity rather than literary quality.'

The indexing is carried out by typing the whole text of each statute on cards; each card accommodates 68 letters, and a statute may require 20 or more cards. The cards are then fed into a computer and these tapes make up the store or 'library'. The tapes are then analysed by the computer, which makes an alphabetical list of all the words in the 'library' and records against each word the numbers of the documents in which it appears. To search for a specific problem, the key words are selected, and the computer then makes a list for each word of all documents in which that word appears. When the lists for all the selected words are made, the computer compares them and prints the full texts of those documents in which all the words appear.

Many programmes are of the type proposed by H. P. Luhn, and known as Keyword-in-Context (KWIC). The KWIC system is used for printing many current bibliographies and indexes, and its supporters point to its undoubted virtues of speed and economy of production. This is because the computer input can be copied directly from document titles by a keyboard operator, and the documents do not have to be scanned and analysed by a qualified indexer. Each title and reference is printed at each point in the alphabetical list where one of its keywords appears. It is, therefore, a multiple entry system which relies on adequate subject information being given by authors in the titles of their articles. As can be seen, it is very difficult to give a proper reference because of the width limitation of the page, and also to avoid using unsought terms ('accepting', 'according').

One method is the ingenious SLIC index (Selective Listing in Combination) devised by J. R. Sharp at British Nylon Spinners. The object, as indicated by the title, was to overcome the type of separation of terms produced by chain indexing, by ensuring that every combination of terms from a subject analysis is listed and not only those that happen to fall together in the analysis. In a subject with five facets, A B C D E, this would produce 16 entries in all, thus:

A B C D E
A B C E
A B D E
A B E

and so on for A C, A D, A E, B C, B D, B E, down to E by itself. The method would repay further study; it seems very apt for machine indexing, though it does produce some unsought and even unlikely combinations, such as KNITTING: WELDING and KNOTS: VISCOSITY in Sharp's own examples.

An alternative line of research has been to use computers for analysing whole texts, either for indexing, as in the work of Horty and Tapper, or for generating index languages, reviewed by Batty.

Some of this research indicates that natural language indexing, while not as effective as controlled language indexing in retrieval, nevertheless compares favourably on economic grounds. Reports vary so much, and some of the test files are so small, that one hesitates to draw conclusions one way or the other.

Generation of index languages by computer has been investigated by the Cambridge Language Research Unit and reported by Karen Sparck Jones. Whole texts are analysed to find out how words occur in similar contexts, and a theory of 'clumps' is being worked out. The limitations of single-hierarchy classifications are emphasised, and a set of related types of multiple classifications has been identified; these are called 'strings', 'stars', 'cliques' and 'clumps', according to the complexity of the relations between the terms in each set. The simplest, a string, is a straightforward linear connection; a star has a central element related to several others like the spokes of a wheel; a clique has several elements all related to one another; and a clump has the most complicated network of interrelationships both within the set of terms and external to it.

Before committing ourselves to the view that the future of information retrieval systems lies in the abandonment of classification and indexing in favour of computers, sometimes taken for granted by computer specialists such as Licklider, we have to consider a little more critically the advantages and the disadvantages of machines. One factor that has been passed over all too lightly is that of cost. Figures for a *research* programme might be expected to be high, but even so one would have to receive substantial advantages in speed, or range of search, to make this an economic figure as compared with a good classified index.

Costs would not be important, however, if the use of a machine enabled us to do more than is possible with card indexes, or if the machine performed tedious and burdensome operations which at present have to be done by human beings. It is expensive to buy a motor-car, but it makes possible journeys that were extremely difficult on foot, and requires less maintenance than a horse. I believe, though I do not consider it by any means proved, that machines offer these possibilities for certain types of retrieval, but not for others. It seems to me nonsense to spend time programming a computer to carry out a search that could be done in two minutes in a conventional index, and it is sometimes forgotten that, unless classification is called in to help, the computer has to search all the library for every enquiry, so that, in practice, no enquiry can be satisfied in less time than it takes to do this. To the resounding claim that a machine can search the whole of the Library of Congress catalogue in two minutes, the only answer is: 'Who wants to search the whole catalogue?'

16

Information Retrieval Through Classification

Overview

This examination of forms of index and of schemes of classification seems to show that, while each form of index is bound to incorporate some measure of relational linkage into its structure, the classified index itself does not appear to hold out much promise for social science documentation, because it depends more than the other forms on an actual scheme of classification; and those in general use are quite unsatisfactory for this purpose. Some fail in their treatment of the subject, some in their lack of the detail and flexibility necessary for documentation, and some in both. This view, moreover, seems to be confirmed by the lack of use of the classified form in published indexes. A few, like CEDESA, use the UDC; but that scheme finds few supporters in social science, even in Europe, though it is very strongly entrenched there and often used for classifying scientific literature, including abstracts of periodical articles and similar very specific subjects.

As a result, there is a conflict between the natural wish to use a classified arrangement because of the obvious advantages it has in bringing together related literature and the disillusionment that comes from finding that the schemes used in libraries do not, in fact, bring these advantages. The specialist examines classification schemes to see how they treat subjects he is expert in and finds them unsatisfactory. Nevertheless, they continue to be used by librarians maven, on occasion, defended or actually extolled. We can hardly wonder if specialists conclude that there must be some professional reason for this, and assume that library classifications are tools peculiar to librarians and are unrelated to the type of classifications that scholars themselves need to use. The formation of the Classification Society in the UK, and later in the USA, has attracted a few contributions from librarians and information scientists, however, and provides a forum for the exchange of views. The first issue of the *Classification Society Bulletin* in 1965 contained a set of bibliographies, and close relations have been established with the Classification Research Group.

There is certainly a grain of truth in this. Libraries should be able to offer the scholar the services of an automatic memory, and he should not have to concern himself with its mechanism, any more than the owner of a television set has to; he can, of course, if it really interests him, but it is not essential. What is essential, though, is that the mechanism should work as its user requires; he should not have to put up with an inefficient apparatus, which might, for example, require him to search through hundreds of works on European economic history in order to find the one that deals with the Common Market. If the classification schemes available do not deal with the literature in the way required by the research worker, it would appear justifiable to reject classification, and to turn our attention to other forms such as the alphabetical or the mechanical index.

Similarly, in the USA 'classification' tends to be equated with the Decimal and the Library of Congress Classifications, the two most widely used. In a report on 'Documentation, indexing and retrieval of scientific information' presented to the US Senate in 1961, Eugene Wall wrote: 'Please note that here the term "classification" is noto used as a synonym for "shorthand description" or the like; rather, it is used in the restricted sense of formal hierarchical arrangement, wherein ideas are included as sub-classes of broader ideas, etc., and are formally arranged, for retrieval purposes, in such a manner.' On this very restricted view of classification, of course, it would indeed be surprising if it were found to be of any value for information retrieval, and it goes far to explain why the *BNB* has found it necessary to develop the very detailed PRECIS subject index system since its adoption, unaltered, of the 18th edition of DC. This has had the very favourable effect of bringing the results of a long research project on classification to the aid of constructing a machine-compiled alphabetical index to a classified catalogue.

Development

During recent years there have been several attempts to work out ,the basic principles of retrieval systems, and a great deal of progress has been made by various teams, notably in India, France and Eng~land, where more attention has been paid to the use of classification. In his attempt at a general theory Vickery shows how these advances in classification theory have proceeded along lines converging on those of research on the use of machines in the USA and the USSR. Ranganathan and his DRTC team have been producing a series of articles 'Non-conventional methods of document retrieval', showing how the Depth Classification schedules of CC can be used for machine-based as well as manual indexing.

It is my firm belief that the nature of an information service makes it inevitable that some form of classification, or codification, will always be required. Certainly, machines can take over many tasks of a routine and repetitive nature and can carry them out much more swiftly and accurately than a human being. If the retrieval process always consisted of finding a specific answer to a specifically stated question, no doubt machinery could take it over. But there is much more to it than this, and if we analyse the process, we see that the searcher may constantly require to think about the results he is getting; in other words, searching the literature is by no means wholly a task of a routine and repetitive nature.

Information, whether gained by direct sense perception or by consulting documentation, is 'assimilated', in Jean Piaget's term, by being incorporated into a structured pattern which already exists in the enquirer's mind. All modern research on the learning process tends to confirm this, and the work of Piaget, J. P. Guilford, Noam Chomsky, L. S. Vygotsky and A. R. Luria, as well as many others, shows that we cannot make sense of the world unless we are able to perform this process of assimilation, to turn what Vygotsky calls 'spontaneous concepts' into 'scientific concepts'. I have given a more extended account of the relevance of theories of learning in my paper on 'User Psychology' to the conference held jointly by the FID and the Italian National Institute in Rome in 1971.

The retrieval process begins when a lack of information shows itself in a human mind and the decision is taken to find out if this information has been discovered and published. The first step that the searcher takes is to formulate in words what he conceives to be the subject on which he seeks information. It is evidence of our deeply rooted habit of defining things by referring them to classes that very often enquiries are formulated in much more general terms than the enquirer really wants, and we should not be surprised by it. Information about other members of the same class will be helpful, because the very fact of membership of a class signifies the possession of similar properties and the involvement in similar relationships. L. B. Doyle puts it very clearly when he says that 'hierarchies have been, and still are, important. They provide familiar conceptual grooves by which people can steer themselves to areas of interest.' Since the need for a search arises from the process of completing a mental picture, the word or words chosen to begin the search are more likely to be related to the general picture than to the piece missing. It is often difficult to describe in precise language that which we do not know; we are aware of a gap in our knowledge, but not of its contents or dimensions. We are, however, usually well aware of the picture we are trying to build, and, in beginning a search, it is natural to think in terms of the general picture, simply because any information relating to it will be welcome. Even if we know some of it already, it may help to clarify our mind or may remind us of another possible line of questioning.

In formulating a request, therefore, the searcher may or may not be able to state his need precisely. If he cannot, the retrieval system should provide some map of the territory he is exploring, to help him narrow his search and avoid diversions into irrelevant matters. Even if he can, such a map may be useful if it calls to mind the relationships with other parts of that territory and with other areas of knowledge outside.

The second step that the searcher takes is to match the subject as he conceives it in his own words with the words of the scheme used to arrange the literature. Many library systems fail here through lack of progress and of contact with experts in the subjects they cover. An enquirer who is not expert in the subject of his search will expect a guide of some authority to the literature he is consulting; one who is expert will lose faith in the value of the guide if it does not contain the terms or the documents he knows to be in current use in His subject. It is true that any scheme of arrangement becomes 'fixed' to a certain extent once it has been written down. But a library scheme is for arranging knowledge, and since knowledge progresses, the scheme must be able to progress also, however difficult this may be. A good example of one problem, the use of a common and a formal name for the same thing, is shown by the terms 'Common Market' and 'European Economic Community', both of which may be used in searches for the same information. Another instance of an emerging subject, International Affairs, is discussed by Ranganathan, who shows how the normative principles of Balance of Power and Geopolitics tend to give rise to more and more literature treating of their interrelationships, forming a focus on the resulting complex and drawing away from the original basic subject, History. Workers in this field will expect to find libraries aware of its existence, and some account taken of it in the schemes of arrangement in indexes.

Having chosen the terms under which he will search and matched them with those used by the index, the enquirer now proceeds to examine the index itself at the appropriate places. An alphabetical index will choose one of two synonyms as its heading for entries, and put in a reference from the other: 'Common Market *see* European Economic Community'. An index to a classified catalogue will refer from both terms to the notation symbol under which the entries are filed, and at the appropriate heading the searcher finds a series of cards referring him to the documents in the library that deal with his subject. The next step, then, is to examine each entry to decide on its relevance to the search. The searcher divides the cards into two groups-those references selected as relevant, and those rejected as irrelevant, or unsuitable or known already.

During the consultation the index should provide the searcher with other leads for his consideration. The European Economic Community may be discussed in, or our understanding of it assisted by, documents dealing with the European Free Trade Area, the post-war economic history of Europe, Commonwealth Free Trade, and so on. These are the subjects that would appear as parts of the same area of knowledge as the Common Market, and would be associated together in the searcher's mind. In the process of 'laying down' daily a series of index entries for documents as they are published, these and any other topics associated with them in the literature must be incorporated into the index in the same relationships. The scheme of arrangement must therefore be able to show-the new relationships that arise as knowledge progresses.

The final stages in the retrieval process consist of locating the documents named by the relevant index entries and reading them to learn what information they contain. The first means that whatever system of indexing we use must contain the addresses of the documents indexed—that is, their location in the library; this may be a shelf number, a citation from a periodical, a document serial number or a classification number. Most libraries store their books in a classified sequence, which, of course, allows the searcher to browse among the books themselves as well as in the index. Indeed, some libraries have no other facilities for browsing, since their only catalogues are author catalogues. Pamphlets are sometimes stored in classified sequence, sometimes in other sequences that oblige the searcher to approach them through an index. Periodicals are sometimes classified into broad subject groups and sometimes arranged in a single alphabetical sequence; in both cases the searcher has to begin his consultation with the library's subject index, unless he can select likely titles and use their published indexes-if there are any. The final stage, reading the document, is normally the task of the research worker himself, but it may often be done by librarians also, in search of material for answering enquiries.

The whole process of information retrieval, therefore, consists of a series of acts of codification and selection: codifying the needed information and selecting words to describe it; codifying the chosen words in terms of the library's stereotype system; selecting from that system those references that appear to have relevance; and selecting from texts the information that actually proves to be what is wanted. Classification and indexing are particularly concerned with the middle stage, though they may also help in the first, and if we return now to the mechanisms by which libraries make their stereotypes, we can, in the light of this discussion, see more clearly which mechanism has most to contribute.

The alphabetical dictionary index, compiled on the principle of 'specific entry' and arranged iri a single alphabetical sequence, provides imgiediate access to cards for relevant literature provided (a) that the searcher has selected the correct word to describe his subject, and (b) that the same word is used in the index itself. If either or both of these conditions do not exist, the index may yet lead to the right matcrial if the cross-references it contains link up the words chosen with those used for index entries. Experience in many different types of library shows that an enquiry may be framed in words that are 'right' from the point of view of a match with the index, but that frequently these words describe a larger area of knowledge or areas closely related to the one sought-the whole picture being formed or the areas next to the gap where information is lacking.

If the index is to do its job properly, it must include a structure of references between specific and general terms, and from each specific subject to other specific subjects within the same general field, if they are sufficiently closely related to be normally linked together in the reader's mind. In practice one rarely finds dictionary indexes that do include all such possible references. The computer-produced Permuterm Subject Index to the *Social Science Citation Index,* which has some alphabetico-classed structure as well, has the following, for which it is hard to find any rationale:

Abuse

sa Drug-Abuse

Alcoholism

Delinquency

Delinquency

Alchoholism

America

Causes

Drug

sa Pharmaceutical

Drug-Abuse (no sa to Abuse)

The alphabetico-classed index does not provide direct access unless the term chosen happens to be regarded as a 'class' term for the purpose of the index. Specific topics have first to be sought in an alphabetical key list showing which terms are class terms and what other terms they include. Once within the right class, the reader is provided with a series of sub-divisions showing the related specific topics. The difficulty is that subjects assumed to be of sufficient generality to be class terms are not themselves classified, but are separated by the accidental position of their names in the alphabet. Ease of access depends, therefore, on the principle by which class terms are selected. In a thesaurus, for example, one would find references between Broader and Narrower Terms, which are class-inclusion relationships. If the term 'Trade' were selected and the enquirer chose 'Economics', he would require a reference from the more general term to the less; under Trade, however, he would find a series of terms describing the various aspects of Trade.

The classified index, arranged in the sequence of the notational symbols, does not provide immediate access for any enquirer, since his first step is to translate the term he chooses into notational symbols. Once he has done this, however, he is directed to a section of the index in which he finds not only the term he chose, but also those related in the ways he is likely to need. The whole purpose of a scheme of classification is to provide as complete a picture as possible of each part of the field of knowledge, those parts that are most closely related being filed nearest together. In order to achieve this, other types of index must build up their series of cross-references-that is, they must rely on a classification scheme even if they do not use its notation as a means for arranging the sequence of entries.

Some argue that this necessarily means the rejection of the classified index; that even if alphabetical indexes have concealed classificatory bases, nevertheless alphabetical order itself is commonly used, in encyclopaedias and so on, and is widely understood; and that any new term can easily be introduced merely by naming it. This argument does not take into account the reader's approach to information retrieval. Either the system of arrangement provides links from reader's terms to indexing terms, or it does not. If it does not provide such links, he is not helped at all; he is merely thrown back on his own resources, and has to think of another word, to start another search. If it does, it is because the index has borrowed from the technique of classification. Lack of classificatory aids means failure for the alphabetical index; on the other hand, importing classification means departing from the alphabetical principle to some extent, while not using theclassificatory system in the most effective way. A number of studies, such as those of Wingfield, Landauer and Meyer, and Lauer and Baltig, have, indeed, shown how the use of classification in categories acts as an aid to the memory, and is far superior to alphabetical headings in recall; Lauer and Baltig report that 'one major finding of this experiment was the consistently greater effectiveness of taxonomic category than first-letter communality among words ... taxonomic category proved to be a very strong cue, whereas first letters at best were very weak cues'. To reject the classified index in favour of the alphabetical, therefore, merely means shutting one's eyes to the fundamental problem, that of providing links between the ideas in the reader's mind and the ideas in the literature indexed. Unluckily, shutting one's eyes to a problem does not make it disappear.

Others argue in favour of classification schemes as they stand, and suggest that documentalists exaggerate the importance of specific entry. If specific subjects are classified under general headings, this will coincide with the approach of the reader who also chooses a general term, and will not raise a barrier for the reader who chooses a related term, since these too will be classified under the same general heading.

This proposition certainly has something to commend it, but there are two major disadvantages.

In the first place, the quantity of literature published means that general headings grow apace, and soon the unfortunate searcher finds that he has to look through scores of entries in order to find the few he wants. An example of this is provided by the Human Relations Area Files, in which documents are summarised by experts and assigned to appropriate categories, a copy of the summary being filed under each category.selected. Some of these categories contain over 1000 entries, which is clearly too many for scanning, all the more since these entries are actually full summaries of the items and not simply index cards. In *Sociology of Education Abstracts* the abstract (No. 398) of a whole issue of the journal *Urban Review* deals with 'bussing' and the 'community school', but neither of these terms, though commonly used as search terms, is in the subject index, which is alphabet ico-classed. In section 0 Administration and Organisation, we find abstract 398 in subsection 004 Integration, and sub-section 013 School and community relationships; in section

3 Goals and Functions of Education, it appears in 301 Social distribution of education, and in 310 Education and social change, where there is a list of 33 abstract numbers with no further indication of actual subject content; it appears in several other sections, Social change, along with 28 other numbers.

In the second place, the reader wanting a specific topic will not find it, even if he formulates it precisely, unless the index contains a reference to the general heading. Thus, the specific term must be used or the reader finding no entry will conclude that the library has nothing dealing with his subject. In the classified index the specific terms appear in the alphabetical file, with a reference to the notational symbol. The use of general headings only will mean that several specific topics will have the same symbol; and when the reader turns to the classified file, he will find that the symbol not only includes all these, but also has another name, that of the general heading itself. This is bound to cause confusion and to forfeit one of the main advantages of using a classification scheme—the clear presentation of a map of any field of knowledge so that the reader is helped to organise his own thoughts.

The solution chosen by the HRAF, says F. W. Moore, 'does not lie in simply dividing these categories up, thereby complicating an already complex system. For this reason we feel that degrees of access through an electronic system is the only practical solution to this problem.' Many others have adopted the same course, and a vast literature has grown up on the use of mechanical and electronic sorting machines for information retrieval. I shall examine this aspect in more detail later, but since it seems likely that manual indexes will be used for many years yet to come, even if only in those libraries that cannot afford computers, and since the great development of library services now taking place throughout the world means that document classification schemes will continue to be used, even if only for library shelves, it is useful to summarise at this point what we require of these schemes to make them efficient retrieval systems for the social sciences. Even in the USA, the chief centre of machine research, the 1961 Minnowbrook Conference on Information Retrieval in the Social Sciences called for research on the various classification schemes available and their prospects of development.

The purpose of a classification scheme is to arrange information, in documents on shelves or on cards in indexes, in a sequence that will be helpful to the user. We have seen that the major schemes can be criticised on several grounds, and this criticism helps us to understand the qualities desired. First, and one of the most important, is the provision of sufficiently detailed sub-division to enable the librarian to classify precisely and accurately even the most specific periodical article-that is, to enumerate in the schedules all the terms that appear in such articles. Second, the scheme must be flexible-that is, it must provide a mechanism for combining these terms in a consistent and logical manner; it requires therefore a series of notational symbols that permit of all these combinations without confusion or 'synonyms'-two subjects receiving the same symbols. So far, I have said little about notation, and it is of secondary importance, but this does not mean that we need give no thought to it; on the contrary, some otherwise useful schemes have failed to win success because their notations are psychologically repulsive. Third, 'the scheme must be able to express clearly and without ambiguity the major categories of terms that appear in social science literature, in particular the various social groups formed by assemblies of individuals and the networks of relationships subsisting between the groups and their members. If possible, the categories should be combinable in ways that reflect the actual literature-that is, the scheme must recognise the two conflicting views on the nature of groups and offer a solution acceptable to both sides. It must recognise, in principle and in actual use, the need remarked on by Swift for coping with the different perspectives of different groups. Finally, the scheme must produce a collocation of subjects having more relation to the current consensus than some of those, in particular the DC, whose outline is based on ancient and superseded theories of knowledge. The problem of `main classes' (or whatever term we use to name our major general headings) has not yet been given the attention it deserves, except by Bliss, whose outline has probably more to recommend it than most of the others. In making a classification scheme we have to have a starting point, and the question `How specific is specific?' has often been asked, in this context as well as in the context of choice of subject headings in alphabetical indexes.

17

Modes of Formation

Basic Views on Knowledge

"The field of knowledge, i.e., the number of specific subjects which have to be related in a classification, it potentially infinite: between any two points in the system an indefinite number of new points might have to be inserted. Moreover, knowledge is multidimensional: the interconnections of each concept spread out in many directions, and usually each subject is a synthesis of several such multiply-connected concepts. Subjects so formed are said to show 'lamination'. A still looser form of combination, 'assemblage', exists when two 'universes of discourse, each infinite and self-contained in some definable sense, may have to be considered in relation to one another'".

In Dr. Ranganathan's system of classification (Colon Classification) compound subjects were built up synthetically from 'elementary' concepts and his notational devices represent such combinations by a system or ordinal numbers. [Read also his conception of Categories, Facets and Phases, discussed below.]

Ranganathan stresses that the Universe of knowledge is not static: "It is a dynamic continuum. Its structure is therefore ever changing. Hence it is not sufficient to know its structure at the present moment. We should also understand its mode of development."

Modes of Formation of New Specific Subjects

"Ranganathan indicated five modes of formation of new specific subjects: (a) by the lamination of terms from different facets within the same original universe, and (b) by the loose assemblage of terms from original universes; new terms were introduced into the structure by (c) the denudation of a class to form a sub-class, by (d) the dissection of a class to form an array of sub-classes, or by (e) the interpolation of a new term in an existing array. This kind of development went on continually. As such changes accumulated in a particular main class, it became necessary to reorganize the ranking of terms in particular arrays. or even in a whole facet. Further, it became necessary to reshape the facet formula of the class. Ranganathan conjectured that such adjustments might occur once in a generation.

Analysis of Subject Terms in Recorded Information

In 'analytico-synthetic classification', as will be seen in our treatment of such schemes of classification in subsequent chapters, the field of knowledge is analysed into elementary terms which are then systematically ordered and combined, thus synthesizing specific subjects. In order to display linkage in an aggregate we are to analyse the elementary terms into Fundamental Categories, which always stand in fixed relationships one to another in specific subjects. Next, we are to lay down rules for the order of citation of these categories and label each category with a distinctive affix whereby it can be recognized.

We may mention here that an analytico-synthetic scheme of classification recognizes an adequate number of main classes, not squeezing them all into 9 or 26 according to the digits available in an established series. It shows sub-divisions of these main classes divided into the major facets relating to the fundamental groupings, Personality, Matter, Energy, Space and Time which permit phase relationships being built up in a clear and recognizable manner. Such a scheme has a notation reflecting faithfully and economically all of these features and gives the maximum autonomy to the classifiers and cataloguers in their daily work.

Categories

"A Category, conceptualistically defined, is a concept of high generality and wide application. Or, it may be defined as the most general kind of existence or reality which any mentionable object can have". (Shera and Egan. The Classified Catalog.)

Aristotelian Categories

'Aristotle used the term Category to express the ten classes of being, or the typical forms of speech used to express being, or finally, the typical judgements regarding being.' The Aristotelian Categories were:

1. Substance
2. Quantity
3. Quality
4. Relation (e.g. double, half, loudest, etc.)
5. Place
6. Time
7. Situation of position (e.g. horizontal etc.)
2. Possession of acquired character (e.g. does or ornament); state (e.g. fever etc.)
3. Action
4. Passivity or passion (e.g. defeat, being cut, etc.)

For Aristotle; the Categories were terms, one or other of which must be affirmed of any subject if we ask what it is. The basic Category, according to Aristotle, was that of substance, for if we ask of any concrete individual, what essentially it is, we must answer in terms of a substance: man, horse, stone, etc. The other categories presuppose substance.

Kant's Categories

"Kant", observe Shera and Egan, "revised the Categories of Aristotle to make them dependent upon the forms of judgment. These forms of judgment involved the fundamental ways of thinking of objects, and his table of Categories is, therefore, explicitly a classification of the possible objects of human thought according to the fundamental ways in which the human mind can conceive or understand objects. The Categories of Kant were:

1. Categories of quantity
   - Unity
   - Plurality
   - Universality

3. Categories of relation
   - Substantiality
   - Causality
   - Reciprocity

2. Categories of quality
   Reality
   Negation
   Limitation

4. Categories of modality
   Possibility
   Actuality
   Necessity."

Disguised Categories in D.C. and U.D.C.

Composite schedules in D.C.

Categories were first introduced into classification in the guise of composite schedules. Dewey, for example, divided chemistry into Physical, Analytical and Systematic, splitting up the subject field by Categories, such as problem, operation, analysis and substance.

Associational devices in U.D.C.

The U.D.C. in its breakdown of the chemistry schedule as pointed out by Vickery, went much further than Dewey. "The 'analytical numbers' 54.01/09 comprise general properties of and operation on chemical substances; the numbers 54-1 to 54-94 are states of the substances; and so on." (Vickery).

It may be pointed out that the formulation of Categories in such schedules as exemplified above, has not been consciously and deliberately carried out. Shera and Egan in Classified Catalog observe "These modes of being, as identified by Aristotle and refined and reclassified by Kant must have been at least vaguely operative in the minds of authors of the Universal Decimal Classification when they added to their expansion and modification of the Dewey system certain supplementary signs or symbols of association and relationship.

Dr. Ranganathan's Fundamental Categories

Dr. Ranganathan developed fully the application of the Aristotelian principle to the analysis of the structure of recorded information. The first explicit use of Categories in classification was made by him. His Colon Classification exhibited from the start a division of classes into Facets or Categories. From his understanding of the way in which knowledge increases (discussed above: Modes of formation of new specific subjects) it became possible for Ranganathan to identify a variety of 'facets' or aspects of relationship which the constituent parts of all knowledge bear to each other. Ranganathan related all facets to one another of fundamental Categories or Concepts—Personality, Matter, Energy, Space and Time. These are, in effect, Aristotelian modes of being, in terms of which any mental concept may be expressed. These Categories are usually written merely as PMEST. Vickery, however, has suggested that there are other fundamental concepts which govern division. Space and Time simply denote geographical and chronological divisions. The foci in the other categories differ from class to class. The Category 'Energy' always denotes an operation, a process, or a problem to be solved; 'Matter' is represented by materials; 'Personality' is best thought of as the core of any subject. When foci from all five Categories are present, the PMEST formula gives us our combination order or order in chain. We begin with Personality, the most concrete Category, and move through the others according to the formula, until we come to time, and most abstract of the five categories concerned.

Thus, the distinctive property of Colon Classification is its emphasis upon the basic way in which a subject may be characterized and its attempt to ignore the traditional hierarchical grouping of such characteristics. Ranganathan's great contribution to classification is his implicit rejection of the physical book as the constituent unit in classification and has substituion of thought-unit or subject-unit. We may however, note that Ranganathan achieved only partial success and it was due to two errors: (1) like the editors of UDC, he attempted to represent all possible relationships within the Universe of Knowledge (Universe of Subjects, as it is now called) and this led him to increasing complexity; and (2) his too hasty adoption of the decimal principle in notation prevented any real escape from the shackles of hierarchy.

Manifestation of Facets: "Time-Facet, Space-Facet-Energy-Facet, Matter-Facet and Personality-Facet may manifest themselves in specific subjects, not necessarily once only but as often as necessary and at successive levels; when so manifesting, they often acquire different names in different specific subjects and the different manifestations of one and same pattern of foci and facet constituted by facets have different names in different specific subjects."—Ranganathan. General theory of classification (in ABGILA, June 1951). The first Energy-Facet, for example, could introduce a second 'round' of Personality and Matter categories the second Energy-

Facet which follows could introduce a third 'round', and so on. Time and Space could figure in the last round.

Levels and Rounds: Levels are the steps of division within a Fundamental Category, generally either P or E. In each of these there may be more than one method of division. Thus in Political Science we have the division into Type of rule [P]: anarchy, monarchy, communism etc. and Parts of rule [P2]; head, executive, legislature, party. These are both an inherent part of Personality but can be clearly separated. They are different levels of personality.

Rounds are recurrences of Personality after the Energy-Facet. We can often divide the Energy-Facet by Kinds of things – these are Personality. So we have this problem recurring a second time round. Thus in chemistry we have the problem [E] Analytical, Chemistry, which divides into Kinds of Personality – macro, micro, volumetric etc. These are rounds.

Phase Relations

In the simplest phase-relation, a specific subject involves two main classes (with or without subdivisions) which are brought into some kind of relation with each other. Its class number consists in order, of the class number of one of the phases (primary phase), a prescribed connecting symbol, and the class-number of the other phase (secondary phase). The problem, however, is to decide which should be the primary phase. The symbols which are used to introduce phases are called 'phase indicators'.

Kinds of Phases: For a long time the idea of phase has been implicit in all modern schemes of classification. Provision had been made for it to a certain extent in notation, but-no name was given to it. The mathematical symbols of the UDC, the zero, double-zero and treble-zero of D.C., the systematic tables of Bliss-constitute an implicit recognition of the existence of phase. D.C.'s provision for dividing a subject 'like the main classification' is in fact a tact use of phase as a mode If division. In UDC, for example, phase relation as specified notationally by adding the second class number after a colon; e.g. English Literature and the Bible is notationally specified as 820 : 22. The D.C. indicates a phase change by the interpolation of a zero between the part of the notation relating to the subject and the part relating to the form (form of presentation). Bliss indicates it by changing his notation to Arabic figures.

Ranganathan first introduced the term 'phase' for the above and isolated a number of different kinds of phase, such as bias, tool, influence, and comparison.

Relational Analysis of Subjects

J. F. L. Farradane has, in recent years, developed a system of classification as an instrument of information work in science and technology. The traditional approach including facet-analysis is to work 'deductively' from the general class to the special, analyzing subjects by applying characteristics of division, but Farradane's method is to work 'inductively' from the particular to the general. He starts with elementary concepts—isolates (noun subject terms) and then establishes relations between these isolates. These isolates must not be confused with the isolates or foci produced in a fully faceted classification, although they are in some ways similar. Certain relations exist between these isolates as conceived by Farradane, viz. causation, appurtenance, reaction, space and time. The symbols used in the indexing system to express such relations between the isolates are called operators and they form the crucial part of Farradane's system. If the isolates are combined, or qualified, by the right operators—those which express the only possible relations between them—a linear symbol called an analet may be constructed. Alphabetical arrangement of such analets by their first factors will provide "a complete logical subject . . . A classification can be constructed by selection of deductive relations arranged in hierarchical form". After making a number of analets within a subject area isolates sharing common relations with others are grouped together and a classification gradually emerges. Farradane claims that his methods result in the only true representation of the structure of knowledge and that his principles provide accurate and adequate indexing and classifying with complete flexibility.

The different kinds of relations existing between items as suggested by Farradane can be expressed thus:

Fixed Relation	:	Causation
		Appurtenance
Temporary Relation	:	Reaction
		Space
		Time

The meanings of these relations are as follows:

Causation	:	A causes, results in, etc. B
Appurtenance	:	A contains, comprises, etc. B
Reaction	:	A is affected by B
Space, Time	:	A is in, on, etc., located by B

If we take the fixed relation—appurtenance—as the basis of our linear arrangement we obtain a hierarchy of the kind:

- Electric engineering
- Electric lighting
- Discharge lamps
- Mercury vapour lamps

These items have, in Farradane's terminology, a fixed relation to one another. 'Electrical Engineering' includes 'Electric lighting', which includes 'Discharge lamps', which includes 'Mercury vapour lamps'. This is, according to Farradane, one of the two most fundamental relations existing between items.

Thought Units are Multi-relational

The thought unit which we shall have to classify will not be limited to a fixed relation; or indeed to any single relation, but will be continuous of all or any of the relations given by Farradane—assuming that they are exhaustive.

Farradane dealing with relations has suggested that fixed relations should precede temporary relations. Dr. Ranganathan, however, has considered Categories rather than relations and has argued for an order of decreasing concreteness. Farradane's order of relations could be stated thus: Appurtenance, causation, reaction, space and time. Dr. Ranganathan's categories, arranged in an order of decreasing concreteness, will lead to the same order of arrangement in the following concrete case :--Plants for human consumption which contains sugar beet which is affected by climate in India in 1960 (In this example 'causation' is not included).

Appurtenance relation is universal and would occur with all items in a set, thus in the above example India stands at the end of a chain going up to world (for example, India—Asia—World).

We cannot set a limit on the lower end of an appurtenance chain because the subdivision into parts can proceed indefinitely.

Theoretically we cannot know the upper limit of a chain either, since new knowledge may uncover appurtenance relations between items not previously held to be related in this way. In fact, however, upper limits can be fixed by convention.

These upper limits, therefore, will determine the main classes of a scheme of classification. In the chain cited above we began at the 'Electrical engineering'. If the upper limit be set at this item, main class 'Electrical engineering' will be established. If, on the other hand, the chain is continued up to 'Engineering', the main class would be pushed a stage higher. It will be seen, then, that main classes in a system of classification are conventionally fixed, that they cannot be fixed at the lower end since the lower end consists of an infinity of entities, that they must, therefore, be fixed at the upper end and in conformity with the prevailing state of knowledge.

Compound and Complex Subjects

We are thus led on to discuss multi-phased subjects in a book. A book may deal with two or three or many subjects, considered separately or in their interrelationships: or with two or more aspects of one or more subjects. When a subject contains foci from more than one class it is a complex subject; e.g. The influence of the Bible on English Literature is a complex subject, since it contains foci from Literature and from Religion. The part of such a subject which is derived from one main class is called a phase, as has been discussed in the foregoing paragraphs. The above example reflects more than one phase and is thus a multi-phased subject.

Similarly, Mathematics for engineers is a complex subject. These represent the interaction of the original subject. The interaction of two normally distinct subjects is called a phase-relation (discussed in the preceding pages.) Phase relations are usually specified by linking on to the original subject (the primary phase) other subjects from the rest of a general classification with other separate subjects and are distinct from facets.

Discipline vs. Specific Subject

In the Editor's Introduction to Dewey Decimal Classification, 17th ed. the concept of 'discipline' is clarified. "The concept of 'discipline' or field of specialization, is basic to an understanding of Dewey's system. The primary basis for D.D.C. arrangement and development is by discipline, while subject, strictly speaking is secondary. There is no one place for any subject in itself; a subject may appear in any or all of the disciplines. No class can be said to cover the scope of marriage, or water or tomatoes, or Brazil; in common parlance, there is no single number for any of these concepts or subjects.

Role of an Alphabetical Index

This leads us to discuss the function of the alphabetical index in bringing together 'distributed relatives'. We have enumerated the functions of an alphabetical index. Dewey uses relative index in displaying the relations and bringing together the distributed relatives.

We may here discuss one highly important function performed by the alphabetical index, viz. the display of many of the relations between subjects which are not displayed by the classified order.

It is well-known that a classified sequence of books on shelves or on cards in a catalogue can display one system of relations, because it is a simple, linear order. For example, if Dyeing of textiles is placed in Textile Technology, it is thus related to the other operations in textile manufacture—to cleaning, spinning, etc. Its relationship to be dyeing of other materials (e.g. leather) is not shown. But consider the index entries in a classified catalogue:

- Dyeing: Leathers: Technology
- Dyeing: Textiles: Technology

The missing relationship is established in the index.

Take, for instance, the following cases in D.C. classification scheme:

- The economic history of India is 330.954
- The political history of India is 320.954
- The social history of India is 954
- The constitutional history of India is 342.54

That all these are related are not shown in the classification which displays only the relationship of Indian economic history to British economic history (330.942), to French economic history (320.944) etc and so on. But while the classification scatters the kinds of Indian history, the index collects them—brings together the 'distributed relations' thus:

- India : Economic history 330.954
- India : Political history 320.954
- India : Social history 954

In Bliss the preferred order collects the kind of history under the country, as it does in Brown. So, German economic history is MGE, German Social history MGH and so on. Here the systematic order displays the relations which are left to the index in Dewey and an index to Bliss should bring out those which are related systematically in Dewey:

- Economic history : France MRF
- Economic history : Germany MGE
- Economic history : Great Britain MUE

18

Classification in Social Sciences

Purpose

The purpose of a general classification scheme is to enable libraries to arrange their documents and indexes in a sequence that will be as helpful as possible to the user. One of the main criticisms directed against librarians by social scientists has been that the schemes found most widely do not, in fact, produce a helpful arrangement; very often they scatter material that needs to be used together, and not infrequently they abolish subjects completely. Many people, for example, pre engaged in the study and teaching of Health Education, but this 'subject has no existence in the Decimal Classification, which is used by most education libraries. Small wonder, then, if the users receive the impression that the purpose of a classification scheme is to enable librarians to carry out some obscure function of their own, part of the 'mystique' of librarianship, which contributes only to the separation of books from readers, and, as a consequence, of librarians from those whom they are supposed to serve. At the Home Universities Conference in 1960 Professor Cormack made a strong plea, on behalf of readers, that librarians might cease from erecting such barriers, that they should regard service to readers as of greater importance than maintaining the integrity of classification schemes and cataloguing codes. 'In classification let us not deify Dewey; let us not make books and readers fit into a Procrustean bed of Dewey's making.'

Such a sentiment is entirely justifiable; but the remedy lies not in abandoning the techniques of classification and indexing, but in abandoning those parts of the techniques that have outlived their usefulness, and now constitute a hindrance, and not a help, to library users. Many librarians do not seem aware of the extent to which antiquated classification schemes damage the reputation of their profession, and in consequence tend to magnify the labours of changing to a new scheme. Certainly, these should not be underestimated; but A, if, as I believe, service to readers is the function to which all processes; are subordinate, then we should surely look for ways which simplify, changes as they become necessary, rather than refuse to recognise the need for change because we are out of contact with our readers.

The Decimal Classification

Overview

The Decimal Classification of Melvil Dewey was the first of the 'modern general schemes and has become widely known through its use by public and school libraries. Very few research libraries use it, though many use the Universal Decimal Classification, which was modelled on the DC in 1895 and has steadily grown away from it ever since. Produced in 1876 for the library of Amherst College, the great contribution made by the DC was its principle of 'relative location'—that is, the numbering of subjects, instead of `fixed location', the numbering of positions on shelves. Relative location allowed subjects to be moved about on the shelves as new books were added. Dewey's scheme also enabled new subjects to be inserted at the appropriate places, which meant that the numbering system toad also to allow of such interpolation, and he hit upon the idea of using decimal numbers for his scheme's notation. He divided the universe of knowledge into nine fields which he numbered from 1 to 9, and made a notation for the sub-divisions of each field by simply adding the necessary figures on the right-hand end. Using a minimum of three figures, his nine fields or 'main classes' and their sub-divisions were thus numbered 100-999, and to these he added a tenth class, numbered 000-099, for general and polygraphic works that could not be fitted into any particular main class.

Librarians were quick to see the advantages of relative location, and the scheme was popular from the start. Its early years coincided with the growth of the public library systems of Europe and the USA, and many new libraries adopted the scheme. Its editorial body has now been established in an office in the Library of Congress, and the 18th edition was published in 1971. The scheme is now in three volumes, with a greatly extended Introduction, and a very real attempt has been made to bring it up to date; indeed, nearly all of the 'specific criticisms I made in the first edition of this book have been met, though one can still find some confusion, cross-classification and entire absence of important subjects.

The outline of the scheme corresponds to an inversion of the three great classes of knowledge proposed by Francis Bacon: History, Poesy, Philosophy. A mid-nineteenth century scheme made by W. T. Harris was the DC's immediate parent, but there is, of course, a long tradition of Baconian influence on classifications of knowledge. Dewey's treatment brings the social sciences into the fourth place in his sequence, at Class 300, and as a result of following Harris and Bacon he separates social science from Philosophy-and Psychology on the one hand (in Class 100), and from History and Geography on the other (in Class 900). Even those scholars who regard History as among the Humanities rather than the Social Sciences would hardly expect to find, separating the two, the whole of Linguistics, Pure and Applied Sciences, Fine Arts and Literature. Probably the separation from Philosophy and still more from Psychology is more serious; indeed, the treatment of Psychology in DC has a very curious history and at no time does it appear to me that the arrangement could have been helpful to psychologists.

Within Class 300 one can find many examples of such failure to introduce any principle of systematic collocation into the scheme. One feature that appears regularly in DC is the use of sub-divisions beginning at 0 for general matters such as the Theory and History of a subject. Thus, 300 is used for Social Science–General works, but since the 15th edition the place 301 has been allotted to Sociology, which by virtue of this position should be regarded as the generalised theory of the social sciences-the position which Durkheim was protesting against in 1904, and which would certainly find few supporters today. Class 301 itself is subdivided primarily into a series of groups and interrelations:

301.1 Social psychology

301.2 Culture and cultural processes

301.3 Ecology and community

301.4 Social structure

Criticisms of poor collocations can be made; for example, Public Administration at 350 is separated, by 360 Social Welfare and 370 Education, from such public services as Communication and Transport in 380; Demography is at 301.32, but Statistics of Populations (Demographic Statistics) is at 312; 390 Customs and Folklore is at the other end of the class from 301, and far from Social Anthropology, which is away in the Science class at 572. Slavery at 326 is regarded as a branch of Political Science, and stands next to 327 Foreign Relations; Forced labour, on the other hand, is an Economic activity, at 331.5. Class 330 is for Economics, but Commerce is provided at 381; Marxism at 335.4 appears as a branch of Economics (with other Economic ideologies), with the sub-division 335.411 for Philosophic foundations, and including Dialectical materialism, yet at 146.3 Materialism, in Philosophy, we still find the note, 'including dialectical materialism'.

If we take the subject 'The influence of hereditary factors in the psychology of delinquent children', we are in a dilemma when we try to classify it by DC, even though all the terms appear to be in tlae scheme. Since the original number for 'Hereditary factors' in Psychology at 136.733 no longer exists, we have to rely on the place at 573.2 under Physical anthropology, where we are directed by the index: Hereditary characteristics *see* Genetic make-up. Similarly, 'Delinquent children' have moved from 136.763 to 155.453 with other types of exceptional children. The scheme thus recognises the existence of the various facets of the subject-psychology, hereditary factors, delinquent children. What it fails to recognise, however, is the importance of the relationship expressed here as 'influence'. We can therefore classify the subject at *either* 155.453 *or* 573.2; in other words, we can classify one half or the other, but not both together, not the aggregate. This failure to recognise the need for precise specifying of complex subjects is actually a failure to recognise their existence, for no rules are laid down as to which heading to choose, and the scheme lacks not only precision but also consistency of application. We might perhaps tolerate a scheme which denied the need for precise classifying–Lewis and Kyle have both on occasion admitted doubts as to Fits suitability in the present state of social science documentation, and ,–the House of Commons project also showed that MPs usually expressed their subject interests in broad rather than specific terms–but it should be recognised that this is a deliberate choice, and not a mere inadequacy, by the insertion of a rule for use in classifying. Such rules appear in other schemes; a general instruction has to be made, as one cannot expect to foresee every complex subject that may arise in the literature, but if the scheme admits the need for composite specification, it is not a difficult matter to provide for it. Such an instruction might take the general form 'Where A and B appear in relation r, the classification symbol should always be ArB, with a reference from B'.

DC does admit the principle of synthesis-classifying complexes by assembly of their elements-in certain fields. The simplest are the division of subjects by geographical location and chronological period. Clearly, one could not possibly enumerate at every subject a complete list of countries and dates, and the simple solution is to provide separate tables of these, with notational symbols that may be attached without ambiguity to any subject number where necessary. Dewey himself recognised the need for such synthesis from the beginning, and called it 'number building'. The method has several advantages: it ensures consistency in classifying, it economises on the size of the scheme's schedules, and it means that certain symbols always have the same meaning whenever they appear in a class number, which makes for ready recognition and fewer mistakes. The geographical numbers are taken from Class 900 History, and usually, though not always, follow the symbol 0. Thus, as 942 is England and 370 is Education, 370.942 is Education in England.

Provision for synthesis does occur elsewhere, particularly in subjects with a quasi-geographical sub-division. There is a section on 'Synthesis of notation (number building)' in the Introduction, in Volume 1. The schedule of exceptional types of children from Education at 371.9 may be used in the Psychology class at 155.45, and a schedule of industries appears in 620 to 699, and these divisions may be used at suitable places, such as 331.892 Strikes:

331.892	Strikes
331.8928	In special industries, divided like 620/699

622 is the place for Mining; therefore:

331.892822	Strikes in the mining industry
and 331.8929	Strikes, divided by country
therefore 331.892971	Strikes in Canada

So that, in this case, the more specific subject 'Strikes in the mining industry in Canada', at 331.8928220971, would precede the more general subject of 'Strikes in Canada', contrary to the supposedly universal DC practice of following the logical principle of 'general' before 'special'.

A more extensive application, though, is in the seven separate Tables in Volume 1, which are applicable as instructed in the schedules:

1	Standard sub-divisions	-01 to -09
2	Areas (geographical)	-1 to -9
7	Persons	-01 to -08

The editors have now tried hard to come to terms with advances in theory and practice, even claiming that they apply facet analysis. One can but sympathise and applaud; indeed, it would be hard to overestimate the value of the contribution made to the science of classification by Melvil Dewey, and DC can truly claim to have inaugurated a new era, so much so that for library purposes all previous schemes have been superseded. However, the structure of subjects written about in the literature has changed so greatly since 1876 that, for all the detail in its schedules and the efficient organisation behind its revised editions and its periodical bulletin *(DC Additions, Notes, Decisions)*, it cannot possibly be recommended for any library aiming at information retrieval and not merely a form of order for the books on its shelves.

Universal Decimal Classification

Overview

If the editors of DC continue to avoid the issue of composite specification, the responsibility has been assumed by the International Federation for Documentation (FID) in its publication of the Universal Decimal Classification. The originators of the UDC, Paul Otlet and Henri La Fontaine, introduced DC to Europe in 1895, urging that it should be used to classify an *international* bibliography of books and periodical articles covering all subjects, on cards. This vast project was actually begun, and the inadequacy of DC soon became apparent. Permission was obtained for its expansion, which has proceeded ever since, several editions of UDC in various languages having already been produced, and a trilingual abridged version in English, French and German. In this country the British Standards Institution has undertaken the production of an English version as British Standard Specification 1000. Intense propaganda for and against the UDC has been carried on ever since its publication, and many specialist libraries and documentation centres have adopted it, because its improvements on DC go far towards overcoming the defects described above. After a detailed examination, however, Kyle has concluded that it cannot be recommended to new users, and that money would be better spent making a new scheme than on revising UDC. This is also the view of Reiner Zekalle, who declares that 'Die internationale Dezimalklassification (DK), das gegenwartig einzige universelle Ordnungssystem mit weltweiter Verbreitung, ist fttr die Klassifizierung der gesellschaftswissenschaftlichen Arbeiten ... unzureichend, ja unbrauchbar.'

Nevertheless, it has many points in its favour. It is far better than DC, is internationally known and used, and its revisions are prepared by specialists. A. C. Foskett, in the most detailed critical examination of the UDC to date, concludes that its faults, rather than its virtues, have tended to be stressed by previous critics, and that it does in practice serve its purpose well enough to justify continued effort to bring it in line with modern thought, both in subject organisation and in classification theory. He has also made comparisons with American scientific and technical thesauri devised for computerised systems, and again suggests that the performance of UDC is better than might be expected. His proposals for future development, like those of Ingetraut Dahlberg, would involve some radical departures from previous practice.

The basic structure is the same as DC, a division of the field of knowledge into nine main classes, with the tenth, Class O, for General Works. The three-figure minimum has been dropped, but notational symbols, which tend to be long, can be split up by inserting a 'point' after every second or third figure to make small groups that are not so repugnant to the user. The main new feature, from the viewpoint of information retrieval, is the systematic attempt to cater for synthesis of complex subjects by means of a series of Auxiliary

Tables, which include tables for Geographical and Chronological sub-division but also go much farther; they are identified by the use of arbitrary signs such as +, /, [], and so on, as well as .00 and .0.'The disadvantage of these, of course, is that they do not have an accepted position in the sequence of numerals or letters, and their sequence has therefore to be laid down, and either memorised or consulted whenever the file is used. But the Auxiliary Tables certainly enable UDC to cope with even the most complex subjects, though in a somewhat cumbersome way. The most used symbol is the colon, which is the sign of relation, and does not actually have a Table as such, since it can be used to join any two (or more) numbers from the scheme. Thus, the example given above from DC, of 'The influence of hereditary factors in the psychology of delinquent children', is dealt with in UDC by the formula ArB, where A is 'delinquent children', B is 'hereditary factors' and r is the symbol of relation, the colon. The colon device has often been claimed to be the complete answer to the problem of expressing relations by means of synthesis, but it is, of course, no more than a beginning, since the same sign is used for all manner of different relations, influence, comparison, cause and effect, and so on, and there is therefore no means of distinguishing between these. Thus, in the index cards issued by the Centre d'Information de Documentation Sociale et Economique Africaine, in Brussels, we find subjects such as these:

Mining research in Spanish Sahara 338:622 (661)

where 338 is Production, 622 is Mining and (661) is Sahara (and *French* West Africa)

and

Economic regulations affecting the cocoa trade on the Ivory Coast
351.824.5:633.74(666.8)

where 351.824.5 is Trade, 633.74 is the cocoa industry and (666.8) is the Ivory Coast.

Clearly, in these examples the colon sign stands for two different meanings, thus introducing homonyms into what is in effect an artificial language. Such a procedure inevitably brings ambiguity, always undesirable, and avoidable if the necessity of distinguishing between different relations is recognised by the use of different notational symbols. Moreover, although the ability to synthesise as many numbers as required undoubtedly enables the scheme to achieve precise specification, the basic structure, taken from DC, still prevents the separation of categories in the scheme, and their combination as the literature requires.

The wide acceptance of the UDC, particularly on the Continent of Europe, testifies rather to the power of the new devices for synthesis than to the intrinsic qualities of the scheme itself. The official view of the FID and the British Standards Institution is that the UDC can be brought up to date and equipped with devices able to cope with modern literature in a manner acceptable to specialists, but it is hard to see how this could in fact be done without a complete revision of the basic structure. As this would amount to altering the scheme beyond recognition, it seems to me that we would do better to follow Barbara Kyle's advice and concentrate such meagre resources as are available on producing a new scheme. This also seems to have been at least implicit in the conclusions of some participants in the *International Symposium on UDC in Relation to Other Indexing Languages*, held in Yugoslavia in 1971. In reviewing this, Neelameghan also relates the development of UDC as a Standard Reference Code for UNISIST, and emphasises the need to base this on a general theory of classification suitable for documentation of 'micro-thought'.

The Library of Congress Classification

The classification scheme drawn up for the collections of the Library of the United States Congress was originally based on the now defunct Expansive Classification made in the late nineteenth century by C. A. Cutter, but it was never intended for universal application, and was based entirely on the books in the Library of Congress. The various subject departments of the library compiled systems for their own collections, and each class was therefore developed, more or less in isolation, by experts in the bibliography of the subject. The independence of classes goes to the extreme length of listing geographical and chronological sub-divisions for each class; little provision for synthesis exists, and the same country may have many different numbers, according to the main class. Its notation also differs from DC and UDC in that it consists of two capital letters followed by numbers used as integers and not as decimal fractions; new subjects are intended to be dealt with by gaps left at what is hoped are suitable points in the sequences of numbers. Each class is revised and new editions are published independently, which leads to the curious result that some classes, such as Medicine, have had frequent revisions, others none.

As we might expect in a scheme based on the collections of a national library which also acts as the library serving the Government, the social sciences are well treated in LC. Kyle remarks that the arrangement would suit well the 'old-fashioned sociologist', and, as Mills shows, the size of the collections has meant that the scheme contains an immense amount of detail and some very specific subdivisions. Even if we are given only the minimum of opportunity to combine concepts-and that only within the same class and almost entirely for geographical division-very specific subjects find a place of their own because they are represented by documents actually in the library.

The scheme begins with Philosophy at Class B, followed by History, extending over C-F; G is for Geography, including Anthropology and Customs, H for Social Sciences, J Political Science, K Law, L Education. Class H was published in 1909 and simply reprinted in 1959-hence the 'old-fashioned' appearance, no doubt – and offers a distinct improvement on DC, in spite of odd omissions such as 'Social Change' and 'Stratification' which appear in neither schedules nor index. Class H is almost a circular affair, which begins and ends with theories, and has groups in the middle with activities on either side:

H Social Sciences

HA Statistics

HB Economics (HC History, HE Transport, HF Commerce, HG Finance, HJ Public finance)

HM Sociology (including Social psychology)

These are then followed by social groups:

HQ Family

HS Associations, Clubs

HT Communities, Classes, Races

after which there is a return to activities:

HV Social pathology. Philanthropy. Charities and, finally, theories of society:

HX Socialism, etc.

An example of failure to modernise the terminology can be seen in HM Social theory, in which HM 101-121 is for Civilization, with three headings among the sub-divisions:

HM 106	Evolution. Biological sociology
111	Degeneration
116	Mutation

while a little further on we find the curious mixture

HM 278	Passive resistance
	Crowds. Tumults. Revolutions
HM 281	Theory
HM 283	History

Classes are included among Communities in HT, with HT 851 for Slavery, which is clearly regarded as more than a merely economic phenomenon; Negro slavery appears under the heading 'General' in the schedule, but there is no index entry under the term 'Negro'.

Education, in Class L, likewise contains some rather strange groupings, and dates from 1929. LA History, LB Theory begin well enough, but Theory is followed by Principles, which is joined with Practice and leads directly into Primary and Secondary education. LC Special forms has the same sort of progression, beginning with Sociology of education and Moral education and going off to Special classes of Persons including Women and Boys. LC 3951-3990 Education of exceptional children has no specific place for the Gifted child, who does, however, appear in the Index with a direction to the numbers LC 3951-90. The rest of Class L, LD-LG, is entirely given over to Individual institutions, mostly American, but including, for example, the names of Oxford and Cambridge colleges. Psychology, as in DC, is far away with Philosophy in Class B, and has very little sub-division, and that of a type that certainly could not cope with psychological literature in a way that would appeal to any contemporary school of psychologists.

For all its detail, then, the LC scheme cannot claim to offer an adequate system for information retrieval. Certainly, it can show in places an approach to division into categories that appear in the modern literature, but this division does not give the impression of being systematic and is by no means consistent. When one finds categories used, but in a confused way, one cannot but believe that the use is unconscious. LC fails to give the individual librarian a method for coping with new subjects or new complexes; all it does is to lay down a list of subjects that, however extensive, cannot hope to enumerate all those that will ever be written about, and the extreme lack of flexibility that comes from absence of synthesis makes it unsuitable for a documentation centre in which specific classification is required.

The Bibliographic Classification

Henry Evelyn Bliss, the compiler of the Bibliographic Classification, spent his whole life on this scheme and its theoretical basis, and his work forms an important part of modern classification theory. In his books on the organisation of knowledge he considered how subjects develop, and attempted to systematise the relations between subjects and between subjects and their parts. He maintained the objective reality of 'natural order', and thought that if a classification scheme accurately reflected this order it would not need radical changes as knowledge progresses. He considered that, although many changes continually take place at the frontiers of knowledge, necessitating frequent revision of the details of classification schemes, the great 'main classes' of knowledge are relatively stable, and that a scientifically based sequence of main classes would therefore last for a long time. This did not prevent him from criticising all previous schemes and making considerable departures from their sequences in his own.

BC is based on four main principles:

1. **Comprehensiveness.** The scheme must cover the whole of knowledge as shown by the current consensus of scientific and educational thought.
2. **Subordination.** The development of subjects from general to specific, called by Bliss 'gradation by specialty'.
3. **Co-ordination.** An important factor, the collocation of related subjects in a manner helpful to readers; alternative collocations are provided for some subjects, in recognition that different groups of users may approach the same literature from different viewpoints.

4. **Composite specification.** This is Bliss's term for the ability to bring together different parts of the scheme in a manner flexible enough to cope with complex subjects. He extended the use of auxiliary tables, as shown in UDC, very considerably, providing - some 45 in all-some general, such as the geographical and chronological tables, some specific to one subject, such as the administration schedules 14a-d for use in Class J Education.

Bliss made a deliberate attempt to find a scientific basis for his sequence of main classes. He had made an extensive study of the history of classifications of the sciences, and his outline may broadly be summarised as Sciences, Social Sciences, Humanities. Thus, the,sciences of Man begin with Class H Anthropology and medicine, and'go on to I Psychology, J Education, K Sociology, L-O History, Q Social Welfare, R Political Science, S Law, T Economics. The terminology is naturally more up to date than that of other schemes, since the full scheme was first published from 1940 to 1953, but once again we find that some important process terms such as 'Social Change' and 'Stratification'are missing from both schedules and index. As can be seen, the order collocates subjects used together very much better than the other schemes, and there is in addition a much more liberal provision of references from one part to another. For example, at IFC Memory and learning, there is a 'See also' reference to JE in Education. An example of alternative collocation is that of the Law of Special subjects, which can be placed either with the subject itself or in the main class for Law, between SL and SS.

The important principle of composite specification is based on the Systematic Auxiliary Schedules, which consist of lists of terms that may be used to subdivide more than one term in the scheme. Most of them use a notation of capital letters, like the scheme itself, but are separated from the main subject number by a comma. A new edition of BC is in course of preparation under the direction of Jack Mills, at the School of Librarianship of the Polytechnic of North London, and is scheduled for publication by Butterworths in 1975. Drafts for several social science subjects are complete, including Statistics, Education, History, Social Welfare, and Political Science. Extensive use has been made of facet analysis for a basis, and the draft revisions seem to have achieved striking success in incorporating this type of structure without too much disturbance of the existing schedules and notation. In some cases alternative schedules are being provided for present users who do not wish to make too many changes-one of the most difficult problems facing the editors of any such revisions. In Education, which is largely based on the London Education Classification used in the Library of the London Institute of Education, perhaps the most important change is the provision of integral schedules for Educational Administration, including central and local government as well as school organisation; in the previous edition this existed only as Auxiliary Schedules 14a-14d, and these were not particularly systematic. The facility for synthesis is retained, of course, by simple combination of notational symbols retroactively-that is, from the last schedules backwards. The primary facet, Educands and Schools, comes at the end at JL; Primary Education is JM, and the first direct sub-divisions begin at JMM, JMN, etc. All the terms preceding these in the schedule can be used as sub-divisions simply by adding the appropriate notation:

JMAB Aims and objectives of primary education, where AB is taken from facet JA Principles and Philosophy of Education, in which JAB is Aims and objectives.

JMC Administration of primary schools, where C is taken from facet JC Organisation and Administration of Schools.

JMK Curriculum in primary schools, where K is taken from facet JK Curriculum.

This notational device, first proposed by E. J. Coates, gives great flexibility with relative brevity; the result is that, within a given facet, the first arrays of sub-divisions can be worked out as required by the literature and will give a sequence parallel to that of the whole classification.

Synthesis is also achieved by using the whole classification to divide certain subjects. In JK Curriculum the first set of sub-divisions is specific to JK, but after JKM synthesis is allowed. Thus, Main Class B is Physics; JKN is Teaching Physics, divided like Class B. These forms of synthesis give the classifier greatly improved autonomy for specifying complex subjects in a post-coordinate manner as required by the literature, and the new edition of BC, when published in full, will represent a real advance over the old, while preserving much of Bliss's own original thinking.

The Colon Classification

The Colon Classification is the work of the great Indian librarian S. R. Ranganathan, and was first published in 1933; it is a testimony to Ranganathan's vast energy that, in addition to all his many other works, he has produced no less than six editions of CC, the latest appearing in 1960. It presents the singular paradox that though little used outside India, it has had an outstanding impact on classification theory, and, like the DC, marks the beginning of another new era in the science of making schemes of classification.

Alone among the great general schemes, CC recognises the absolute necessity for complete and precise specification of subjects for the purpose of information retrieval, no matter what the cost in, for example, the length of the resulting notational symbols. As he says in the Preface to Edition 6: 'Documentation service is really exhaustive, expeditious, pinpointed, bibliographical service to specialists, with emphasis on nascent micro-thought. Such a service needs as its basis the use of depth classification in international abstracting periodicals, in national documentation lists, and in special bibliographies prepared, from time to time, by research libraries.'

By 'depth classification', Ranganathan means the provision of a scheme that is sufficiently detailed and flexible to allow a classifier to deal fully and accurately with any topic, no matter how specific. To do this, he published CC in two stages: Basic Classification and Depth Classification. The Basic Classification, which is that published as Edition 6, is intended for use mainly for books ('macrothought') in general libraries; the Depth Classification, which will appear as a series of separate fascicules, is intended for classifying pamphlets and articles ('micro-thought') in specialist libraries and documentation centres. These are being published in very great detail in *Library Science with a Slant to Documentation,* and include Management, Demography, Economics, International Trade, Banking and Investment. Ranganathan himself has opened an attack on the problems of classification in the social sciences with an analysis of their emergence and scope. He has a brief review of their treatment in the other general schemes, and goes on to relate each branch to his 'Spiral of scientific method' to show which has a legitimate claim to the description 'science', and which should be included as 'auxiliaries', though they have as yet a doubtful claim to 'science'; these include Geography and History. His sequence now includes SZ Social Sciences as a class of Partial Comprehension, and, similarly, TZ Geography and History, UZ History, Political Science and Economics.

Ranganathan has not paid much attention to the problem of Main Classes and their sequence, going so far as to say that these should be postulated and that we should not waste time trying to find some objective basis. His choice resembles that of Bliss, but the broad general outline differs: Sciences, Humanities, Social Sciences. This means that Biology and Medicine, the last of the sciences, are followed by Useful Arts, Spiritual Experience, Fine Arts, and so on. Q Religion and R Philosophy lead back to S Psychology, T Education, U Geography, V History, W Political Science, X Economics, Y Sociology, Z Law. This order could certainly be criticised, but it has, like BC, much more useful collocation than the other schemes; personally, I prefer the broad BC sequence Science, Social Science, Humanities, but it would not be hard to make out a case for the CC outline.

Ranganathan's technique, explained in great detail in his *Prolegomena,* is based on the traditional logical method of division of a subject by separating out the species of a genus by 'characteristics' in which one species differs from another. This method had certainly been used in the other schemes; but it was used inconsistently and without a sufficiently clear distinction between the sets of divisions arrived at by the use of several characteristics. CC keeps these sets clearly separate from each other, allowing each set to be divided continuously by the same characteristic without hindrance or interference from the others. Moreover, Ranganathan has developed a theory that each set of sub-divisions, or 'facets', can be produced by the use of characteristics related to five fundamental ideas. These produce five basic facets, or categories of terms, and these he calls Personality, Matter, Energy, Space and Time. He has never given a wholly satisfactory explanation of these categories, but they can be quite readily understood by illustration, from certain classes. The Space facet of a subject is shown by geographical sub-divisions, the Time facet by chronological sub-divisions, the Energy facet by processes and activities, the Matter facet by raw materials and the Personality facet, the primary facet, by that set of divisions that give the Main Class its unique definition; in a Technology, for example, the end product constitutes the Personality facet.

These facets are kept separate by means of punctuation marks, a comma for Personality, a semi-colon for Matter, a colon for Energy, a full-stop for Space and Time. Thus, the Personality facets in Edition 6 include:

Class X. Economics		Class Y. Sociology	
4	Transport industry	Persons	
41	Land	1	By age and sex
42	Water	3	By residence
43	Air	31	Rural
5	Commerce	33	Urban
512	Retail	4	By occupation
518	Wholesale	5	By birth and status
62	Banking	51	Royalty
621	Central	592	By caste
6212	Federal reserve	7	By race
7	Public finance		
72	Tax		
75	Public loan		

The Energy facets include:

X	Economics	Y	Sociology
2	ProBuction	2	Physical character and feature
3	Distribution	3	Activity
8	Management	4	Social pathology
9	Personnel management	45	Crime
		8	Equipment

The notation symbol introducing an Energy facet is the colon. The subject 'Personnel Management in the Federal Reserve Bank' receives the notation X6212 :9 and the subject 'The Incidence of Crime in Urban Populations' receives the notation Y33 :45. This class has just begun to be revised for Edition 7.

This illustrates how each facet can be divided without interfering with the others. The same facility exists for synthesis of subjects from different main classes, and in CC, unlike UDC, the different relations are represented by different signs, in the same way as the different facets. Thus, the subject illustrated before, 'the influence of hereditary factors in the psychology of delinquent children' can be precisely specified as

S2-65 Og G:61

in which S is Psychology, S2 is Adolescent children, -65 is Criminal, Og is the relational symbol meaning 'influenced by', G is Biology and G:61 is Heredity. This is a complex notation, doubtless, but it expresses accurately a complex subject.

Similarly, where the same term may appear in several classes, CC makes every possible effort to use the same sequence and notational symbols. The Personality facet in S Psychology, a list of Individuals, resembles very closely the P facet in T Education, and several numbers are also repeated in Class Y Sociology. At certain points the classifier is directed to use sub-divisions listed elsewhere; for example, S8 Social psychology is to be divided like the P facet of Class Y Sociology, and Y2 Family is to be divided like R4 Ethics from Class R Philosophy. This effects considerable economies in the scheme and has in addition some mnemonic value, but it must be admitted that, however desirable the principle, the practice does not always work out satisfactorily. T:8 School management is to be divided, with a few additions, like the E facet of Class X Economics, where X:8 is the subject Management itself. This place is, of course, mainly for the management of business enterprises, and its sub-divisions are not by any means suitable for Schools.

The notational symbols, though worked out with great care to give the shortest possible combinations for complex subjects, are often themselves difficult to sort out and often prove psychologically unacceptable. It is easy to exaggerate the importance of such defects, but Ranganathan himself seems to dismiss them too easily, and tends to underestimate their influence on the scheme's popularity.

Whatever doubts we may have about CC, however, there can be none about the power of the method of facet analysis. We do not need to accept the idea of 'fundamental categories', although these have in fact proved useful in the construction of schemes for special subjects, particularly in industrial technology, where CC's own lack of detail has made it necessary to start from the beginning in most cases. A. Neelameghan and his associates in the Classification Research Circle at the Documentation Research and Training Centre, Bangalore, continue the development work headed for many years by Ranganathan himself, and their results appear in their journal Library *Science with a Slant to Documentation*. These are by now often some way in advance of CC practice, so that, even if the scheme does not itself find general acceptance, the work and the ideas on which it is founded continue to influence profoundly every phase of current research on classification and indexing. Neelameghan has also taken over the Secretariat of the FID Committee CR for Classification Research, and it may be that some rapprochement between CC and UDC will eventually be forthcoming.

This survey of the treatment of social science subjects by the main general classification schemes shows that none of them offers a wholly satisfactory answer to the needs of research workers. Each has its advantages and disadvantages as an established system, and with many new libraries being set up throughout the world, it is clear that the need for a good general scheme remains as urgent as ever. We need to have good reasons for rejecting schemes that have given moderate satisfaction for many years. Very optimistic forecasts are given by the protagonists of the several schemes in the useful survey edited by Arthur Malt by. Nevertheless, my belief is that none of them can be recommended as it stands for libraries with emphasis on social science literature; and where the users are research workers who need to retrieve specific information, they are all quite unsatisfactory.

This does not at all mean that the situation is hopeless; on the contrary, the experience gained by librarians and documentalists in the study and use of these schemes has produced a considerable body of theoretical literature, while the advent of punched card and electronic sorting machines has led to an even greater quantity of writing from a totally different point of departure. Maltby's symposium includes a contribution by R. R. Freeman, based on several years of research, on the contribution of classification to machine-based systems. The latest work of these groups shows a marked tendency to converge towards a general theory, and there are good reasons to hope that progress towards a new general classification scheme will not be long delayed. The major obstacle, even now, is mere lack of the necessary finance, and as the demand grows stronger all the time, some agency is certain to undertake the work in the end. Social scientists have much to gain by it, in the increased efficiency with which their literature will be organised in libraries and documentation centers.

19

Practical Classification

Example 1

Watson (J). ground work of economic theory; 1937

10 Step 0: Raw Title

Ground work of economic theory.

Note: 101 there is no ellipsis sensed in the title. A perusal of the book also shows that the Raw Title is a tell-tale title.

102 Therefore the Full Title is the same as the Raw Title.

11 Step 1: Full Title

Ground work of economic theory.

Note: 111 The word "of" is a preposition. This is only an auxiliary word. It is not essential to the indication of the subject of the book. It may therefore be omitted.

112 The term "ground work" is a puff. It is not essential to the indication of the subject of the book. It may therefore be omitted.

113 There is o derived composite term in the full title, needing to be broken into fundamental constituent terms.

12 Step 2: Kernel Title

Economic Theory

Note: 121 "Economic Theory" is the focal term in the Basic Facet. It therefore denotes the Basic Class. We shall symbolize it by (BC).

122 There is no other focal term in the Kernel Title.

13 Step 3: Analysed Title

Economic Theory (BC).

Note: 131 There is only one kernel term in the kernel Title.

132 Therefore, re-arrangement of kernel terms does not arise.

14 Step 4: Transformed Title

Economic Theory (BC).

Note: 141 The focal term "economic Theory" is not the standard term in practice or in any of the schemes of classification.

142 Its standard equivalent term current to -day is "Economics".

15 Step 5: Title in Standard Term

Economics (BC)

Note: 15C In CC the equivalent of the term "Economics" in ordinal language is "X"

Note: 15 D In DC, the equivalent of the term "Economics" in ordinal language is "33"

Note: 15U In UDC, the equivalent of the term "Economics" in ordinal language is "33"

16 Step 6: Title in Focal Numbers

CC	UDC	DC
X(BC)	33(BC)	33(BC)

Note: 161 As there is no focal number other than the basic class number, there is no occasion for the insertion of any connecting symbol anywhere.

17 Step 7: Title in Synthesised Focal Number Class Number

CC	UDC	DC
X	33	33

Step 18: Verification by Reverse Translation

FOR CC NUMBER

181 Facet Analysis

X is the Basic Facet.

There is no Isolate Facet.

182 Digit By Digit Translation

X=Economics

Which is equivalent to "Ground work of economic theory".

For UDC and DC Numbers

181 Facet Analysis

33 is the Basic Facet.

182 Digit By Digit Translation

33=Economics.

Which is equivalent to "ground work of economic theory"

Example 2

Ghosh (Bindu Bhusa). Problems of agricultural finance in India; 1937.

20 Step 0: Raw Title

Problems of agricultural finance in India.

201 The Basic Class "Economics" is implied. This should be supplied explicitly.

202 The time isolate "brought up to 1930s" is implied as shown by a perusal of the book. This should be supplied explicitly.

203 The term "Agricultural finance" is a derived composite term. It comprehends the fundamental constituent terms "Finance" (for) "Agricultural industry". It must be broken into them.

21 Step 1: Full Title

Problems of finance for agricultural industry in economics in India brought up to 1930's.

Note: 21 The words "of", "for" and "in" and the term "brought up to" are prepositions. They are only auxiliary terms. They are not essential to the indication of the subject. They may therefore be omitted.

212 The word "Problems" is a puff. It is not essential to the indication of the subject. It can therefore be ommitted.

22 Step 2: Kernel Title

Finance. Agriculture industry. Economics. India. 1930's.

Note: 220 The kernel term "Economics" denotes the focus in the Basic Facet. Therefore, the symbol (BC) should be added after it.

2211 The kernel term "1930's" denotes the focus in the Time Facet.

Therefore, the symbol [T] should be added after it.

2212 The kernel term "India" denotes the focus in the Space Facet. Therefore, the symbol [S] should be added after it.

2213 The kernel term "Finance" stands for "Financing". It therefore denotes the focus in the Energy Facet. Therefore, the symbol [E] should be added after it.

2214 There is no kernel term denoting a focus in Matter Facet.

2215 The kernel term "Agricultural industry" denotes the enterprise. It denotes the focus in the Personality Facet. Therefore, the symbol [P] should be added after it.

23 Step 3: Analysed Title

Finance [E] Agricultural industry [P] Economics (BC) India [S] 1930's [T].

231 There is not more than one manifestation of any one fundamental category. By the Postulate of Sequence (section H21), the facets should be arranged in the sequence (BC) [P] [E] [S] [T].

24 Step 4: Transformed Title

Economics (BC) Agricultural industry [P] Finance [E] India [S] 1930's [T].

Note: 241 CC wrongly uses the term "agricultural economics" for "agricultural industry". Therefore, the term "agricultural industry" may be retained.

25 Step 5: Title in Standard Terms

Economics (BC) Agricultural industry [P] Financing [E] India [S] 1930's [T].

For Colon Classification

251 All the focal terms have ready-make numbers.

26 Step 6: Title in Focal Numbers

X(BC) 8(J)[P] 6[E] 44[S] N3[T]

Note: 260 The descriptive symbol after the focal numbers should be removed.

261 By Postulate of Connecting Symbols (see section H5), ":" should be put before the Energy focal number 6; "." Should be put before the Space focal number 44, and "," should be put before the Time focal number N3, respectively.

262 By Postulate 1 for Omission of Connecting Symbols (see section H51), comma need for be put before the Personality focal number 8(J).

27 Step 7: Title in Synthesised Focal Numbers

Class Number

X*(J): 6.44'N3

Step 8: Verification by Reverse Translation

281 Facet Analysis

X	is Basic Facet.
8(J)	is personality (Enterprise) Facet.
6	is Energy (Problem) Facet.
44	is Space facet.
N3	is Time facet.

282 Digit by Digit Translation

X	Economics
X8	Industrial economics
X8(J)	Agricultural industry.
X8(J):6	Financing of agricultural industry
X8(J):6.4	Financing of agricultural industry in Asia.
X8(J):6.44	Financing of agricultural industry in India.
X8(J):6.44'N3	Financing of agricultural industry in India brought upto 1930s.

For universal Decimal Classification

251 In DC and UDC we have the following:

332.7 Credit (Private Credit)

Including theory and forms of credit; comprehensive works on credit and institutions.

332.71 Agricultural credit

Loans for promoting agricultural operations.

"Financing" is not exhausted by loans. Therefore the above isolate cannot be taken to be the same as "financing".

252 UDC does not provide for [E] in the subdivision of "338 Industrial Economics and Production". Therefore the Isolate Number for " Financing" has to be got by Subject Device.

Step 6: Title in Focal Numbers

33 [BC] 81 [P] 658.4 [E] 54 [S] 193 [T]

The focal number 658.14 for "financing" belongs to a different (BC), viz, 65, which represents "Business and Business methods".

Therefore, it should be preceded by the connecting symbol colon at the stage of synthesizing. This amounts to be late in UDC.

262 The connecting symbol for [S] is bracket-pair. This too amounts to a postulate in UDC.

263 The connecting symbol for [T] is similarly quote-pair, that is, as pair of inverted commas. This too amounts to a postulate in UDC.

264 After every three substantive consecutive digits, a dot should be inserted. This a convention in UDC.

27 Step 7: Synthesised Title in Focal Numbers Class Numbers

338.1:658.14(54)"193".

28 Step 8: Verification by Reverse Translation

281 Facet Analysis

33	is basic Facet.
8.1	is Personality Facet.
658.14	is Energy Facet.
54	is Space Facet.
193	is Time Facet.

282 Digit by Digit Interpretation

3	Social sciences
33	Economics
338	Industrial economics and production economics
338.1	Agricultural industries
338.1:658.14	Financing agricultural industries
338.1:658.14(54)	-do- in India.
338.1:658.14(54)"193"	-do- brought upto 1930's

For decimal Classification

261 In Dc there is no provision for synthesizing two class numbers. Therefore, the energy isolate number 658.14 has to be left out.

261 In DC the connecting symbol for [S] is 09.

263 In DC the isolate number in [T] is not a common isolate number. For each country a separate schedule of [T] is given. For India, the appropriate isolate number is:

03: British rule, 1774-1947

27 Step 7: Synthesised Title in Focal Numbers Class Number

338.10954.03

28 Step 8 Verification by Reverse Translation

Facet analysis and digit by digit interpretation are similar to those for UDC with the exception that the facet 658.14 does not occur. The resulting translation is "Agricultural industries in India brought upto 1940's". This is of a greater extension than the subject of the book for the following two reasons:

1 The [E] is missing; and

2 The isolate in [T] is of greater extension than necessary.

Principles for Facet Sequence

When no fundamental category manifests itself more than once in a subject, the sequence of its facets is uniquely determined by the Postulate for Sequence. But, that postulate is not sufficient when any fundamental category manifests itself in a subject more than once. We enunciate in the succeeding subsections a few principles for guidance in such cases. It may be stated at the outset that the sequence should be determined by taking only two facets of manifestations at a time.

Commodity-Raw Material-Transformation-Principle

If facet A is a commodity got out of the raw material forming facet B by the process of transformation forming facet C-all of the same subject-then the three facet should be arraged in the sequence A,B,C.

311 A commodity facet will always be taken as a manifestation of Personality.

312 The raw material facet may be either an intermediate commodity or merely the matter-constituent of the commodity. In the former case, the raw material isolate should be taken as a manifestation of Personality; in the latter case as a manifestation of Matter.

For example, consider the subject. "Weaving yarn into cloth". This belongs to the basic class "Textiles". Here "Cloth" is [P]. So also "Yarn" is [P]. "Weaving" is [E]. The sequence of these facets within the basic class textiles should be

Textiles (BC) Clothe [P] Yarn [P2] Weaving [E]

3141 Let us add one more facet "Cotton" to the subject in 314. "Cotton" is the material constituent of yarn. Therefore it is [M]. Then by Cow-Calf Principle, "Yarn" should be tied, as it were, to "Cotton". Thus, "Cotton" also will belong to the First Round. The Sequence will thus be

Textiles (BC) Cloth [P] Yarn [P2] Cotton [M] Weaving [E].

315 Let us take that the cloth is made of cotton and lace. Let us further take cotton to be the dominant raw material. Then "Lace" may be taken as [M2]. The sequence will then be

Textile (BC) Cloth [P] Yarn [P2] Cotton [M] Lace [M2] Weaving [E].

Wall-Picture Principle

If two facets A and B of a subject are such that the concept behind B will not be operative unless the concept behind A is conceded, even as a mural picture is not possible unless the wall exists to draw upon, then the facet. A should precede the facet B.

Illustration

This is best illustrated by examining the sequence between two manifestation of the fundamental category Energy. For example let the manifestations be "Disease" and "Cure". The concept of "cure leans for its very existence on the concept of "Disease". So also let the manifestations be "Disease" and "Prevention". Here also the concept of "Prevention" leans for its very existence on the concept of "Disease". This is true of each of the manifestations enumerated in succession' as isolates in the scheduled for Handling Facet in relations to "Disease" in the schedules for the (BC) Medicine in CC. Therefore, assuming that "Disease" belongs to the first round, the Wall-Picture Principle fixes the sequence of these two isolates as

Medicine (BC). Disease [E] Cure [2E].

Energy-Energy Sequence

The Wall-Picture Principle is usually helpful in determining the sequence of the energy facets in a subject. This sequence should first be determined. Once it is done, the first energy isolate ends the First Round; and therefore it is itself [E]. The second energy isolate ends the Second Round; and therefore it is itself [2E]. And so on. We can also say that the First Round stars after the (BC); the Second Round starts after [E]; the Third Round starts after [2E]; and so on.

The first step in facet analysis after separating out (BC) and all the [S] and [T] is to fix the sequence of all the [E] taking one pair at a time.

Personality-Energy Sequence

3231 Example 1

The Wall-Picture Principle will be of use in determining the sequence between a [P] and a [E]. For example "Function" is energy facet. It is capable of being taken with the (BC) History. "President" is personality facet capable of being taken with the same (BC). The concept "Function" cannot become operative unless the concept of "President" is conceded.

History (BC) President [P] Function [E]

Similarly, "Morphology" is energy facet capable of being taken with the (BC) Medicine. "Heart" is personality facet capable of being taken with the same (BC). The concept "Morphology" cannot become operative unless the concept "Heart" is conceded. Therefore, the Wall-Picture Principle fixes the sequence of these two facets as

Medicine (BC) Heart [P] Morphology [E]

3233 Example 3

So also "Teaching technique" is an energy facet capable of being taken with the (BC) Education. "Secondary (educand)" is a personality facet capable of being taken with the same (BC). The concept "Teaching technique" cannot become operative unless the concept "Secondary (educand)" is conceded. Therefore, the Wall-Picture Principle fixes the sequence of these two facets as

Education (BC) Secondary (educand) [P] Teaching technique [E]

Actand-Action-Actor-Tool-Principle

If in a subject, facet B denotes action on facet A by facet C, with facet D as the tool, then the four facets should be arranged in the sequence A, B, C, D.

Illustration

For example, let the subject be "Tubercular disease of lungs". Here "Disease" is the Action. "Lungs" is acted upon; it is therefore the Actand. "Tubercular bacillus" acts on the lungs. It is therefore the Actor. Thus the three isolate should be arranged in the sequence

Medicine (BC) Lungs [P] Disease [E] Tubercular bacillus [2P]

Assignment to Rounds

Since an energy isolate ends a Round and what succeeds it is the next Round, the Actand-Action-Actor Principle is usually helpful in assigning a [P] or a [M] to the appropriate Round. In the example in section 321, assuming that "disease [E]" ends the First Round, and therefore the second Round comes immediately after it, the [P] "Lungs" has been assigned the First Round; and the [P] "Tubercular bacillus" has bee assigned to the Second Round. Therefore "Lungs" is marked as [P]; and "Tubercular bacillus" is marked as [2P].

Cow-Calf Principle

If a facet A and another facet B belonging to the same subject are not to be separated though they are distinct from each other and thus separable, A and B should be kept together in the same Round, even as a milch cow and its unweaned calf are not separately sold out though they are distinct entities and thus separable, but are kept together in possession of the same owner.

Personality-Personality-Tie

The Cow-Calf Principle will be of use in tying together, as it were, two personality isolates. For example, let the subject be "Functions of the President of India". Here obviously "Functions" is [E]. Let us assume that it belongs to the first Round. "President" is [P]. "India", which stands for the "Indian State" is also [P]. "President" is taken with "India" even "President" should be tied together, as it were. They should be assigned together to the same side of the [E] isolate "Function"-that is to the same Round. We have already seen in section 313 of this chapter that the [P] "President" should be assigned to the first Round.

Personality-Matter-Tie

The Cow-Calf Principle will be of use in trying together, as it were, a personality isolate and a matter isolate. For example let the subject be the "Construction of aluminium rail coach." Obviously "Construction" is [E]. Let us assume that it belongs to the First Round. "Rail coach" is [P] and "Aluminium" is [M]. "Aluminium" is to the "Rail coach" in the inseparable relation of a calf to its cow. Therefore, the isolate "Rail coach" [P] and "Aluminium" [M] should be tied together, as it were. They should be assigned together to the same side of the [E] isolate "Construction"-that is, to the same Round. By the Actand-Action-Actor Principle, "Rail coach" [P] precedes "Construction [E]. That is, it belongs to the First Round. Therefore, by the Cow-Calf Principle, "aluminium" [M] also belong to the First Round. By the Postulate of Sequence (see section H21) the "Rail coach" [P] should precede "Aluminium" [M]. Thus the resulting sequence will be

Engineering (BC) Rail coach [P] Aluminium [M] Construction [E]

35 Whole-Organ Principle

If, in a subject, facet B is an organ-that is an organic part-of facet "A", then A should precede B.

This Principle may be looked upon as a particular version the Wall-Picture Principle

Personality Isolates

The Whole-Oran Principle is of use in determining the sequence of two personality isolates falling in the same round. For example let the subject be "President of India". Here "India" stands for the State of India; and it is a [P]. "President" is also a [P]; and he is an organ of the State, according to the Constitution of India. We have already seen in section 331 of this chapter that they both lie in the same round.

History (BC) India [P] President [P2]

In other words, "India" is a personality isolate of level 1; and "President" is a personality isolate of level 2.

Matter Isolates

By convention, we regard a property as a matter isolate. A property is inherent in the material of which it is the property. It may therefore be regarded as an organ of the material. Moreover, by Cow-Calf Principle, these two should not be separated. By the Whole-

Organ Principle the material should come first and the property should come thereafter in one and the same Round.

Example with Rounds

Pandya (N). Helpless children in the chemical factories. 1955.

40 Step 0: Raw Title

Helpless children in the chemical factories.

Note: 401 The (BC) "Economics" is implied. This should be supplied explicitly.

402 The time isolate "brought up to the 1950's" is implied. This should be supplied explicitly.

403 A perusal of the book shows that the space isolate "India" is implied. This should be supplied explicitly.

404 The energy isolate "Labour" is implied in the isolate term "children". This should be supplied explicitly.

41 Step 1: Full Title

Helpless children in labour in chemical factories in economics in India brought up to 1950s.

Note: 41 The terms "of", "in" and "brought up to" are only auxiliary terms. They are not essential to the indication of the subject. They may be omitted.

412 The term "helpless" is only a puff. It is not essential to the indication of the subject. It can be omitted.

42 Step 2: Kernel Title

Children Labour Chemical factories Economics India 1950's

Note: 420 The kernel term "Economics" denotes the focus in the Basic Facet. Therefore, the symbol (BC) should be added after it.

4211 The kernel term "1950s" denotes the focus in the Time Facet. Therefore, the symbol [T] should be added after it.

4212 The kernel term "India" denotes the focus in the Space Facet. Therefore, the symbol [S] should be added after it.

4213 The kernel term "Labour" denotes the focus in the Energy Facet. Therefore the symbol [E] should be added after it.

4214 The kernel term "Chemical factories" denotes the focus in the Personality Facet. Therefore the symbol [P] should be added after it.

4215 The kernel term "Children" denotes the focus in another Personality Facet. Therefore the symbol [P] should be added after it.

422 Let us now consider [E] and [P].

4221 There is only one [E] in the subject. Therefore there cannot be more than two rounds. For [E] alone can end one round and start another. This is implied in the Postulates for Rounds of Energy and for Round of Personality and Matter. (See sections J51 and J52).

4222 There are two [P] in the subject, viz, "Chemical factories" and "Children". We have to fix their positions in the sequence of facet.

4223 Let us consider the sequence for "Labour" [E] and "Chemical factories". [P]. The concept "Labour" [E] cannot become operative unless the concept "Chemical factories" [P] is conceded. Therefore by the Wall-Picture Principle, the sequence should be

Chemical factories [P] Labour [E].

Or again, "Labour" [E] is Action and "Chemical factories" [P] is Actand. Therefore by the Actand-Action-Actor Principle, we get the same sequence.

Chemical factories [P] Labour [E]

This means the kernel term "Chemical factories" belongs to the first Round. Therefore the symbol after the focal term "Chemical factories" can be left simply as [P].

Labour [E] Children [2P].

423 The kernel terms "India" in [S] and "1950s" in [T] should be put in the last round. It is the Second Round in this subject. The is prescribed by the Postulates for Space and Times Facets (see section J41).

Step 3 Analysed Title

Children [2P] Labour [E] Chemical Factories [P] Economics [BC] India [S] 1950s [T]

431 By the Postulate for Basic Facet (See section H31), The Kernel term "Economics" in the basic facet should be put first.

432 By the result in note 4223, the kernel term "Chemical factories" in [P] should second, and the kernel term "Labour" in [E] should be put find.

Step 4 Transformed Title

Economics (BC) Chemical Factories [P] Labour [E] Children [2P] India [S] 1950's [T]

Note: The kernel term "Chemical factories"[P] should be changes to the standard term "technology industry" [P].

442 The focal term "Children" [2P] should be changed to the standard term "Child" [2P].

443 The kernel term "Labour" [E] should be changed to the standard term "Personnel management" [E]. This now generally used in the place of the old term "Labour". Therefore the Canon of Currency calls for this change.

These standard terms are given in the schedules of CC.

Step 5 Title in Standard Terms

Economics (BC) Technology Industry [P] Personnel Management [E] Child [2P] India [S] 1950s [T].

Step 6 Title in Focal Numbers

X(BC) 8(F) [P] 9 [E] B [2P] 44 [S] N5[T].

Note: 46C1 By the Postulate of Connecting Symbols (See Section H5) ":" should be put before the Energy focal number 9; and "." Should be put before the Space focal number 44 and (') should be put before the Time focal number N5 respectively.

46C2 By Postulate 1 for Omission of Connecting Symbols (see section H5), comma need not be put before the personality focal number 8(F).

47C Step 7 Title in Synthesised Focal Numbers

X8(F):9B.44'N5

48C Step 8 Verification by Reverse Translation

48CI Facet Analysis

X	is the Basic Facet.
8(F)	is the First Round Personality (Enterprise) Facet.
9	is the Energy (Problem) Facet.
B	is the Second Round Personality (Type if personnel) Facet.
55	is the Space Facet.
N5	is the Time Facet.

48C2 Digit by Digit Interpretation

X	Economics
X8	Industrial economics
X8(F)	Economics of technology Industry
X8(F) :9	Personnel management in technology industry.

X8(F) :9B	Child labour in technology industry
X8(F) :9B.44	-do- in Asia
X8(F) :9B.44	-do- in India
X8(F) :9B.44.'N5	Child labour in technology industry in India brought up to 1950's

which is equivalent to "helpless Children in Chemical factories (in India). 1955"

For UDC

452U But occasionally ., it deviated from that postulate. "Economics" is one of the basic subjects in which it does not follow that postulate. Of course, its DC core is responsible for this deviation.

453U In steps 4 and 5, this deviation gets reflected. Of Course, this will persist in the class number. As a result, the sequence of the classes also will become different from what it would be if the postulate had not been deviated from.

454U According to the schedules of UDC, the title in focal terms should be

Economics (BC) Labour [E] Child [2P] Technology industry [2P2] India [S] 1950's [T]

455 The kernel term "Economics" in (BC) has a ready-made number.

456 The kernel term "Personnel Management" in [E] has a ready-made number. It is directly attached to the focal number in (BC).

457 The kernel term "Child" in [2P] has a ready-made number. It is directly attached to the focal number in [E].

458 The kernel term "technology industry" in [2P2] is itself a focus in another (BC). It is not part if the Schedule for the (BC) "Economics".

46U Step 6: Title in Focal Numbers

33(BC) I[E] 3[2P] 66[2P2] 54[S] 195[T]

Note: 46U0 The descriptive symbols after the focal numbers should be removed.

46U1 By postulate 1 for Connecting Symbols, the Space isolate number should be enclosed within brackets; the Time isolate number should be enclosed within inverted commas.

46U2 As a result of the used of the enumerative, non-analyticosynthetic DC core, non connecting symbol admits of being put either before the energy isolate number "1" or the personality isolate number "3".

46U3 By Convention, a "." Should be placed after each set of three consecutive substantive digits.

46U4 As the focal number in [2P2] belongs to a (BC) which is different from the (BC) of the subject classified, a colon has to be inserted before it.

47U Step 7 Title in Synthesised Focal Numbers

331.3:66(54)"195".

48U Step 8 Verification by Reverse Translation

48U1 Facet Analysis

33	is the Basic Facet
1	is Energy Facet
3	is Second Round First Level Perosnality (Kind of Personnel) Facet.
66	is Second Round Second Level Personality (Enterprise) facet.
54	is Space Facet.
195	is Time facet.

48U2 Digit by Digit Translation

3	Social Sciences.
33	Economics
331	Labour.
331.3	Child labour.
331.3:66	-do- in chemical industries.
331.3:66(5)	Child labour in chemical industries in Asia.
331.3:66(54)	Child labour in chemical industries in India.
331.3:66(54)"195"	Child labour in chemical industries in India brought up to 1950s

which is equivalent to "helpless children in chemical factories (in India). 1955".

4D For Decimal: Classification

1. Decimal classification differ from UDC to some extent.

2. For [2P], its schedule gives
   3 Labour by critical age groups (instead of Child labour")
   31 Child Labour.
   38 Child and youth labour in speific occupations (divided like 620-698).

38 "Divided like 620-628" gives as the isolate in [2P2]
   66 Chemical technology.

4 We have therefore either,
   41 To choose the kernel term in [2P] as the co-extensive one "Child" and omit the kernel term in [2P2]; or
   42 To choose the kernel term "Chemical technology" in [2P2] and the more extensive kernel term "Critical age group" in [2P].

51 IF we make the second choice, we get
   3313866 Labour by critical age group in chemical technology, where 8 functions as the connecting symbol between the class numbers 331.3 and 66.

52 If we make the first choice, we get
   331.31 Child labour,

61 If we make the first choice, the class number is more extensive than the subject classified because of the omission of [2P2].

62 If we make the second choice, the class number is more extensive than the subject classified because of the focal number in [2P] being more extensive than the kernel term [2P].

63 This dilemma is quite common in DC as we have seen already, in sections F31 and F712.

7 The focal number in [S] is 54; and its connecting symbol is 09.

8 The focal number in [T] is 04, This means, "British period", which is more extensive than "1950s".
   331.31095404
   331.3866095404

5 Example with Levels

Srinivasan (G A). Ordinary linear differential equation of the second order made easy.

50 Step 0: Raw Title

Ordinary linear differential equation of the second order made easy.

Note: 501 The (BC) is "Differential and integral equations". It is implied. It should be made explicit.

502 A perusal of the book shows that it deals with the graphical solution of such equations. Therefore the term "graphical solution" should be added.

51 Step 1: Full Title

Graphical solution of ordinary linear differential equation of second order in differential and integral equations.

Note: 511 The preposition "of" is only an auxiliary term. It is not essential to the indication of the subject. It may therefore be omitted.

512 The term "made easy" is a puff. It is not essential to the indication of the subject. It may therefore be omitted.

52 Step 2: Kernel Title

Graphical solution Ordinary. Linear. Second order. Differential equation. Differential and integral equatios.

520 The kernel term "Differential and integral equations" denotes the focus in the Basic Facet. Therefore, the symbol (BC) should be added after it.

5211 The focal term "Graphical solution" denotes the focus in the Energy Facet. Therefore, the symbol [E] should be added after it.

5212 Each of the terms "ordinary", "linear", and "second order" differential equations, denotes a focus in a Personality Facet. Therefore, the symbol [P] should be added after each of them.

5221 In the study of "Differential and integral equations", these are separated out, in the first instance, into isolates such as

"Ordinary diff eqn" "Partial"

"Simultaneous" "Integral"

"Total differential" etc.

These may be taken by convention as the manifestations of the fundamental category Personality.

5222 Again, each of these groups is again separated out by there degrees into the isolates "Linear", "Quadratic", etc. By convention, we shall take these as organs of the first remove of the "Ordinary", etc.

5223 So also, each of these organs of the first remove is again separated out by their order into the isolates "First order", "Second order", etc. By convention we shall take these as organs of the first remove of the "Linear", etc. This implies that they are organs of the second remove of "Ordinary", etc.

5224 By the Cow-Calf principle, the Kernel terms "Ordinary", "linear", and "Second order" should be tied together, as it were, and kept on the same side of the Energy kernel term "Graphical solution".

5225 Thus "Ordinary" is first level Personality that is, [P]. "Linear" is second level Personality - that is, [P3].

5226 In adapting the conventions mentioned above, a knowledge of the subject is necessary.

53 Step 3: Analysed Title

Graphical Solution [E] Ordinary [P] Linear [P2] Second order [P3] Differential and integral equations (BC).

531 By the Postulate for Basic facet (see section H31), the kernel term "Differential and Integral equation" in the basic facet should be put first.

532 By the result in 523, the kernel terms "ordinary" [P], "Linear" [P2], "Second order" [P3], and "graphical solution"[E] should be put in succession after the kernel term in (BC).

54 Step 5: Transformed Title

Differential and Integral equations (BC) Ordinary [P] Linear [P2] Second order [P3] Graphic solution [E].

541 All the kernel terms are standard ones.

55 Step 5: Title in Standard Terms

Differential and Integral equations (BC) Ordinary [P] Linear [P2] Second order [P3] Graphic solution [E].

For Colon Classification

551C All the kernel terms have ready-made numbers.

56C Step 6: Title in Focal Numbers

B33(BC) 1[P] 1[P2] 2[P3] 6[E]

561C By Postulate 1 for Omission of Connecting Symbol, comma need not be put before 1[P].

56C2 By the Postulate of Connecting Symbols, comma should be put before 1[P2] and 2[P3], and colon before be removed.

57C Step 7: Title in Synthesised Focal Numbers Class Number

B331,1,2:6

58C Step 8: Verification by reverse Translation

58C1 Facet Analysis

B33 is Basic Facet

1 is the First Level Personality (Equation) Facet.

1 is the Second level Personality (Degree) Facet.

2 is the Third level Personality (Order) Facet.

6 is the Energy (Problem) Facet

58C2 Digit by Digit Translation

B	Mathematics
B3	Analysis
B33	Differential and integral equation
B331	Ordinary differential equation
B331,1	Linear differential equation
B331,1,2	Second order linear differential equation
B3331,2:6	Graphic solution of second order linear differential equation which is equivalent to "ordinary linear differential equation of the second order made easy (graphic solution)".

According to UDC

551U The kernel term "Differential equations etc." in (BC) has a ready-made number.

552U Each of the kernel terms "Ordinary" in [P] and "Linear" in [P2] has its kernel number attached directly to the focal number in (BC). This direct attachment can be used only for [P]. Therefore "Linear" [P2] has to be translated into its Strict Focal Number by attaching its normal focal number to the focal number of its (BC).

553U The kernel term "Second order" in [P3] has its focal number attached directly to that in [P2]. Therefore, it can be represented by its normal focal number alone.

554U The kernel term "Graphical solution" in [E] is found in an altogether different (BC). Therefore, it has to be translated into its Strict Focal Number by attaching its normal focal number to the focal number of its own (BC).

56U Step 6: Title in Focal Numbers

517.9 (BC) 7[P] 517.94[P2] 191[P3] 518.4[E]

56U1 As the Strict Focal Number in [P2] has to be started from the focal number in the (BC) itself, colon has to be inserted before it.

56U2 As the Strict Focal Number in [E] has to be started from the focal number in its own (BC) which is different from the (BC) of the subject being classified, a colon has to be inserted before it.

57U Step 7: Title in Synthesised Focal Numbers

UDC Class Number

517.91:517.94191:518.4

58U Verification by Reverse Translation

58U1 Facet Analysis

517.9	is the Basic facet.
1	is the First level Personality (Equation) Facet.
517.94	is the Second Level Personality (Degree) Facet.
191	is the Third Level Personality (Order) Facet.
518.1	is the Energy Facet.

58U2 Digit by Digit Translation

5	Pure Sciences.
51	Mathematics.
517	Analysis
517.9	Integral equations, etc.
517.91: 517.94	Linear differential equations.
517.91: 517.94191	-do- of second order.
517.91: 517.94191: 518.4	Graphical solution of second order linear differential equations

which is equivalent to "Ordinary linear differential equations of second order "graphical solution".

For Decimal Classification

551D In DC, focal numbers are not provided for the focal terms in [P2], [P3], and [E].

56D Step 6: Title in Focal Numbers

517. 38 (BC) 2[P] ?[P2] ?[E]

57D Step 8: Verification by Reverse Translation

58D1 Facet Analysis

517.38 is Basic facet.

2 is Personality (Equations) Facet.

58D2 Digit by Digit Translation

5	Pure Sciences.
51	Mathematics.
517	Calculus
517.3	Integral Calculus
517.38	Differential equation
517.382	Ordinary differential equations (including linear and non-linear)

Examples with Round and Levels

Pandya (N). Lock-out of helpless children in the chemical factories. 1955

61 The title of this book differs from that in example 4 only in the addition of the term "Lock-out". Therefore, the only new problem is to accommodate this new isolate term.

62 Factors such as Industrial Relation, Strike, and Lock-out denote a state of the personnel in Personnel Management. No such term is a manifestation of Time, Space, Energy, or Matter. Therefore by the Postulate of Isolate Facets (see sec. H12) each of them is taken to be a manifestation of Personality.

63 Consider the sequence of the kernel term "Children" and "Lock-out". By the Wall-Picture Principle, their sequence is fixed as Children. Lock-out.

64 "Children" has already been assigned to the Second Round. Therefore, it follows that "Lock-out" also falls in the Second Round. Since "Children" belongs to First Level Personality in the Second Round, it follows that "Lock-out" has to be taken to belong to the Second Level. Thus, the symbol to be added after it is [2P2].

65 Step 5: Title in Focal Terms

Economics (BC) Technological Industry [P] Personnel Management [E] Child [2P] Lock-out [2P2] India [5] 1950s [T].

For Colon Classification

66C Step 6: Title in Focal Numbers

X(BC) 8(F)[P] 9[E] B[2P] 79W[2P2] 44[S] N5[T].

67C Step 7: Synthesised Title in Focal Numbers

X8(F):9B,79W.44'N5

For UDC

651U The kernel term of each of "Children" [2P] and "Lock-out" [2P2] has its focal number directly attached to focal number 1 in [E]. This direct attachment can be used only for [2P].Therefore, "Lock-out" [2P2] has to be translated into its Strict Focal Number by attaching it number to the focal number in (BC) and [E] taken together.

66U Step 6: Title in Focal Numbers

33(BC) 1[E]3[2P] 331.895[2P2] 66[2P3] 54[S] 195[T].

66U1 As the Strict Focal Number in [2P2] has to be started from the focal number in the (BC) itself, a colon has to be inserted before it.

67U Step 7: Synthesised Title in Focal Numbers

331.3:331.895:66(54) "195".

Other Examples

Eight other examples of practical classification based similarly on postulates and principles will be found in the following places:

71 Five examples in the Annals of library science 5, 1958, 40-43.

72 One example in the Annals of library science 6, 1959, 39-41.

73 One example in Ranganathan (S R). Library manual, ed. 2, 1960, sec 773.

74 One example in the Annals of library science 7, 1960, 77-89.

81 Step 1: Full Title

Full Title: Title derived, by an examination of the document, from Raw Title by Filling up all the ellipses found in it, and breaking down each derived composite term into its fundamental constituent terms corresponding to the five fundamental categories and, if necessary corresponding to the characteristics leading to the various isolated, so as to bring out all the relevant facets including the basic facet.

Note: 811 The full title will necessarily have terms denoting the focus in each one of the different facets of its subject.

812 It may also have other auxiliary terms such as articles, prepositions, and conjunctions used to make the title expressively meaningful. This will depend on the natural language of the title.

8121 As an alternative, a language, such as Sanskrit, German, and Russian, may absorb the auxiliary words into the essential words and contain only morphological variants of the latter.

813 The full title may also have certain explanatory or redundant "puff" words belonging to the Raw Title. For example, in "text book on labour problems", the term "Text Book" is a puff. The term "problem" also is a puff.

814 All the auxiliary terms and puffs should be removed.

82 Step 2: Kernel Title

Kernel Title: Title derived from the Full Title by removing all the auxiliary terms and puff, and by replacing all the essentials focal terms in their respective nominative forms.

Note: 821 Each focal or essential term is called a Kernel Term. It is one of the bare term in the name of the subject.

822 After the kernel term denoting the basic class, the symbol (BC) should be inserted. (See sec H11 Postulate of Basic Facet).

823 For each of the other kernel terms, the fundamental category of which its concept-correlate is a manifestation should be found out. (See section H 12 Postulate of Isolate Facets).

8231 After each kernel term, the symbol for the corresponding fundamental category should be inserted in forms such as

[P], [M], [E], [S], [T]

824 It two or more [E] occur, each such symbol should be amplified so as to show the Round to which it belongs, viz, into [E], [2E], [3E], etc. (see section J51 Postulate of Rounds of Energy).

825 Each [P] and each [M]should be amplified as to show the Round to which it belongs, viz, into

[P], [2P], [3P], etc. and [M], [2M], [3M], etc.

826 If [P] or [M] occurs more than once within a round, that symbol should be amplified so as to show the Level to which it belongs, viz, into

[P], [P2], [P3] if in round 1;

[2P], [2P2}, [2P3] if in round 2; and so on. (See section K4 Postulate of Levels).

8261 Levels should be indicated similarly for each of [M], [S], and [T] if its occurs more than once within a round. (See section K4 Postulate of Levels).

827 The marking of the rounds and the levels will have to be done according to the postulates and the principles governing the sequence of facets. The postulates have been stated in the

earlier chapters. The principles have been stated in section 3 of this chapter.

83 Step 3: Analysed Title

Analysed Title: Title derived from Kernel Title by adding after each kernel term the symbol denoting the nature of its manifestation. (See section H1 Postulation of Fundamental categories: H11 Postulate of Basic Facets; and H12 Postulate of Isolate Facets).

Note: 830 The symbols in the Analysed Title form a help in rearranging the kernel terms in accordance with the postulates and the principles governing their sequence. The rearrangement called for may be stated as follows.

831 (BC) should be put first. (see sec H21 Postulate of Sequence).

832 The should follow in succession [P], [P2], [P3], etc. (see sections j53 Postulate of Sequence within a Round and K41 Postulate of Sequence of Levels).

833 Then should follow in succession [M], [M2], [M3], etc. (see sections J53 Postulate of Sequence within a Round and K41 Postulate of Sequence of Levels.)

834 Then [E] should follow. (see section J53 Postulate of Sequence within a Round)

835 Then should follow in succession [2P], [2P2], [2P3], etc. (see section J53 Postulate of Sequence within a Round and K41 Postulate of Sequence of Levels).

836 Then should follow in succession [2M], [2M2], [2M3], etc. (see section J53 Postulate of Sequence within a Round and K41 Postulate of Sequence of Levels).

837 The [2E] should follow. (see section J53 Postulate of Sequence within a Round).

838 Then should follow successively, in a similar manner, the kernel terms of round 3, round 4, etc.

8391 At the end of the last round should follow successively [S], [S2], [S3], etc; and [T], [T2], [T3], etc. (see section J41 Postulate for Space and Time Facets and K41 Postulate of Sequence of Levels).

84 Step 4: Transformed Title

Transformed Title: Title derived from Analysed Title by rearranging the kernel terms in accordance with the postulates and the principles governing their sequence and retaining with each its won descriptive symbol.

Note:

841 The kernel terms in the Transformed Title have all been taken largely from the Raw Title.

842 These terms are not likely to be standard terms.

843 It will be convenient to have the kernel terms replaced by standard terms.

844 But the movement to arrive at standard terms in any language is too recent to have provided standard terms for every discipline.

845 In their absence, we have to use as standard the terms used in the schedules of the preferred scheme of classification.

846 This expedient, it must be stated, does not however affect the results of the work done in the idea plane in reaching the steps 1, 3, and 4 and the work done in the verbal plane in reaching step 2. They are all independent of the scheme of classification used.

85 Step 5: Title in Standard Terms

Title in Standard Terms: Title derived from Transformed title by replacing each kernel term by its standard term, but retaining with each its own descriptive symbol.

Note:

851 The transition from step 4 to step 5 is entirely in the verbal plane.

852 As stated in note 843, reduction to Title in Standard Terms is only a convenience in the move towards the next step.

853 Reach kernel term should now be replaced by its ordinal number as provided in the preferred scheme of classification.

854 If a kernel term does not have a ready-made number, the scheme is like to have prescribed a device for arriving at its number. In this way, it should be possible to complete the replacement of each kernel term by its equivalent ordinal number.

8541 In CC, the Canons of Scheduled Mnemonics, Seminal Mnemonics, and Alphabetical Mnemonics, and the Chronological, Geographical, and Subject Devices are prescribed for the purpose.

86 Step 6: Title in Focal Numbers

Title in Focal Numbers: Title derived from Title in Standard terms by Replacing each kernel term by its focal number, but retaining with each focal number its own descriptive symbol.

Note:

861 The transition from step 5 to step 6 amounts to translation from natural language to ordinal language.

862 We should now remove each descriptive symbol and insert in its place the connecting symbol appropriate to the focal number following it, as prescribe by the postulates or the rules concerned. (see section H5 postulate of Connecting Symbols, H51 Postulate 1 for Omission of Connecting Symbol, J71 Postulate 2 for Connecting symbol, and K61 Postulate 3 for Omission of connecting Symbols).

87 Step 7: Class Number

Synthesised title in Focal Number or Class Numbers: The ordinal number derived from the Title Focal Number by Removing the descriptive symbols and inserting before each focal number its appropriate connecting symbol as prescribed by the postulate or the rules concerned.

Note:

871 The transition from step 6 to step 7 is entirely in the notational plane.

872 The focal number in the basic facet is the Basic Class Number.

873 The focal number in each of the other facets is an Isolate Number.

874 If desired, a ninth step also may be taken as shown in the next subsection.

88 Step 8: Verification

Verification by reverse Translation: This is done by

1 Analysing the class number into its facets;

11 Naming each facet;and

2 Giving a progressive digit by digit interpretation ignoring the staged when no intelligible concatenation of digits occurs.

Bibliography

Autry, Brick. "A Curious White Elephant: The Library on the Reservation." *La Confluencia* (July 1977): 1, 3-4, 44-45.

Ayras, A. "Library Problems in Finland's Northern and Northeastern Developing Regions." *Scandinavian Public Library Quarterly* 10, no. 3 (1977): 97-104.

Baba, A. M. 1988. *Dewey Decimal Classification, Universal Decimal Classification, and Colon Classification: development, structure, comparison.*

Batty, C. D. 1967. *An introduction to Colon Classification.* Hamden, CT: Archon Books.

Bhargava, G. D. and S. P. Sood. 1975. *Colon Classification: theory and practice.*

Blei, Norbert. "Three-Day Run on a Navajo, New Mexico Spirit Trail." *American Libraries* 6 (February 1975): 96-104.

Blumer, Thomas J. "Library Service for American Indian People and American Indian Library Association." *Library of Congress Information Bulletin* 43 (September 10, 1984): 296-98.

Bury, S. 1986. "Ranganathan's theories embodied in both Colon Classification and the second edition of Bliss' bibliographic classification." *Herald of Library Science,* 25 (Jan/Apr), 1-13.

Cedar Face, Mary Jane. "Southern Oregon Digital Archives: Preserving a Unique Bioregion and Its Ethnohistory." *College & Research Libraries News* 65, no. 4 (April 2004): 193.

Chilcote, Sandy M. "Report from Labrador: Access to Indigenous Language Materials." *International Leads* 5 (Spring 1991): 3.

Cohen, Shayne Del. "Library Aide Services in Fallon, Nevada." *American Indian Libraries Newsletter* 1, no. 2 (1977): 8-9.

Cunningham, Cindy Altick. "Native Americans and Library Service: Washington Examples." *Alki* 11 (March 1995): 6-7.

Cunningham, William D. "Anto Wicharti: The Responsibility of State Libraries to Provide Direction and Programs in Library Service to Indians." *Library Journal* 94, no. 22 (December 15, 1969): 4496-99.

Dorr, Jessica, and Richard Akeroyd. "New Mexico Tribal Libraries: Bridging the Digital Divide." *Computers in Libraries* 21, no. 9 (October 2001): 36-42.

Edinger, Anne. "Tribal Librarians Focus on Cultural Materials." *Tribal College Journal* 14, no. 1 (2002): 53.

Ellis, Brian C. "Jayronomo: Smoke Signals from a Public Library." *Oklahoma Librarian* 22 (April 1972): 8-9, 45-46.

Evans, Duane L. "Students Establish Community Library." *Kansas Library Bulletin* 38 (Winter 1969): 15. [In Potawatomi community building]

Falconer, Sandra. "Iwi Archivists as Recordmakers?" *Electronic Library* 21, no. 5 (2003): 461-64.

Grant, Lana. "Library Services to American Indians." *Library Administration and Management* 5, no. 4 (Fall 1991): 210-11.

Heyser, Richard G., and Lotsee Patterson Smith. "Public Library Service to Native Americans in Canada and the Continental United States." *Library Trends* 29, no. 2 (Fall 1980): 353-68.

Husain, S. and M. T. M. Khan. 1990. "Conceptual Changes in the Fundamental Categories in C C 7." *Herald of Library Science*, 29 (Jan/Apr), 45-50.

Kaula, P. N. 1985. *A treatise on Colon Classification*. New Delhi: Sterling Publishers Private Ltd.

Kumaravel, J. P. S. and S. C. Shunmuganathan. 1989. "Colon Classification - edition 7: some observations." *Herald of Library Science*, 28 (July), 210-212.

Lee, Deborah. "Aboriginal Students in Canada: A Case Study of Their Academic Information Needs and Library Use." *Journal of Library Administration* 33, no. 3/4 (2001): 259-92.

Lincoln, Tamara. "Cultural Reassertion of Alaska Native Languages and Cultures: Libraries' Responses." *Cataloging & Classification Quarterly* 35, no. 3/4 (2003): 265-90.

McIsaac, Marina Stock, with Radford Quamahongnewa and Ruth Finneman. "Native American School Library Professionals: An Unmet Need." *School Library Journal* 30, no. 5 (January 1984): 38-41.

Mickinock, Rey. "The Plight of the Native American." *Library Journal* 96, no. 16 (September 15, 1971): 46-49.

Moorcroft, Heather, and Alex Byrne. "Intellectual Property and Indigenous Peoples' Information." *Australian Academic & Research Libraries* 27, no. 2 (June 1996): 87-94.

Ongley, David. "Guidelines Adopted for Alaskan Public Libraries." *Sharing Our Pathways: A Newsletter of the Alaska Rural Systemic Initiative* 6 (November/December 2001): 6-7.

Ornstein, Sarah. "Multimedia Library Offers Unique Learning Experience." *Pequot Times* 11, no. 9 (2002): 8.

Parkhi, R. S. 1972. *Library classification: evolution of a dynamic theory*. Delhi: Vikas Publishing House Pvt Ltd.

Philbrick, Roger P. "To Serve Native Americans, Understand and Involve the People Themselves." *Wisconsin Library Bulletin* 70 (July-August 1974): 152-54.

Plotnik, Arthur. "Cheryl Metoyer-Duran: Taking the Dream to WHCLIS." *American Libraries* 10 (October 1979): 551.

Ranganathan, S. R. 1962. *Elements of library classification*. Bombay: Asia Publishing House.

Ranganathan, S. R. 1965. *The Colon Classification. Rutgers Series on Systems for the Intellectual Organization of Information (ed. Susan Artandi)*.

Ranganathan, S. R. 1971. *Colon Classification, ed. 7 (1971): a preview*. Bangalore: Sarada Ranganathan Endowment for Library Science.

Richardson, Bernard E. "By Red Rocks: Notes on Library Service to Native Americans." *Road Runner* 17, no. 3 (1974): 1-17.

Satija, M. P. 1989. *Colon Classification, 7th edition: a practical introduction*. New Delhi: Ess Ess Publications.

Seymour, Flora W. "Indians and Reading." *Library Journal* 60 (November 1935): 893-94.

Shields, Gerald R., and George Sheppard. "American Indians: Search for Fort Hall's Library Service." *American Libraries* 1 (October 1970): 856-60.

Sullivan, Robert. "Nga Taonga Tuku Iho Kei Roto i Nga Whare Matauranga o Aotearoa: Collection Management in the Field of Traditional Maori Knowledge." *New Zealand Libraries* 48, no. 1 (March 1995): 5-10.

Szekely, Chris. "Library Services for Maori People." *Wilson Library Bulletin* 67 (April 1993): 46-48.

Teixeira, Lauren. "Magic of Community: The Telecommunications Revolution and Native American Heritage." *Wilson Library Bulletin* 69, no. 1 (1994): 34-37.

Testerman, Karen L. "Dream Realized: Woksape Tipi Library Opens." *Indian Country Today,* January 20, 1997: S-1.

Zaidi, S. M. 1989. "Comparison of the Colon Classification edition seven (basic and depth version) volume 1: schedules for classification with relevant parts/sections of edition six (amended); a brief survey." *Herald of Library Science,* 28 (July), 204-210.

Index

G

H

I

J

K

L

M